The Box

Palewell Press

The Box

Susan Jordan

The Box
First edition 2024 from Palewell Press,
https://palewellpress.co.uk
Printed and bound in the UK
ISBN 978-1-911587-87-3

All Rights Reserved. Copyright © 2024 Susan Jordan. No part of this translation may be reproduced or transmitted in any form or by any means, without permission in writing from the Author. The right of Susan Jordan to be identified as the author of this work has been asserted by her in accordance with the Copyright, Designs and Patents Act 1988

The overall cover design is Copyright © 2024 Camilla Reeve
Images used on the front cover were downloaded from www.shutterstock.com
The photo of Susan Jordan on the back cover is Copyright © 2024 Susan Jordan
A CIP catalogue record for this title is available from the British Library.

For all the people I've met who have had experiences similar to Jo's. I hope they too find someone who believes in them.

Acknowledgements

I'd like to thank those friends who were kind enough to comment on all or part of the later drafts: Tanya Atapattu, Adrian Barker, Sue Proffitt, Jane Shemilt, Janet Smith and Mimi Thebo. I'd also like to thank friends who read parts of it at a much earlier stage: Victoria Finlay, Emma Geen, Sophie McGovern and Peter Reason. My thanks and respect, of course, to all those whose stories have contributed towards the creation of Jo. Thanks to Andrew Kay for his help with the cover image. Lastly, thanks to Camilla Reeve at Palewell Press for liking the book enough to publish it, and for all the work she has done on it.

Contents

Richard 1
Jo 5
Richard 8
Jo 16
Richard 23
Jo 30
Richard 37
Richard 42
Jo 48
Richard 52
Jo 62
Richard 66
Jo 72
Marian 80
Richard 84
Jo 87
Richard 93
Jo 101
Jo 109
Richard 115
Jo 122
Richard 131
Jo 135
Marian 143
Richard 151

Jo	157
Richard	162
Richard	168
Jo	176
Fran	183
Richard	189
Jo	195
Jo	200
Richard	204
Jo	209
Richard	215
Jo	221
Marian	227
Richard	234
Richard	242
Jo	252
Jo	258
Richard	265
Jo	270
Richard	279
Author's Biography – Susan Jordan	288
Support and Advice	288

Richard

He stood gazing along the estuary of the Teign, the dirty shingle swallowing his shoes, a breeze lifting his fine hair. In his pocket he felt the stone: smooth, polished, a ridge along one side. Jo's stone, that he'd once meant to give to her, before their lives had rolled away from one another. It comforted him to feel it there. The early evening light dipped low over the water in a transient blaze. Above the river the dying sun, behind shreds of cloud, had a fierce glow that for a moment lit the world with meaning. The poignancy of it caught at his heart.

He hadn't brought the box; he was only exploring. Black and shiny, it rested on the clean white mantelpiece of his B & B room, standing out stark against the pale cream wall. Wherever he'd looked in the small room it had caught his eye, reminding him of what he had to do. He felt an urgency to get it done with, as though that would seal over the wound of his loss, but he wasn't ready to let Kate go yet. This wasn't the place; he could see that now. He'd thought it might be but secretly hoped it wasn't. If only he could have asked her where she wanted to be. Why wasn't she there? Her absence hit him again as violently as if he'd just discovered it.

Upstream the estuary narrowed into the distance. Still gazing at it, he took crunching strides towards the stretch of water that lay like flat silk. As he came close, he saw himself twinned in the river and felt a sudden sharp longing for Jo, Kate's twin. He'd wanted her to be there when he gave his wife to the water. Needed her to be there, if she could, but he knew it would be too much for her.

He saw Jo's white hands with prominent finger joints, just like Kate's except that the nails were bitten right down, the sleeves of her jumper drooping over them, her long brown hair twisted back anyhow with a comb clip, her large brown eyes that pleaded and then looked away. Kate's eyes had confronted. Both Kate and Jo had been thin, quick, angular, though Kate had rounded out with motherhood. Rick, their son, had been good for her.

When he'd told Rick where he was going his son had tried desperately to be scientific, screwing up his pale only-just-ten-year-old face to ask how hot the fire would have been, how long it took, how much ash you got. He'd let Rick weigh the box in his hands: it was heavy, but not as heavy as either of them had expected. Richard hadn't let Rick look inside, remembering that when his own mother's ashes were buried he'd been shocked to notice fragments of bone among the dark gritty residue. On Rick's face he'd seen an utter disbelief that mirrored his own: that this, and only this, was what remained. Kate wouldn't like being shut in a box; she'd hated being confined. She'd be far happier dissolving into sun-burnished water; he promised her he'd do it as soon as he could. Two months since the funeral: no time at all and a chasm of empty days.

Funeral: he word's finality fell like a shadow. He'd had to go through it twice. Marian, Kate's mother, had insisted on holding a service in her local church, despite being an atheist. She'd wanted Kate be buried in the churchyard there – of all the impracticable ideas. He'd let Marian have her service, but this one had been far more of an ordeal than the funeral he'd organised. His memory skirted round the edges: the blustery day in early May, sodden grass and drooping bluebells in the churchyard, the tangle of umbrellas as the few people huddled into the church doorway. Inside the church, the smell of damp and incense and old books, the white lilies donated by the WI; the young vicar's unexpectedly punkish haircut. The space beside Marian where Jo should have sat. None of it had felt real. Kate had had little connection with her mother's Dorset village and she'd no more been a Christian than Marian was.

Before that, back in Edinburgh in the soulless crematorium chapel, he and their friends had done their best to honour Kate in her way, with huge bunches of tulips – red, yellow, purple, pink, any colour but white – and a length of vibrant fabric, one of her designs, draped over the coffin. Kate's friend Ella had read a simple, heartfelt rhymed poem that she'd written and another friend, John, had played and sung *The Carnival is Over*. Richard had played the song on YouTube again and again afterwards, luxuriating in sweet grief. When his time came to speak, he'd found that for a moment he had no voice; his throat stayed obdurately closed. Then the words had flowed as he conjured up the Kate he knew.

In the chapel they'd all commemorated the person they loved, then waited in silence to hear the words that delivered her body to the flames. Jo hadn't been there but had sent a few faltering lines to be read out. They began: 'I don't know what to say,' as though she too had been beyond speech, but then described her closeness to Kate – the mysterious closeness of twins that he'd never fully understood. It had struck him how eloquently she wrote, how in her own grief she'd managed to speak for all of them.

A breeze was creasing the water, frilling it with white. Now that the sun was lost in cloud, the river softened from deep metallic blue to a familiar English grey. The tide was coming in; the toes of Richard's shoes were dark from the lapping waves. He stepped back, shading his eyes, and gazed across the river at a huddle of trees and houses nested between the hills. Perhaps this wasn't the place: Kate wouldn't want to be overlooked. Farther down the estuary, or perhaps on another river, there must be a more private spot. He'd tried elsewhere and thought this little nature reserve spreading out into the water would be the best, but he would have to come back in order to be sure. Despite all the places in Edinburgh that they'd loved together, he knew it had to be Devon. Kate had been happy there as a child, and had stayed in Totnes with her aunt and uncle. Her face had always come alive when she spoke about it.

He felt for his phone in his pocket and the edge of his hand caught against Jo's stone. Shading the screen from the light, he scrolled through to find her number. There was no signal down here but he started a text: Sorry you couldn't make it to the funeral.

No, that wouldn't do. If he made her feel guilty she'd never want to help him. He deleted it and put the phone back in his pocket.

The sun was lower now. Through the sparse cloud its yellowing light seemed almost within reach. Richard shaded his eyes, trying to watch it obliquely. When he looked away, a disc of sun had imprinted itself on his vision. He blinked, then turned and walked reluctantly back the way he'd come, before the tide came right in and the light died.

Jo

She'd been at the bus stop in Muswell Hill for thirty minutes, long enough to have walked home, but having waited so long she couldn't give up. The people perched inside the shelter on the narrow plastic seat shuffled and muttered to each other. An elderly woman smiled at her but she dodged away from conversation. She stood just under the roof of the shelter, keeping a distance from feet and bags, not caring about the little rivulets that ran into her eyes and down her cheeks. They washed away the smell of old clothes, stale bodies, that lingered on her after a day in the charity shop. She recoiled from the smell every time another bag came in, but told herself – as she'd been told – that the job would do her good. You can't just sit at home, they'd said, you'll get ill again.

Her shoulders sagged with relief now the day was over. The other volunteers had kept trying to talk to her. Jim, who had a learning disability, smiled each time he shifted bags and heavy boxes and stood expecting a smile back. Khadija, from Syria, couldn't stop talking about having got refugee status – a miracle, she'd said. Jo had wanted to feel happy for her but all the time was thinking of her sister. Eileen, nearly ninety and eager to be useful though she couldn't do much, had sat behind the counter chatting to every customer who came in, and had switched her attention to Jo when the shop was quiet. Jo escaped whenever she could, hiding her shame at having nothing to say that the rest of them would want to hear. It was easier to go and iron the clothes, alone in the back room among the bulging black bags and piles of orphaned books. Every so often Estelle, the glossy, bossy woman who ran the shop, had looked in, the red, yellow and black plastic strips that covered the doorway slapping her back as she pushed through.

'Just making sure you're all right, dear. Got those T-shirts for me yet? Make them nice and smart, won't you?' Estelle had once owned a dress shop and 'smart' was her favourite word. Jo had seen Estelle trying not to look at the scars that marked her arms like gradations on a scale of pain.

It was calming to think of Richard: the way he'd accepted she couldn't face the funeral. She wished other people could just let her be the way she was; Mother's cool disapproval had jabbed like a knife between her ribs. It wasn't so much about Jans; Mother had implied Jo was letting *her* down. It hadn't been Mother who told her Jans had died – to Mother she was still Jancis, to Jo always Jans, though she knew Kate was the name her sister had preferred. It was Richard who had rung, his own pain making him careful of hers. She hadn't cried then, she'd been too shocked, but now tears flooded up, for herself and Richard as well as Jans. All she'd taken in at the time were the words: *Ruptured brain aneurysm. Not always fatal, but ... Only forty,* he'd kept repeating. *Only forty. Just before her – your – birthday. I'm so sorry. I'm so sorry.* In their silence they'd shared the incredulity, the unimaginable hole left in both their lives. At that moment Jo hadn't found it jarring that he'd called her Kate; her death was bigger than her name.

Two buses arrived together. People crowded on to the first one, ducking against the rain. Jo squeezed past them to the one behind, where the driver was reluctantly opening the doors. A man had his foot on the step and she stood ready behind him, fishing in her bag for her pass. When his Oyster card bleeped on the reader she stepped up behind him, pushing back the overhanging sleeve of her denim jacket, making sure she got on quickly, trying not to hold people up. The bus moved off with a jerk before she had time to find a seat and she nearly fell across a plump, wary-looking woman guarding a lapful of carrier bags. She moved carefully down the bus to the one remaining seat, in the corner by the window at the back, and squeezed in beside a teenage lad who lounged, legs stretched out, tapping at his phone screen with one finger. The bus smelt of people and wet clothes; through the window she could see nothing but steam and trails of rain. It didn't matter: she knew the route and the bus's voice kept telling you where you were.

As soon as she sat down she felt her phone buzz. Often she ignored it for days and then didn't find anything new when she looked, but without thinking she pulled it out of her pocket. Richard – just when she'd been thinking of him. A long text saying he'd like to see her: something about wanting to remember Kate and the time before that, Jo's time with him. She didn't often think about that time; to her he and Jans had belonged together. Jo hadn't lasted long with him: she shuddered now as she thought of him touching her, and the breakdown that had started not long after. She hadn't wanted to be with anyone then; it had been a relief when he moved on to Jans, though she had liked him as a friend.

'Bounds Green *Station*,' the bus's voice announced, with its odd emphasis. Jo pressed the bell and battled her way towards the central doors, squeezing past a huge man who stood in the doorway with an outsize suitcase in front of him. She wouldn't see Richard - not yet, anyway. His text felt like an intrusion. Leave me alone, she wanted to say, you're bad news. I'm bad news.

Richard

Coming back to Edinburgh, the box of ashes in his suitcase wrapped in Kate's marbled silk scarf, Richard felt he'd failed her, though giving her half-heartedly to the wrong place would have been far worse. You know it wasn't right, he said to her in his mind. He'd been to the estuary again yesterday, but farther up, one of the few places on that side where you could get down to the water. The noise of a train on the line behind him, so close he could almost have touched it, had jarred through his body. The spot was perfect otherwise, a grassy bulge into the river shaded by trees, near a long narrow rind of shingle, but noise had always disturbed Kate. Perhaps this wasn't the right estuary; it had to be a place that she'd loved and been happy in. Perhaps nearer to Teignmouth. He'd been there with her a long time ago and didn't find it as magical as her childhood memories, but that wouldn't matter if it was right for her. He'd have to ask Jo what she thought, even if that risked her anger and upset.

They'd already passed the pitted red cliffs of Dawlish and the jaunty moored boats in the Exe estuary, beached on mud at low tide. Kate and Jo had called it the Extuary; they'd always played with words. They'd sometimes invited him to join in, though he was nowhere near as quick as they were. In his mind he could hear Kate saying the word 'Extuary' and see her mischievous smile. Somewhere in the background Jo smiled too, like her but more uncertain.

Remembering Kate's smile brought the rest of her to life. Her body against his, her bony arms and firm thighs, her dark spicy perfume, the warm flutter of her breath against his cheek: she was so real he had to glance round to make sure she wasn't there. Her presence kept catching him at unexpected moments, then left him as suddenly as it came. I remembered your word, he whispered secretly to her, now seeing nothing more than the grey imitation leather seat beside him. I know you're still there. The image of the black box, cosseted in the delicate purple scarf, replaced her with such immediacy it left him gasping, as if the sea outside had drenched him through the window. It couldn't really be her in there; his mind must have played a trick. It was like the dreams he kept having where she'd gone away somewhere and was on her way back.

After Starcross the line ran inland. The flat fields with their glassy patches of floodwater calmed him, even though they were an inescapable sign that the climate was tipping out of balance. He leant back in the broad seat, wiping his handkerchief over his face, and stretched out his legs, relieved there was no-one to see him. He'd been lucky enough to get a cheap upgrade to first class; it gave him a table to himself in an almost empty carriage draughty with air-conditioning. He didn't pick up the fresh copy of *The Times* that had been put out for him but sat staring as the steward refilled his cardboard cup with coffee. At least seven hours till he could wheel his case up the slope at Waverley station; seven hours of forgetting and remembering that Kate wasn't there.

He left a message on Rick's phone, reassuring him that he'd be home today. The memory of Rick's pale bleak face squeezed at his heart; he longed to be back with his son even though their shared pain was as jagged as broken glass. Rick needed him; he mustn't let himself turn away. As he thought of seeing his son his eyes shut of their own accord, as if a heavy curtain had come down. He rested his head back against the seat, his mind blank with the enormity of what they faced.

He emerged from the below-ground gloom of Waverley Station into early evening light. At the top of the slope a kilted piper, who'd once told Richard he came from Bristol, was packing up his pipes. Deflating, they gave an agonised wail; Richard had an urge to comfort them. Turning the corner into Princes Street, he had the familiar sense of being a foreigner in the city. The tall, dark stone buildings, which he'd always loved, reminded him instantly that this wasn't England. The Gothic style had a faintly European feel and at the same time was unmistakably Scottish. Kate had wanted to live in Edinburgh after they came back from Paris – eight years ago, when Rick was still a toddler. She'd needed to be as far away from her mother as possible, and had been determined make a home there. Coming back now without her, he didn't feel it was home to him. As he bought his ticket on the bus, his flat Yorkshire voice sounded unmusical against the soft Edinburgh trill.

His case felt heavy as he pulled it round the corner, the wheels grating behind him, from Newington Road into one of the many terraces of stone houses, then down past the wide road junction by the Olympic Pool towards the little street of 1930s semis where he and Kate had chosen to live. Lifting the case over the step up to the gate, he noticed a strip of paint on the gatepost that had begun to peel. He stopped and with all his concentration slowly tore it off, exposing grey wood underneath, then studied the grain with minute care. For a moment he succeeded in emptying his mind of everything else. Then, out of habit, he glanced up at the bedroom to see if Kate was there. The evening sun blazed against the house's upper windows, so bright he couldn't see in; the hurt of the light reminded him that she wasn't.

Feeling like a stranger, he rang the bell instead of taking out his key. His sister Fran opened the door, eyebrows raised enquiringly, her hair fluffy round her face, her glasses smeared with fingermarks. He followed behind her as she turned towards the kitchen. Her pale green T-shirt was rucked across her plump back and her arms had a bulge of flesh above the elbow that he found almost obscene. They were so much fatter than Kate's arms, older too. Fifty-three, he reminded himself, five years older than he was. The roots of her hair under the yellow-orange dye were practically white. Kate had been barely forty, and beautiful – to him at least. Why should it be Fran who was left? Immediately he felt guilty for wishing her away.

'Journey OK? Everything all right?' she said in her slow, kind Yorkshire accent, not asking the rest. Her voice was like his, a foreigner's here.

He heaved his case into the hall and shook his head. Wearily he rubbed his hair, feeling how thin it was getting, and looked down into her face, which was wrinkled with concern. She was short and stocky like their mother; like their father he towered over her. Her soft plump body and lightish hair were familiar, reassuring; at the same time something in him screamed for her to go away.

'Where's Rick?'

'Playing football.' She smiled fondly.

'Is he OK? Should I go and get him?' He stood poised in the hallway between his case and the door. Fran had swept the wooden floor, clearing away the last specks of grass and mud that had dropped from Kate's shoes.

'No,' she said, in the soothing voice he'd heard her use on the phone with distraught people at the charity where she worked. 'He's with Robbie and his dad. He'll be back soon enough. I don't think he really wanted to go.'

He could picture Rick stiff with effort, pressing his lips together and clamping his thin arms against his sides. It's all wrong, he wanted to say to him, it shouldn't have happened. You don't have to force yourself to do these things. The rush of tenderness made him feel hot.

'Tea or coffee?' Fran asked, still quietly kind.

'Wine. We always have – had – a glass at this time.' They hadn't always, but now he enshrined the habit as a sacred ritual.

He and Fran lay back awkwardly in the living-room chairs. Kate had chosen them but the wooden arms, low seats and long sloping backs had never accommodated his shape, and short-legged Fran had to stretch out to touch the floor. He fidgeted, trying to make himself comfortable for Kate's sake. He'd taken off his shoes and was rumpling the Turkish rug with his feet, sliding it about on the wooden floor the way Rick did. That had always annoyed Kate, he remembered, and stopped. Beside their chairs were newspapers that Kate had read and dropped, now shepherded into tidy piles by Fran; in the high bookshelves along the white walls were gaps like missing teeth where Kate had taken books with her to the studio. He'd always liked her art books, big hardbacks with shiny jackets that easily tore and cracked. The evening before she died she'd leafed through one of them with him, pointing out in the paintings a detail in a corner, a shape he hadn't noticed, a colour he couldn't name. He couldn't remember who the artist was and felt an urgent need to ask her.

He took a sip of his wine and stood the glass on the floor beside him. Fran had made a point of saying it was Cabernet Sauvignon, in case that wasn't to his liking. Kate would have opened what she wanted and assumed he'd like it.

They sat in silence for a while, then Fran said, turning her half-empty glass in her hands, 'You mean you... brought them back?'

He blinked for an instant, not registering what she meant. He couldn't think of Kate as 'them.'

'What?... Oh, it wasn't the right place.'

'So what are you going to do?'

'It wasn't the right place, I said.' He braced himself, a small boy fighting his big sister, though she'd asked gently enough.

'OK.' At one time she would have nagged him, like their mother. He saw her look down into her glass, stopping herself. 'I'm sorry. It's just so much easier to be practical about things.'

'Yeah. You and me both.' His face softened into a smile.

The burden of practicality suddenly felt too much. On the far wall the bright silk screen prints that Kate had made when she was a student looked alive behind their glass. He'd loved the care and skill that went into her work – such a contrast to her carelessness around the house. Dangling across the back of the chair where Fran was sitting was a turquoise scarf that Kate had thrown there weeks ago. He didn't think he could ever put it away.

Fran went to start cooking and he let her get on with it. He preferred not to see her rooting around in his and Kate's kitchen, opening the cupboards they'd chosen together, searching through Kate's collection of spices – who else would have arranged them by colour? – splashing the patchwork of tiles that he and Kate had gathered over time from antique shops in different parts of the city.

There was not much light left and Richard let the room fade around him. He couldn't bear to touch the curtains. Indigo with a subdued pattern of fuchsia and white, they were one of Kate's first designs when she'd moved on from printmaking to textiles. Now the fabric was faded along the inner edge. Natural dyes did that, Kate had said the last time she drew them, lifting the corner meditatively, enjoying the effect. She should have been standing by the window now, looking out at the garden in the dimming light.

Rick must be on his way home. Richard tried to picture himself as a lone father but somehow Kate was there, looking after things in her quick, determined way. He finished his wine and poured himself more from the bottle that Fran had left beside him. It softened the sharp edge of Kate's absence, till he could almost make himself believe she really would be back. Easy to keep drinking until his mind melted into a soft blur, but he couldn't let Rick down. Several times he thought he heard the clack of the metal letterbox – Rick never rang the bell – but when it came Fran got there before he did.

'Hi, Rick,' she was saying as though she said it all the time, 'Good game?'

'Yeah,' Rick muttered vaguely, catching Richard's eye. His eyes looked heavy, dark-ringed, and Richard thought he was thinner.

'Hi, Ricks,' Richard said, stepping forward to hug him. He nodded amicably to Robbie's father, who was standing outside the front door. As his arms came round his son, he felt the boy stiffen till all his bones seemed to stand out. He let go and saw Rick looking at him, the question unspoken.

While Fran dealt with Robbie's father – she was so capable, his sister – he said quietly to Rick, 'I haven't been able to scatter the ashes yet. I thought that was going to be the right place, but it wasn't.'

'So is it… Are they…? I don't like having that box here.'

Of everything that Rick might have said... The unexpected hurt struck him right in the chest. *That box:* the words felt brutal, sharp-edged as the box itself.

'That's OK.' Richard swallowed and tried to sound reassuring, even though the burning ache had almost made him double over. 'The box won't be here for long. Mum needs to have somewhere she can be happy, then we can feel better about it too.'

Rick nodded. He wriggled out of Richard's arms and headed towards the kitchen. How do you ever talk properly about these things? Richard wondered. It felt beyond him. He lifted his case, which he'd left in the hall, and carried it in his arms up the stairs into his and Kate's bedroom. Before Fran came this time he'd been sleeping in the spare room, sliding into the small bed between piles of books and boxes and Rick's old toys. Until this weekend she'd gallantly made do with the sofa, but now he was giving her the spare room. Tonight he'd be sleeping with Kate's half of the bed empty beside him. He hadn't even changed the sheets.

As he opened the bedroom door he had a strong impression of purple, Kate's favourite colour: the bedclothes, the curtains, scarves draped over the dressing-table mirror among the necklaces. The bed was as they'd left it when he took Kate to hospital, the duvet pushed back, showing its deep red underside, the sheet rumpled by both their bodies. Waking early, they'd liked to make love in the morning. That morning, though, she'd woken screaming with pain.

He rested the case on top of the duvet and lay on his front beside it, breathing in the faint smells of both of them that still remained: Kate's perfume, her hair on the pillow, her sweat and femaleness, his maleness, the warm scents of sex and humanity. He hadn't cried much before, but the lump of loss that had been growing inside him rose up till he thought he was going to vomit. He caught hold of the pillow, shaken by dry, jerky sobs that didn't soften into tears.

Fran called up to him, 'Richard! Supper's ready.' Then Rick, pushing his voice as hard as he could: 'Dad! Dad!'

Panting, he levered himself up into a sitting position and rubbed his hands over his face. It had felt unbearable, like wanting to be sick and dreading it at the same time. As he stood up he rested his hand on the corner of the case where the box was. Touching it felt like reaching for Kate again.

Jo

'After great pain a formal feeling comes, Jo wrote at the top of the page. *The nerves sit ceremonious as tombs.'* Emily Dickinson knew what it was like. Then she started, writing fast as if talking, but placing the words carefully on the lines. She soon stopped. Writing felt too distant; she needed to talk to Jans. You shouldn't have died, she said to Jans in her head. It should have been me: that's the first thing I thought when I heard. You never wanted to hear about the voices, did you? The voice, the worst one, said, *Why didn't you die? You shouldn't be alive.* I didn't tell anyone, she said to Jans. The doctors tried to medicate the voices away but it didn't work. Maybe it was *his* voice – the man's. People talked about forgetting things that are too bad to keep in your mind, but she'd always known there was something. This wasn't that kind of forgetting. It was more that all her memories had gone far away so that nothing could really touch her. The medication did that and it was meant to help. But she knew it was all hiding here inside her. It had been hiding inside Jans too.

You didn't want to die and I did, she said to Jans in their secret voice. Jans had known when she'd tried, just as she'd known when Jans wasn't there any more. That morning she'd picked up the bead bracelet Jans had given her, the same as the one she'd given to Jans, and the thought had come, very still and clear: you'll never give me anything again. It was 11.30, just about the time Jans died. Early that morning she'd woken up feeling sick, with a terrible headache right inside her head. It only lasted a couple of minutes but Jans had been with her, so real she felt she could touch her.

Afterwards, in the drop-in, some of the women had said they were sorry and hugged her as if they cared. 'You've lost your sister,' they kept saying, not understanding what it was like to be a twin. Then they started talking about their own losses – husbands leaving, children being taken away, their pain so big they had hardly any space for anyone else's. They'd asked questions, though; people always wanted to know what happened. Jo had told them as though it had nothing to do with her, her head knowing but her inside not feeling. Later she'd cut her arm to make herself feel it, just a fine cut. She'd watched the tiny red globes creep out like a row of insects and smeared them away: her blood and the pain inside it.

It bothers me, she said to Jans, Richard wanting to see me. Perhaps he wants to think I'm you.

She sat back, chewing the end of her cheap fountain pen. Using a fountain pen made the writing feel more real, and today the ink hadn't leaked over her fingers. It was good to write, a relief that was like cutting except that the feelings bled into the words. Only sometimes the words didn't come, and she couldn't make them. She couldn't remember how many of these journals she'd written, all in the same kind of notebook, but she'd started more than ten years ago. Back then at the day hospital they'd sat in a circle on creaky plastic chairs while Caroline, the occupational therapist, encouraged them to put something, anything, on paper. What agony that first session had been, staring at the turquoise lines on the bright white page, then hearing other people read out their carefully rhymed poems or chunks of naked distress. Being afraid she might sound more literate than the others had made it harder.

When she read out her first piece the following week, mumbling into the paper, Caroline had come over to her afterwards and said with slightly patronising surprise, 'That was really good. You write well.'

She'd wanted to say having a breakdown didn't make you stupid, but instead clenched her fists and chewed her bottom lip. She'd already told Caroline she had an English degree from UCL. English and philosophy, to be exact; there were some things she liked to be exact about. She had a feeling Caroline didn't believe her.

'Why don't you try keeping a journal?' Caroline had persisted. She had an eager, sympathetic face with a lot of teeth. 'It might help you. It's an outlet, at least. You don't have to show it to anyone.' People often said that when they wanted to read what you wrote.

Later on, after the day hospital, Jo had bought the first notebook. It had a shiny black cover, with elastic across the corners to keep it shut. She'd liked the feel of it and that had made it easier to write, especially once she stopped thinking about Caroline. She didn't care what she wrote or how, but some things still shrank from being skewered to the paper.

She untangled herself from the balding armchair where she'd been sitting curled up with her jacket on. The flat was always colder than the weather outside and she didn't put the gas fire on unless she had to. The room wasn't at its worst: perhaps Emmeline, who called herself Jo's ex, wouldn't have a go at her about it. Unopened junk mail, stained with coffee and food, was scattered on the blotched wooden table; several mugs, some with mouldy dregs of coffee, clustered at the base of the armchair; more junk mail and free papers littered the worn carpet; a bag of shopping that she hadn't emptied was propped beside the kitchen door. She hadn't smoked for four weeks now, so at least Emmeline couldn't complain about the ashtrays. She didn't want to think about the kitchen: several days' washing-up shoved into the stained white porcelain sink that had gradually filled with rank-smelling water; more dishes and saucepans on the worktop, the food dried on them; the top of the cooker spattered with old brown grease. Emmeline wouldn't think much of that. If Jo offered her coffee, Emmeline would scrub the mug out first and refill the kettle in case the water was stale.

She just had time to pick up the mugs and kick the bag of shopping into the kitchen without turning the light on. The tiny window over the sink, which looked out over a brick wall, might just as well not have been there. The old plastic draining rack was full up and emptying it felt too hard; the washing-up would have to wait. If Emmeline felt like doing it, she was welcome. Jo was wandering up and down the narrow kitchen, looking for a place to put the mugs, when she heard the squeak of wood against wood as the badly-fitting door was pushed open. Emmeline still had a key. Jo thought of asking her to give it back and immediately felt ungrateful.

'Jo?' Emmeline called. 'Where are you? You OK?'

Jo dumped the mugs on the cooker; one of them tipped over, adding a trail of coffee to the grease. 'In here.' She positioned herself in the kitchen doorway so that Emmeline couldn't get in.

Emmeline moved forward to hug her, engulfing her with her large breasts and unfashionably loose sweatshirt. She was taller than Jo and seemed twice as wide; close to, she had a faint smell of oniony sweat – she didn't believe in deodorants. Her body was always warm; despite wanting to resist, Jo took comfort in it. Emmeline was solid: the fat she carried was firm and resilient, not flabby. From the beginning every bit of her had told Jo that she was to be relied on: she worked as a carer and seemed incapable of being anything else.

Jo could feel Emmeline pulling away from the hug. When she let go, Emmeline stepped back and looked at her sympathetically, head cocked on one side. Under her simple short haircut her round face looked both boyish and maternal. For a moment Jo felt an ache of longing, a sharp spike of desire for Emmeline's mix of male and female.

'I'm so sorry,' Emmeline said. 'How awful. I would have come round before, only—'

'No. I didn't want to see anyone. I told you.' Jo wiped the back of her hand across her face, willing Emmeline to stop.

'It's not good to cut yourself off from people.'

'I went to the charity shop. And the drop-in.'

'That's great.' Emmeline smiled encouragingly; it reminded Jo of the hospital OTs.

'And I saw Damian.' Damian, her community psychiatric nurse, had been quietly matter-of-fact and not suppressed his gentle humour, which made her like him. When he'd grasped her hand with his slim dark-brown one she hadn't minded, even though she didn't think he was supposed to.

Emmeline nodded and sat down in the other armchair. The two chairs, both worn, looked completely unrelated. The landlord had always said he was going to replace them. The older one, which Jo favoured, was square in shape and had once been red. The other one, covered with plastic leather, now torn, in what Jo called shit-brown, was taller and wider: Emmeline said it was more her size.

Jo hovered for a moment, working out how to manage the coffee. Then she dived into the kitchen.

'No coffee for me,' Emmeline called to her. 'I've just had.'

She took her time about coming out again. Emmeline was sprawled back in her chair, looking completely at home. She'd taken off her trainers and put them together beside the chair. Jo had given her the striped socks several Christmases ago and they were wearing thin underfoot. Looking at Emmeline's weighty, ungraceful body now that desire had gone, it felt strange to her that the two of them had been together. After the hospital she'd fled into Emmeline's arms for comfort: a woman was safer than a man. She'd always known when she was attracted to a woman; her feelings about men were harder to grasp.

'I heard from Richard,' she said. 'He wanted to meet.'

Emmeline's open mouth was a caricature of horror. 'So of course you said no.'

'Yeah, I said no,' Jo said flatly. 'I couldn't hack it – yet.'

'Yet?'

'He's not as bad as you think. I left him because...' She had run away – literally – as soon as he started touching her body. Back then she'd thought it was about him. Now she suspected it was about something else, those things that had happened a long time ago.

'He abused you. That's what you said.'

Jo looked down at her hands, picking at the skin on the sides of her thumbs. Her face and neck felt so hot Emmeline would be bound to notice. 'He didn't abuse me,' she muttered into her T-shirt, trying to hide her face. 'I think...' She hadn't meant to say anything.

'Just don't go there if it upsets you,' Emmeline said soothingly. 'Bereavement can knock you off balance, make you think funny things.'

She expected Emmeline to ask if she was taking her medication.

'And you be careful of Richard; you don't know what he wants. He's your sister's husband, he's nothing to do with you.'

Jo had given up trying to explain about them not being separate, about Jans being part of her. People who weren't twins didn't get it. She stared at Emmeline, biting her thumb as a burning wave rose up inside her, making her afraid she was going to be sick.

'Easy now, easy.' Emmeline had come over to her and was stroking her back. 'Just take it easy. You've had a big shock. You couldn't have expected a thing like this to happen.'

Jo shook her head helplessly as the pain contorted her face. She wasn't crying; it was too terrible for that. She bit her thumb harder and clutched at her middle, rocking backwards and forwards as she tried to stop the onrush. *After great pain a formal feeling comes*, she repeated to herself, *the nerves sit ceremonious like tombs.* Perhaps it was better not to feel.

The agony subsided and left her gasping. Emmeline tried to hug her but she pushed away the well-meaning arms.

'I can stay tonight, if you like,' Emmeline said. 'Kirsty won't mind. Maybe you shouldn't be here alone.' Jo wished Kirsty had come too. It would have made Emmeline's solid presence less monolithic, less immovable, but she was tempted to sink back into the safe familiarity. She waited till her breathing had slowed and said, 'It's OK. I'm not going to do anything, if that's what you're worried about.'

'I'm glad to hear it.' Her help rejected, Emmeline had retreated into her professional manner. 'Just ring me if you need to. You know you always can.'

'Thanks.'

'And I wouldn't go contacting Richard, if I were you. You don't want to make trouble for yourself.'

Jo felt too tired and weak to argue.

Richard

He'd given up trying to sleep. It had been the same every morning since he'd been home – more than a week now: barely a quarter to six. The thin early light, filtering through the curtains, flattened colours and reduced the furniture to murky shapes. He tried to keep to his side of the bed, but when he woke during the night he found he'd flung his arm across the space where Kate would have been. As he sat up he noticed two dark oblongs on her bedside cabinet – the photos she'd always kept there. He knew them so well he rarely looked at them: him and Kate in the garden here, with Rick sitting uncertainly astride his first tricycle, and Kate and Jo aged about twelve, standing with their arms round one another under the apple tree in the garden in north Oxford. They were so alike then he'd had to study the picture before he could make out which was which. The only difference between them was the faint upcurling smile that he recognised as Kate's, beside Jo's more serious look.

He shook off the duvet and crept downstairs to make coffee. Rick wouldn't be up yet and Fran wouldn't wake till her alarm went off. Even treading sideways, he hit the one creaking step and had to stop himself grunting in annoyance. By the time he was at the bottom, Rick was padding behind him.

'Dad,' he whispered. 'Dad, are you all right?'

Richard turned. Children could take care of their parents with heartbreaking skill; he didn't want Rick to have to do that. Rick was rubbing his hair, which was sticking up, his pyjamas still crumpled from bed.

'Did I wake you?'

Rick shook his head. 'I had a dream about Mum coming back. She could only stay till two o'clock then she had to go away again.'

'I have dreams like that. Maybe she does come back.'

'Do you think so?' Rick asked seriously.

'I don't know. At least she knows we won't forget her.'

'Yes.' Rick paused as though about to say something weighty. 'Dad...'

'What, son?'

'Tell you later. Can I have breakfast now, before Fran does that thing with the milk?'

Richard didn't ask what he meant but moved towards the kitchen. 'It's a bit early; you might want more breakfast later on.'

'That's OK.' It was only when Rick grinned that the nickname suited him. Otherwise he seemed too solemn for it. Like his father and grandfather before him, Richard had passed his name on to his son. His father was Dickie; he had briefly been Richie; he and Kate had wanted to call Rick Dickon because they both liked *The Secret Garden*, until they realised other children might tease him. Kate had told Richard how she and Jo had shared the book in their own secret garden behind the apple tree. She'd shown the garden to him once, years ago, but by then it was overgrown with bindweed and nettles.

The gentle staccato of Fran's alarm became more insistent. She'd never been good at waking up but had nobly made the effort to join Richard, though he would just as soon have been left on his own. He guided Rick into the kitchen and sank gratefully into the familiar routine of getting breakfast with him: orange juice without bits, Coco Pops, milk poured on at the last minute so that the cereal didn't go soggy. Rick was a careful eater. Richard and Kate had taken turns with his breakfast, depending on which of them was working at home that day. Rick could have got his own but both of them had valued the time with him.

While Rick ate, Richard made coffee. In the quiet he noticed the scrape of the spoon in the bowl and the soft lapping and slurping noises. Often they didn't talk much but this morning their silence had an expectant quality, as though Kate would appear in a minute. Hearing the shuffle of Fran's fleecy mules, Richard turned his head sharply.

'Fran!' He tried not to sound accusing. The shock of seeing she wasn't Kate had left his whole body tingling, even though he'd known it would be her.

'Hi,' she grinned sleepily. 'Hi, Rick. You're up early.' Rick nodded, his spoon on its way to his mouth. 'Any tea?'

'Tea? Oh, sorry. I forgot you don't have coffee.' He'd filled the bigger cafetière, the one he and Kate had used when they were both there for breakfast.

Fran smiled understandingly. 'That's OK. Don't worry about me.' She retied her shaggy pink dressing gown over her pyjamas and rooted about in the bread bin. 'Shall I make you some toast?'

Don't fuss over me, Richard suddenly wanted to shout, but Rick became animated. 'Can I have toast? That bread you brought?'

'Of course, love.'

'Thanks, Fran,' Richard said. And don't call him love. He's your nephew, not your son. His sister had often irritated him but never as much as now. He knew it wasn't fair, but he couldn't stop himself resenting her for not being Kate.

Fran turned on the radio. The brisk voices of the *Today* programme injected the day with busyness.

'Do we have to have that?' Rick said, saving Richard the trouble. 'I want music.' He jumped up to get a CD from the pile on top of the cookery books.

Richard didn't know what the music was. The relentless beat felt like an intrusion but he said nothing. If Rick needed music to get him through the day, he must have it. Once the beat started up it left less room for thought. He didn't recognise the first couple of tracks, but with the third one, faster and more frenetic, for an instant he saw Kate and Rick dancing round the kitchen. She used to do that sometimes, needing exuberance after a day's meticulous work, sweeping Rick up with her and sometimes Richard too. Out of the corner of his eye he noticed Rick bite his lip and get up, ready to run out. He took hold of him by the shoulders, signalling to Fran to turn off the music. She accidentally turned it up as she went to get the toast.

Richard flapped his hand furiously in the air. 'Turn it *off*,' he mouthed. He stared as Fran rushed over to the CD player, gingerly holding the edges of a piece of hot toast.

'Oh God, that's better.' He held Rick firmly until he felt the boy's body begin to relax into quiet, heaving sobs. He was just about able to cope with his own grief, but his inability to stop his son's pain nearly brought him to the floor. He felt his throat ache and stiffen and hot slow tears fill his eyes. 'It's OK,' he said to Rick. 'It's better to cry about it.' That was what people said, at least. He didn't know why he found it so hard himself.

Rick's sobs eased slowly and Richard saw Fran watching the two of them with a frown of sadness and sympathy. She'd been fond of Kate, different though the two women were. She cares, Fran does, he thought, warming to her again. If anyone had to be there, he was glad it was her. As he released his hold on Rick she moved close and put an arm round each of them, her dressing gown coming apart again, her glasses slipping down her nose.

'You're not going yet, are you?' Rick said. Richard had hoped she'd be leaving that day.

'Well, I do have to get back to work. I could stay another day, though.' She looked up questioningly at Richard and he nodded.

After Rick had gone to school, Richard sat in front of the computer in the glorified shed that he and Kate had used as an office when the weather wasn't too cold. He had to finish a complicated website for a country house hotel and was already behind with it. The websites were a sideline: bespoke computer networks for companies were what interested him and earned the money. Except that right now they didn't interest him at all. Staring at the screen, waiting for the work to absorb him, he was aware of the space behind him where Kate's drawing desk was, the tilted surface still supporting a pencil sketch for a new fabric design. His body felt for the presence of hers, as it always had in the silence when they worked there together. For a moment he was sure she was there; he could feel her with his back, hear the way she sighed as her concentration settled. He swivelled his chair round to look. On the dusty floor, beside the smaller table that held her paints, lay her Chinese slippers, one with the grubby cotton sole turned upward, the other balanced on its side. She must have kicked them off and put on her shoes to walk across the wet lawn. In the first moment after he came back from the hospital he'd seen those shoes in the hall, plain black leather with grass still on them, and the thought had come: she'll never wear them again. It seemed as unreal now as it had then.

He knelt down by the slippers and stroked them gently with his forefinger. Like the scarf in the living room, they were not to be moved. The cotton uppers were creased as though her feet were still shaping them and in the sun the fabric felt warm and living. For a moment a spasm in his chest took his breath away and he waited for it to subside. Breathing again, he moved back to the desk. Through the window he could see the grass needed cutting; summer already and it was growing fast. He didn't feel moved to do it.

As he started to work Jo's face came to him, almost Kate's but unmistakably not. The need to see her hadn't gone away. She'd texted back to him: Not now. What do you want?

What did he want? The little gestures that would remind him of Kate. The way she pushed back her hair or, thinking, caught the tip of her thumb between her teeth. Had it not been for Jo's terror when he began touching her, he might still have been with her. He wouldn't have left her because of that, but she'd taken herself away and refused to answer his calls, as though he no longer existed for her. The first time Kate answered instead he'd thought it was Jo – their voices were so alike, except that Kate didn't mumble the way Jo did. Before long he'd started ringing for Kate, trying not to think about Jo in her cold, untidy room at the top of the under-furnished house. But she'd always been there, a quiet and sombre presence in their lives. Once, years later, when she was going through her worst time, she'd been convinced Richard was going to attack her, and had told him so. Kate had simply reminded her she didn't have to believe the voices, and later Jo had sent him a postcard frantic with apologies for what she called her 'horribleness.'

He picked up his phone and looked for her number. Before he'd thought about it he'd tapped the screen and put the phone to his ear. Straight away the standard message came back: 'The person you are calling is not available. Please leave a message after the tone.' It didn't surprise him that she didn't pick up: she didn't choose to be in touch with many people. If he asked to see her, would it upset her uncertain balance? She'd know he'd called and might feel he was persecuting her. Yet to leave the call hanging, unexplained, would disturb her too. He left a short, noncommittal message and cut it off almost before he'd finished.

He thought a postcard might be better: she'd always collected them. The one she'd sent him apologising for her madness had been Whistler's gloomy study of his mother. He'd tried not to read anything into it, but knowing her mother he couldn't help making the connection. Leafing through the pile of cards he kept in a desk drawer to send to clients, he rejected Mark Rothko's dark reds as too depressing and an Indian miniature of a god and goddess as too erotic. He held up several to see if they would do and decided on Vermeer's Little Street in Delft – the tall redbrick house had once reminded him of north Oxford. Jo had said something about Proust which seemed to mean she liked it.

'Thanks for your message,' he wrote in his backward-sloping lefthanded writing. 'Take your time. No hurry to meet, early days yet.' He realised he didn't mean it; he needed to see her. 'Hope you're OK,' he wanted to add, 'and not alone too much,' but he knew how sensitive she was to being patronised. He ended: 'Take care' – which might sound patronising in itself – and left the card beside the computer keyboard; posting it would give him an excuse for going out later.

He forced himself to turn back to the website, praying that for a short while at least work might help him believe everything was normal.

Jo

The pain had found her in the night. It was thick and black like tar, and when it disappeared it left a hollow ache inside her. Dr Greenland never liked her talking about it; he'd take it as sign that her symptoms were worse and want to up her medication. To Jo it wasn't a symptom; it was what she felt. 'How are you in your spirits?' he always asked. 'How is your mood? Any negative thoughts?' Once she'd tried to tell him about Mother: how she never talked about Father or told them where he was. Her coldness when they weren't expecting it. 'We took your history,' he'd said. 'I'm treating your illness now.' At one time she'd believed the illness was separate, nothing to do with her, but whenever she remembered about what had happened it made her feel worse. A black curtain came down and then there was nothing.

She'd always noticed how Dr Greenland never looked at her when she was talking. He'd be busy typing his notes, and then would sit back staring at the wall as though he couldn't bear to have her in the room. He was squat and square, with a face like a bulldog; the dark hairs on his fingers were so distinct she thought she could count them. When he asked about the voices, she'd tell him they were OK and the medication helped. That way he wouldn't raise the dose.

They weren't OK, though. The horrible one had been talking to her again last night: *You should be punished. It was your fault. You deserve to die.* Then the black tar had come, and the hollow feeling as she thought of Jans not being there. Your depression, Dr Greenland called it. Your depression that you're trying get over. Go swimming, do voluntary work, go back to the drop-in. She'd wanted to do art therapy but there were no places left in the group, and anyway Jans had been the artist. Her textiles, the colours and patterns. Maybe that's what kept you sane, she said to Jans. You were lucky.

Jans had so much to offer, everyone said. They'd never said it about Jo. She felt like someone sitting on the pavement with a few coins in a paper cup, waiting for people to put more in. Perhaps that was why Emmeline had wanted to take care of her, but sometimes Emmeline felt like a huge hen squashing her chick. She'd always seemed bigger than Jo, not just in size. Jans was half an hour older, but she wasn't bigger like that. As children they'd taken care of each other. When Jo left Richard it had seemed natural that Jans had ended up with him; she wasn't frightened of him. Jo suspected now that she hadn't really been frightened of him either, but Emmeline had kept telling her it was him so that she could protect her.

She lay down again, staring at the ceiling. Nine o'clock, and she was supposed to be at the charity shop by ten. 'You will have to be reliable,' Estelle had said, blinking at her through heavy mascara. 'This is still a job, even if you don't get paid.' Estelle had stumped about the shop in high heels, twitching the garments straight on the rails and lining up the rows of books. Jo felt a surge of fury towards her and hoped it wasn't the illness. She hadn't told the people in the shop about Jans, though she'd taken a couple of weeks' leave. Nobody saw her there in the back room, except when they came in to get something. If anyone found her crying, she'd just say she was having a bad day. They knew about those. Letting them know Jans had died would feel like exposing burnt flesh to their probing fingers.

She kicked off the duvet and slid out of bed. Pulling back the red brushed nylon curtains, so old they were tearing from their hooks, she heard the prickle of rain against the glass. The room smelt damp from the leaking gutter. Outside the weeping panes of the sash window that didn't open, the wet leaves of the plane tree clung to the top of a slowly-moving bus. They were her trees, that one and the one opposite; their living green made the flat bearable. Behind them the tall Victorian terraced houses stood back from the road, their dark brick frontage hiding the lives of people she never saw.

Another sodding day. Right now Jans's death made it only slightly worse than usual. Breakfast, salvaged from the kitchen, was black instant coffee, her medication and a slice of bread with the mouldy edge torn off. She sat at the table by the tall window, staring out above the greyed net curtain that had been hung halfway up. She'd never known why the living room needed it more than the bedroom. She put the mug down and a long splash of coffee added to the stains scattered across the table's dark varnish. It was now half past nine and she should already have left. Fuck Estelle. She fished a pair of moderately clean pants out of the laundry basket and hunted on the floor for the rest of her clothes.

After a perfunctory wash, a struggle into her clothes and a brief attempt to comb her hair, she heaved her rucksack and denim jacket from the sideboard and stood by the door. This was the hard part. As she pulled the door open, tearing a hole in her sanctuary, the sweetish, musty smell from the hall rose up the stairs. She hesitated and nearly went back inside again, then, screwing up her face against the world, slopped downstairs in her still unlaced Doc Martens, the only shoes she had. The grey cord carpet, split into a grinning mouth on the edge of each step, didn't look too unfriendly.

On the doormat, which was always crooked because no one straightened it, the white shapes of today's post stood out in the dim light. Normally she stepped over it and waited until Eric Gaines, the elderly man in the flat downstairs, left her letters by her door. She took them in but rarely opened them. This morning the post was right by the front door; as she kicked it to one side she saw Richard's writing on what looked like a postcard. Shit. He wasn't going to leave her alone. She crouched down and pulled out the card from under the junk mail. He didn't say much but he still wanted to see her. She turned the card over. The picture didn't mean anything at first, but then she remembered: something to do with north Oxford, Mother's awful house off the Woodstock Road and Richard coming there. To her room. 'I wouldn't go contacting Richard,' Emmeline had said. Jo shoved the card into her jeans pocket and stepped out into rain that had been going on for days.

All the buses came except the one she wanted. It was now nearly ten and she imagined dully what Estelle would say. She was used to people lecturing her about not having done things; Damian did it all the time, in his nice way. It made her cringe like a scolded child but it didn't make her do them. From under the bus shelter, perched on the red plastic seat, she watched the people coming out of the Tube station, knowing she wouldn't recognise anyone. She'd lived there for years – she didn't want to count how many – and never felt she belonged. Bounds Green didn't seem like a real place; it was just somewhere by the North Circular on the way to other unreal places: Arnos Grove, Lower Edmonton, New Barnet.

Near the station were two Middle Eastern supermarkets that never seemed to close. The bright lights from their windows illuminated the boxes of aged vegetables outside. The fatty stench of the butcher's department made the displays of Polish chocolates in front of it unappetising. She looked at the shops without interest, mildly dreading the next time she would have to go in there for supplies of squashy sliced bread, tins of soup and oily, plastic-wrapped cheese. These, with a few apples and the odd bar of chocolate, were mostly what she lived on. The men at the counter called her 'dear' with an ingratiating smile that made her flinch.

When the bus came she hauled herself up the stairs and sat at the front, watching the rain obliterate the view from the windows as the driver stopped and started along the snug terraces near Alexandra Park. In her pocket she felt the edges of the postcard against her body. She pulled it out and read Richard's message again. 'Take your time,' it said. Despite herself she liked that. He'd never set about being kind to her the way Emmeline did; he'd simply shown he liked her, perhaps even cared about her. But liking so easily turned into something else. She'd found it strange that Jans could cope with sex when she couldn't. In their teens Jans had always been out at parties or with transient boyfriends while Jo stayed at home listening to anguished music, biting her nails, sometimes cutting when things got too much.

It was twenty past ten when they got to her stop. Jo hitched on her rucksack, pulled her jacket round her and crossed the road to the charity shop, which stood between a French patisserie and an expensive shoe shop. Muswell Hill was like a town of its own, much more of a place than Bounds Green. Once she would have enjoyed the cafés and bookshops; now they intimidated her. Her charity shop sold clothes that had been worn by well-off people.

Estelle was arranging a cardigan on a dummy in the window. Jo tried to slink past her, hunching her shoulders in anticipation. Estelle stepped back and looked at her with a concern that was more like annoyance. 'I was wondering if you were all right, only with you I'm never quite sure. We've had a lot come in today already and I could do with some help. I don't suppose you could manage to ring us next time you're going to be late?'

Jo rushed past her into the little room, choked by the blistering hurt. The room had no proper door; the hanging strips of plastic slapped her as she fought through them. If it hadn't been for 'with you' she might have managed to say something back, but the fear of being seen to be 'ill' stopped her. People like you, she wanted to say to Estelle, people like you are horrible. Your spiky black eyelashes and dyed black hair and blood-red lipstick that seeps into the lines in your upper lip. You only care about other people who are normal, like your precious fucking daughter. Hot tears were spilling down Jo's cheeks. It was like Mother who didn't care, who'd liked Jans more but even so not really that much. Now Jans was gone. The loneliness struck her with the force of a physical pain. She sat down hard on a black bag of clothes, pressing her hands over her face to stifle the sound that threatened to come out.

As soon as she could bear it, she wiped her hands down her cheeks and went over to the small sink in the corner where people filled the kettle. She splashed her face with cold water and, not bothering to find the towel, wiped it on a T-shirt that didn't smell too much. She wasn't going to come back to the shop. Nobody could make her. She felt in her pocket for Richard's card. The corners were bent over and there was a diagonal crease along the top, but something about the picture – the tall stepped gables, the domestic simplicity of the servants in the courtyard – was calming. It wasn't Oxford; the houses didn't have the shut-in coldness of Mother's house in Polstead Road. Mother's house: it was Mother's and not hers or Jans's, just as the house she lived in now was the landlord's and not hers. And Mother was always Mother: she'd never liked being called 'Mum' or 'Mummy'. The other girls at school thought that was strange, just as they thought it was strange that Jo and Jans never invited them back to tea. 'Desolate' was the word that came now.

Jo pressed the back of her hand against her mouth, catching the skin between her teeth. If she'd had a blade she would have cut. Beyond the curtain she could hear Estelle and a customer comparing notes about their grandsons' bar mitzvahs; it made the shop feel even more alien. 'My daughter,' Estelle was saying, with such love and pride Jo wanted to punch her. Mother had never talked about her or Jans in a voice like that, except Jans after she died.

'I'll just take those through,' Estelle said to the customer. 'Thank you very much for thinking of us.'

Jo jumped up and started rooting through one of the black bags, her back towards the entrance. Two more bags were pushed through the plastic strips. 'How's it going?' Estelle called from outside. 'We could do with some new stock out here.'

Jo said nothing.

'I said, we could do with some more stock.'

Jo picked up a few garments and an imitation cut-glass ashtray that she had priced last time and shuffled backwards through the curtain with them.

'Is that all?' Estelle said scornfully, examining the ashtray. Then she stared at Jo's face and said, 'Are you all right?'

Jo was gazing at the pale wood floor.

'What is it, dear?' Estelle said. She actually sounded kind, which made Jo want to cry again.

'My sister.' The word weighed her mouth down. There was so much she couldn't say.

'Is there something the matter with your sister?'
'She... died.' 'It felt shameful to say so.
'Sorry, what was that? I didn't catch it.'
'She died,' Jo mumbled again.
'Oh, dear God, you never said.' Estelle's eyes widened behind the heavy mascara. 'I am sorry. When somebody has, you know, problems like you've had, well... I never thought something awful might have happened.' She shook her head. 'Your sister, that's terrible. I'm so sorry. I wish you long life.'

Jo had heard Estelle say that to an old man who had lost his wife; it must be something Jewish people said. As if he'd wanted a long life any more than she did.

Estelle brushed her lips past Jo's cheek and patted her shoulder. 'Look, you go home, darling,' she said, just as Jimmy barged through the door with a large box that the driver had unloaded from the van. 'You don't have to worry about the shop.'

Jimmy grinned at them; Jo couldn't make her face move in response. She shoved past him into the back room and picked up her rucksack.

'Bye,' she said to Estelle, with a muttered 'Thank you' that fell onto the doormat. She wasn't sure if she'd be able to go back; Estelle's kindness hurt too much.

Richard

Another Wednesday. He looked back in his diary: twelve weeks since the funeral. He felt as though he'd missed the summer; already July had an autumnal feel. Each time the day came round it felt heavier than other days. He'd never been one for anniversaries, preferring to remember things when he remembered them, but now the same memories returned inexorably with the day: that Wednesday when Kate had woken with such a dreadful headache, barely conscious and screaming with pain.

In the ambulance the paramedics had done what they did with such focused urgency that he'd grasped at once how serious it was. From A & E they'd rushed her straight into the operating theatre. Almost before he could take in what was happening, he'd found himself sitting in the hospital corridor, trying not to picture them opening her skull or siphoning away the leaked blood. The hospital smell of antiseptic became the odour of fear. They'd told him the operation would be risky but he'd refused to think of her not surviving. Of course she'd come through: she had to.

A haze of numbness still hung between him and what had happened next, what the doctors had said all those hours later. Something about having tried their very best and being very sorry; he couldn't remember any more. All he could remember was the sickly feeling he'd had from drinking too much tea, and the way everyone had bustled past him without noticing as he blundered through the swing doors into the ward.

During the hours of waiting he'd tried to distract himself by doing the crossword in a paper someone had left. He hadn't managed a single clue: the machinery of his mind had refused to work. Then the doctors led him into the room. It had come to the point where there was no more distraction: Kate lying there not looking like Kate, her head bandaged, the leads dangling useless from the machinery beside her, her pale face set in its unmoving composure, the coldness of her cheek when he kissed it. He hadn't cried, the shock had been too great. Since then grief had been lodged inside him like an undigested meal.

His first thought at the time had been: what about Rick? He'd been thinking it ever since. It was probably too soon to be going away again after he'd been to Devon, but he'd been offered a big job he hadn't felt able to refuse. He'd only be in London a couple of days, but still it felt like a dereliction. If he was honest, it was also a relief. Whenever he was with Rick, the enormity of their shared loss stood like a massive boulder between them, which stopped them being natural with each other. But Fran was coming and that meant Rick would be just about all right. He seemed easier with her unselfconscious affection.

The weather felt colder than it should have been in July; in the misty grey light the garden still seemed asleep. Getting up early and watching it come alive, being able to glimpse the sunrise behind the rowan tree in the corner as the colours changed from faint pink to glowing orange to dazzling white, had always felt like a blessing. Now it was more like a light show that someone had put on, nothing to do with him. He'd come down to the shed, feeling the dew soak into his canvas shoes, to try to work before Rick got up, but as he sat down at the desk the unimportance of what he was doing overwhelmed him.

He caught sight of Jo's postcard beside the computer. It had obviously taken her a while to get round to posting it and the back was stained with coffee. She'd chosen a Samuel Palmer drawing from the Ashmolean, a luminous woodland scene that Kate had loved too. Knowing Jo he'd expected something bleaker, but it seemed to speak again of their time in Oxford. 'OK,' she'd written, each cramped word swimming in a pool of space. 'If you want to meet I don't mind. Can you come to BG?' He had to work out that BG meant Bounds Green; despite his having written to her there, the name of the place never stayed in his memory. He'd been there once and vaguely remembered a faceless high street full of kebab shops and litter.

He stood the postcard against the handleless blue-and-white mug that held his pens, and tried think of work. Once he started, the day's small worries would begin to fill the dark crater inside him that the early morning had blown open. He tried again but knew he couldn't stay there for now. Better to go back and see to Rick; work wouldn't go away.

At lunchtime he made himself go out for some bits of shopping. He didn't understand why Scottish people called shopping 'messages' but he liked it, the way he liked hearing people say 'pieces' for 'sandwiches.' He'd been going to have lunch with his sort-of-friend John, but John had told him about an hour ago that he couldn't make it. It happened sometimes, especially with people who hadn't really been friends of his but, as couples, joint friends of his and Kate's. Or friends of Kate's. They meant well, but often he and they found each other hard going. John thought it was bad for people to get upset and would have talked to Richard about their supposedly shared interest in IT.

Sometimes he thought the only proper friend he had was Mark, whom he'd known since university. Mark was now a Buddhist monk named Viryavanto – Richard would only call him V. Although he looked strange with his ochre robes and shaved head and eyebrows, V was refreshingly real. He never minded talking about difficult things.

Instead of heading down past the rows of houses to the big Sainsbury's at the bottom, he turned the other way towards the smaller shops. Emerging from his quiet cocoon of house and garden, he was jangled by the random noise of voices and traffic, the fumes of cars and buses revving at the traffic lights, the people striding past him, intent in their own worlds, the blaring colours of the shop signs, the jostle of nationalities, cultures and goods for sale – Japanese, Chinese, Syrian, Tibetan, a butcher's shop, a vegan café, a print shop, a betting shop, an optician. Nothing out of the ordinary – he and Kate had been down here hundreds of times – but today it felt like an affront. What right had they to be there? Then he wondered: had losing her really made him such a curmudgeon?

He walked on to the small Sainsbury's and made straight for what he needed – bread, milk, apples, some ham for his own lunch and fish fingers for Rick's tea. At least the layout of a supermarket this size didn't have the bewildering illogicality of the larger one. Why should shampoo be shelved near ready meals or alcoholic drinks near pet food? He recognised one of the women at the counter and for a cowardly moment thought of using the self-checkout instead. She smiled and nodded to him, showing him she was ready, and he stepped forward, holding out his basket like an offering. Her name badge told him she was called Sheetal. She had a kind face, he realised, her brown skin creased in a concerned frown under dyed black hair with the white roots beginning to show. Kind because she was kind: she didn't know anything about him, so she couldn't have felt obliged to be kind. He smiled at her with appreciation. Outside the shop he stood for a moment wiping his eyes. The noise in the street sounded less harsh.

He'd forgotten Rick was going to Robbie's after school. Robbie's parents, Graham and Sarah, had taken him under their wing and were happy to feed him fish fingers and baked beans, almost the only things he would eat these days. When Rick came in, still in his football gear, Richard was pottering in the kitchen, directionless without his son to focus on. The ordinary domestic things he used to do with Kate felt insurmountably hard; even filling the dishwasher seemed to take more strength than he had.

Knowing Rick would have eaten, Richard had made himself a sandwich from the ham he'd bought and the new loaf of bread – he hadn't got round to eating at lunchtime. Half the sandwich was still there on a plate by the draining board. He put out some biscuits for Rick and poured him a glass of milk, which he downed almost in one. Kate would have given him fruit but Richard had forgotten to buy oranges. Rick wouldn't eat apples or pears.

'Good game?' he asked, knowing Rick would never tell him things until he was ready. He ran his finger across his top lip to show Rick he had a milk moustache.

Rick quickly wiped it off; he hated looking babyish. 'All right.'

Richard thought of all the times he'd said 'All right' to his parents, meaning 'Leave me alone' or 'I don't want to talk.'

'Listen, Ricks,' he said. 'I've got to go to London next week. Just for a couple of days. I'm sorry I have to be away again.'

'Yeah?' Rick shrugged, then stared at Richard. 'It's not... the box?'

'No, no, it's for work. A good job that means I won't have to do so much later on. Maybe it'll pay for a holiday.'

'Spose so.' Rick's face told Richard nothing. 'Will Fran be coming?'

'Yes. Is that OK?' Richard reminded himself to be grateful to her. She'd done her best not to let them down and made no fuss about using up her annual leave.

Rick leaned down and started unlacing his football boots; Richard had forgotten to tell him to leave them in the hall.

'I like Fran. Can you ask her to bring that bread she gets?'

'You're sure you don't mind, son? It's just a one-off thing. I don't know why they need to meet with me, but there you go.'

Rick straightened up, looked directly at his father and said in his most grown-up way, 'It's cool, Dad, you don't have to worry. We can look after ourselves.'

'I'm sure you can.' Richard smiled, more touched than he'd expected. He felt the familiar dry tightness in his chest and coughed to relieve it. Rick grinned back at him, so like Kate in that moment that it was almost a hallucination. Then, just as Richard drew breath to say something, Rick was gone from the kitchen, leaving mud on the floor and an empty glass clouded with milk. The room felt strangely uninhabited as Richard made himself more tea. Only the evening light, filling it with softness, kept him company.

Richard

After his meeting, which lasted all morning, Richard wandered out into Covent Garden market, idly looking round stalls that sold hand-made jewellery, printed scarves and colourful expensive toys. Having eaten a fancy baguette in a café open to the central square, he dawdled to the Tube station, half not wanting to go to Bounds Green. As the train jolted through the stations on the Piccadilly Line he wondered if it might have been kinder simply to leave Jo be. But she wasn't a child; much as he'd wanted her to, he hadn't compelled her to meet him. He sat back uneasily, watching the reflected faces superimposed upon the dark of the tunnel. They all looked ghastly pale, even the Indian man next to him, who accidentally trod on Richard's foot as he stood up and apologised profusely.

Emerging into suburban daylight on a street corner harried by constant traffic, he was struck by the soullessness of the place. Everyone seemed to be in transit, hurrying in the way that London people always seemed to hurry; nobody looked at anybody else, nobody seemed happy. He remembered his own brief time in London, alone and rootless, before he'd met Jo and then Kate in Oxford.

He found the burger bar by the smell of frying and the pictures of meals in the window; their lime greens, golden yellows and cherry reds made the food look completely artificial. Pushing open the glass door he was assaulted by a waft of meat and hot fat, with pine disinfectant from the spotless floor. At first he didn't see anyone who looked like Jo. In a far corner near the counter a woman in a faded denim jacket was bent over the table, writing in a notebook, a glass cup of black coffee beside her. Strands of lank brown hair kept falling forward and she pushed them back without looking up. Her hair was the colour Kate's had been before she'd dyed it blonde. As he came closer, he saw the way the fingertips bulged above the bitten nails and thought he recognised the shape of the head. The curve of the back was familiar too, but he'd forgotten how much thinner Jo was than Kate. It made her seem painfully young.

He stood behind the chair opposite her and said her name softly, so as not to startle her. She didn't raise her head, though he thought she'd heard him.

'Jo,' he said again, almost cajoling.

This time she looked up. She stared at him as though she didn't know who he was.

'Can I get you a coffee?' The one beside her had gone cold; a disc of scum floated on the dark brown liquid. 'Black?'

She nodded, still staring, and her face softened into a faint bewildered smile. He'd seen Kate smile like that sometimes when he'd caught her unawares.

While he waited for the coffees, he saw her pull the notebook towards her. The black cover was bent and looked well-used. She thrust it into her rucksack, which she then stuffed under the table, and stared at him again, her chin resting on her hand. She must think he couldn't see her; he knew he shouldn't be looking.

He sat down on the bright green plastic chair opposite hers and realised she still hadn't said anything. 'I hope this is all right,' he said, feeling clumsy. 'I thought it would be good to meet. You know...'

She looked away. 'I don't know. Emmeline told me I shouldn't see you.'

He had no idea who Emmeline was. 'But you came. You're here.'

He reached out his hand, but before they could touch she pulled hers away as though it might burn her. 'Sorry,' he said, 'I shouldn't have done that.'

'It's OK. Anyway, it's not really me you want to see. It's only because I'm like Jans.'

It jarred him that she'd called Kate Jans, going back to the time before her sister had changed her name. Jans sounded so awkward and Jancis was just as bad, which was why she'd chosen Kate. 'It's not only that,' he said. 'I wanted to see you.'

'Why would you want to see me?' Again the questioning look, quickly put away. She started biting a nail.

'We used to be friends. You know, in Oxford. We used to talk.' If only he hadn't tried to do more than talk.

'I hated Oxford. That house.'

'It was a bit bleak, but it could have been wonderful. Those great big rooms, the beautiful Victorian plasterwork. The ceiling roses were amazing.' The deep cream paint must have been at least thirty years old, even back then, and the furniture had seemed to be family discards, unloved and randomly placed, but the house had had an unmistakable grandeur. 'It's a pity your mother was so…'

Jo shrugged; for a moment he saw naked pain in her eyes. 'She still is. She does things in the WI and tells people how to bring up their children. As if she knew.'

Once more he wanted to reach out to her, but this time he stopped himself. Although Kate had apparently been the favourite, she had been just as touchy about their mother. He found it hard to understand how any mother could be like that and had always put it down to class. His mother had been a shopkeeper's daughter. She had been incurably fussy and intrusive but he had always known she cared.

'Must have been twenty years ago,' Richard said, 'when I met you on that coach.' She'd seemed so shy that he'd been surprised she talked to him. 'Strange how these things happen.'

'You mean it's strange how you met Jans,' she said, chewing her bottom lip then biting viciously at her thumbnail. The old name again. He didn't say anything.

'And you,' he said. 'Back in Oxford, when I was doing that Master's at Brookes and people like your mother still looked down on the place because it used to be the Poly.'

She shrugged again as if to say, So what was the big deal, meeting me?

'It is good to see you, Jo,' he said, reaching out for her hand again before he could stop himself. He felt hers stiffen as his fingertips touched it.

'Is it?' She gave him a sideways look.

He'd known it wouldn't be easy but hadn't expected it to be as hard as this. 'I thought you might want to talk about her too.'

She winced and he felt clumsy again. 'You don't know what it's like, being twins.'

'No.' He couldn't say: and you don't know what it's like, being married. He thought of the photo of the two sisters by the apple tree, how wrapped up in each other they seemed.

'Listen, Jo. There's something I... I just wondered if... Would you like another coffee?' He couldn't manage it without more caffeine.

She nodded and gulped the remains of hers. As he got up she sat with her chin propped in her hands, staring at the plate glass door.

For a while they drank their coffee as if that were their sole reason for being there. Then Richard said, 'You know after the... after the funeral—'

Jo looked distressed. 'I couldn't go, I thought you understood that.' She took a swallow of coffee as though it were medicine. 'It wasn't like I didn't want to. Jans understood, I know she did.'

'And so did I, even if your mother—'

The bleak look on her face wrung his heart. Her hands, which could have been Kate's apart from the bitten nails, clenched into fists on the table.

'I didn't mean you should have. What happens is that – afterwards – they give you the person's ashes and, well...'

'So you've got them? You've got my sister there? That's horrible.'

Richard had stopped feeling there was anything horrible about it, but suddenly he saw the box again as he'd seen it in that first appalled moment.

'I'm sorry, Jo. I know this is difficult. What I wanted to ask you was – I mean, I don't know how to find the right place. I thought maybe in Devon, by a river somewhere?'

She looked blank, then troubled.

'I went to the estuary near Teignmouth but that wasn't right. The trains...'

For a moment Jo almost smiled. 'No, she never liked hearing trains. Even in Port Meadow.'

'There are places she and I went to, but none of them seem like where she needs to be. There must be places that you know. I'd really like it to be somewhere you felt was right for her.'

'We used to go to Devon on holiday,' Jo said. 'We had an aunt and uncle there. We went to different bits. There are lots of rivers.'

She seemed at a loss, Richard thought, but then they both were. It was loss that had brought them together. 'So perhaps if you think of anywhere...'

'I don't know,' Jo said, shaking her head.

'And, if you wanted to, I'd like you to be there when I... we... Only if you wanted to.'

'I don't know...' she said again and bit a nail, but meditatively this time.

He watched her fish under the table for her rucksack, then stand up, feel inside it and swing it onto her back. She seemed to have left him already.

'It wasn't you,' she said out of nowhere, turning towards him and giving him another intense look. 'You didn't do anything bad to me.' She turned her head to the side, leaving him no chance to say anything. 'Goodbye.'

'Bye, Jo. We'll keep in touch. You can always text me. And let me know if you think of anywhere.' She looked so alone and so unhappy that he would have liked to give her a hug. But even as he thought it he felt her withdraw. 'It's been good to see you,' he said.

She strode out of the burger bar, not looking back at him. It was Kate's stride.

Once the glass door had shut behind her he sat down again, elbows on the table, fists pressed into his cheeks, gazing blankly at the lighted display above the counter. The place was almost empty. The thin, black-bearded man who had served them pulled down his Afghan hat and leaned his forearms on the counter. Whistling through his teeth, he stared hopefully at the door. He seemed to be another loner.

Richard didn't know who he felt most sad for: Kate, Jo or himself.

Jo

Once outside the door, Jo took Richard's postcard out of her bag. The corners were bent right over, which made it seem more friendly. It felt good to hold on to something of him, even though she'd pulled away from his hand. He'd been nice to her just now – nicer than she'd expected. He hadn't patronised but she knew he'd been careful of her. And she'd let him know it wasn't him. *You're stupid*, the voice said, the worst one, right behind her left shoulder. *You'll be punished for that*. A man, contemptuous yet seductive. It didn't say anything more but she heard it laughing faintly, the way it always did when it wanted her to know how bad she was.

The rain was starting again, fat splotches that hit the pavement hard and soon merged into a general wetness, giving the street a fresh, almost muddy smell. Like all her previous ones, Jo's latest umbrella had been left on a bus. She couldn't face the journey to the Lost Property Office, or the interrogation by a clerk who would be fed up with her for losing it – just like Mother. The rain soaked into her hair and her jeans felt damp over her thighs.

She hadn't told Emmeline about seeing Richard; she'd realised in time that she didn't have to. Emmeline wasn't her partner or her care worker and didn't always know best, especially if it had anything to do with men. Jo felt guilty for being disloyal, but despite the voice she strode forward with something like confidence, watching the round toes of her Doc Martens, scuffed white and never polished, land firmly on the pavement.

She'd been to have coffee with someone like a normal person. Not just someone – Richard. And she'd said things – things she hadn't been going to say. As she brushed her hair back she realised her hand was shaking. She wished she had a cigarette, even though she'd told Damian she was giving up. Unhooking her rucksack, she ferreted in it for some gum and chewed hard as she walked along.

She hadn't felt normal enough to meet Richard in a proper café. Muswell Hill would have been more his sort of place, but there she might have bumped into Estelle or one of the people from the shop. Tomorrow she could tell them she'd had coffee with her brother-in-law, as though that was the sort of thing she often did – but then again perhaps she'd hug it to herself and not say anything. He'd talked about his Kate, after all (she wasn't sorry for having called her Jans), and about Oxford – pieces of her life which were nothing to do with them.

She was usually late for things but she was glad she'd managed to get there before him. Writing in her journal she'd felt safe; as she walked along now she groped behind her to make sure it was still in her rucksack. Unlike Emmeline and the OTs, Richard hadn't asked what she was writing, or thought writing meant there was something wrong with her.

He looked older, she thought. Older and worn down. Behind his glasses she'd seen the grey rings under his eyes. His fine dark hair, which always used to flop down into his eyes, now lay across his scalp in thin streaks. Unlike her he'd got fatter, which made him look kinder as well as older. For some reason she didn't feel small with him the way she did with Emmeline. *You think he likes you*, the voice said mockingly, *What use are you to him? To anyone?* Then the laugh again.

'Shut up,' she nearly shouted, but knew better than to do it in the street. She folded her lips together and bit the top one hard. 'Leave me alone,' she screamed in her head, and started counting the footsteps as she walked faster towards the house. Seventy-seven, seventy-eight. *You're useless. Admit it now, you're a waste of space. You ought to die.* Eighty-one, eighty-two, eighty-three. *What good are you to anyone? Look, there's a bus. Just throw yourself in front of it.* Shaking her head vigorously against its persuasion, she strode up to the house.

Eric Gaines must have heard her open the door. He came out and smiled at her. Half his teeth were missing and the rest were cracked and yellow. He'd once told her proudly that he hadn't been to a dentist for twenty years. He was bald at the front but his iron-grey hair fell to his shoulders in lank strands. He was wearing an orange sweatshirt with IT'S ALL IN THE MIND printed on it. He'd never said he'd had mental health problems but Jo could tell he had; he reminded her of some of the people she'd met in hospital. From his room came an overpowering stench of smoke and unwashed body.

'Hello,' he said. 'I left your post upstairs, by the door. Had a good day?'

He was poised for a chat but she nodded and ducked her head, loping up the stairs two at a time. Once inside the flat, she pulled the door shut and stayed squatting against it. She was still holding Richard's card; she'd stared at it so much that the image meant almost nothing now. Oxford, her and Jans in the house, Proust – hard to believe she'd once read Proust; Richard, when he was still a friend.

Until now she hadn't let herself remember what Richard had said: Jans's ashes. Jans couldn't be ashes. She was still a person, still part of her, Jo. She pictured the ashes in some sort of classical urn that made Jans seem terribly old and far away, as though she'd died decades before. She couldn't believe Richard had asked her where Jans should be scattered – she was used to people not taking her opinions seriously – but he'd sort of understood. He wanted her to help him get it right, for her sake as well as Jans's; he knew it mattered to her. He wanted something from her, she wasn't sure what.

It would have to be by a river, maybe an estuary or maybe farther upstream. Open sea wouldn't be sheltered enough. There were so many places and just now they were all a blur: her and Jans running together along river banks, splashing about in green water, watching boats glide by and waving to the people in them. The memories were tiny, distant as if seen through the wrong end of a telescope. It was hard most of the time to believe she'd ever been that happy. There had been no voices then, and for a long time, until the tortured teenage years, she'd almost forgotten the rest.

You won't get away, the voice said. *You'll never escape.* Then hands flashed into her mind, so vividly that for a moment she thought they were there in front of her. Enormous hands, white and bony with flat freckled wrists, covered in ginger hair that looked wiry, like a brush. She saw blue shirt cuffs, unbuttoned, and a big silver watch. It was just the hands, there in the air above her. All her nerves stood on end as she felt them touching her, creeping across her body. She braced herself against the door and sucked in a scream, her palm close over her mouth.

She couldn't move from the doormat until the shaking had stopped. Then she ran into the bedroom and curled up under the duvet, still with her boots on, her heart pounding with more fear than she'd thought she had in her.

Richard

He heard the football slam into his father's favourite apple tree and saw Rick scoop it up, ready to kick it again. Hands in his pockets, trying not to lose his temper, he went out into the garden. 'Mind the tree,' he said. 'Grandad takes care of it. Trees can get hurt, you know.'

Rick shrugged, lifted the ball, waited a moment and then lobbed it towards him. Richard pulled his hands from his pockets and caught it in a neat save. He'd been a passable goalie, even played for his university once.

'Well done, Dad.' Rick grinned at him. Richard tossed the ball back, quickly losing interest. He'd been coming out to talk to Rick, or at least try. He felt he ought to, and here at his father's house he was less weighed down by their habitual life.

As Richard drew breath, not sure how to begin, Rick said, 'Dad, why did we have to come here? I don't like the country. There's only cows and things. How boring is that?'

'You used to like coming here.'

'You mean when Granny was alive.'

Richard nodded and bit his lip. He didn't want to think about his mother's death. 'And since then.'

Rick said nothing but threw the ball as hard as he could towards him. Instinctively he leaned back and caught it close to his chest.

'Nice one,' Rick said.

Richard shrugged. 'Perhaps we could go for a walk? You know, along by the river.'

'You're always going on about the Fells. I don't see what's so special about a lot of hills. Why doesn't Grandad come too?'

'He's got things to do. Just us?'

Rick wriggled. 'Can't we go into Appleby? There are shops there.'

'We'll go there another day, for tea. With Grandad.'

They strolled to the back gate and then along the lane that led towards the river. The hills stood huge above them, covered with scrubby grass. Richard felt the familiar exhilaration at their size and uncompromisingness.

Rick had stopped beside the hedgerow. 'Dad, what are these white flowers? They smell funny.'

'Cow parsley.'

'Cows don't eat *parsley.*' Rick was scornfully superior, the way children are.

'No. That's just what it's called. Didn't Mum ever tell you?' Perhaps they weren't cow parsley, now he thought about it, but hogweed.

'Oh dad, you never know when I'm joking.'

'Sorry, son. Sense of humour failure.' Laughing no longer came naturally to him.

Rick was scuffing the gravel on the path with his toe.

Richard walked on. 'Do you want to talk about things a bit, so that, you know, they aren't all shut up inside?' He wished he could follow his own suggestion.

'Like in a box, you mean?'

The shiny black box seemed to hang in the air between them.

Rick looked paler, his face contracted. 'It feels too bad to talk about,' he said. 'I don't want it to make me feel that bad.' Rick put a hand over his stomach and Richard was afraid he was going to be sick.

'We don't have to talk,' Richard said. It was a relief: too soon to try and not the right way. He felt horribly clumsy. He put his arm round Rick's shoulders and felt them hunch as if to push him away. Then Rick relaxed and hugged him fiercely. There was nothing more to say.

They walked on across the fields with the hills behind them, Rick sneezing at the cow-parsley or hogweed. When they came to the river he said, 'Dad, you know you said you were going to put the... Mum's... in a river. Well, why not this one? It's sort of peaceful here, and you like it.'

'I like it, son, but it's not right for her. She wouldn't belong here. I've asked Jo if she can help me find somewhere in Devon. That's where they used to go on holidays, where we used to go.'

'Jo? You mean Mum's mad sister?' Rick made a clownish face that was supposed to be mad.

'She's your aunt, Rick, and she's not mad. Maybe she'll come up to see us later on.'

'Oh, does she have to? She's miserable and she smells of smoke, and she didn't play with me. I'd much rather Fran came.' Rick had met Jo only once, when he was much younger and she was only just out of hospital.

'Fran will still come. You know that.'

"Race you down to the river,' Rick said, and beat him easily. Still panting, Richard helped him look for stones, which they flung into the water, making noisy splashes. He had to admit it felt better than talking.

The cottage was dark and smelt of dog and fried bacon – his father didn't believe in opening windows. He could see Rick was disappointed by the special tea they'd been promised: the chocolate cake was pale and dry and the scones had too much baking powder, which left their teeth feeling fuzzy. They had to be careful not to drop crumbs on the green Dralon chairs. Perhaps it was time to take his son home.

While Richard was still drinking his tea, Rick hitched himself up onto the thick stone windowsill. Richard recognised the patchwork cushion as one his mother had made. He had one too; Kate hadn't been keen on it and it had been relegated to a kitchen chair. He thought now of all the careful, loving work that had gone into it.

'Grandad,' Rick said.

Richard's father grunted, one of his all-purpose grunts that Richard found hard to read. He was watering the plants on the other window-sill, his mauvish fingers stiff but gentle as he fingered the earth in the pots. Richard remembered how his father had often seemed kinder to things than people.

'Grandad, why did you move here? Was it because of Granny?'

'No, it was me wanted to come here. She would have been happy staying in York. But there you go.'

'But isn't it boring?

The old man turned round to Rick, watering can in hand, and smiled. His face moved slowly these days, the skin creased into thick folds. 'Not to me. Mind you, I think Joan – your granny – got bored with it sometimes. That was when she still knew where she was, of course.'

Richard didn't want to hear any more. His father was explaining to Rick how his granny had gone into a care home. Richard remembered that before she went there, she'd thought Rick was her son and then said she didn't know who he was, which had upset him. In the end it had been a relief that she'd died. Nobody said it was a tragedy, though they used the word often enough about Kate. His mother had done her conscientious best, caring for husband and children, needing to be needed. There had been a gentleness about her which Fran seemed to have inherited. He felt quietly sad for her.

'Don't you get lonely?' Rick asked.

'Well, it's never the same, being on your own after all that time. More than fifty year, we were married. But you sort of get used to it. Funny we should end up in the same boat, your dad and me, but that's life. You get on with it and you don't make a fuss.'

Richard might just as well not have been there. Unnoticed by either of them, he took down the dog's lead from the back door. Wilkie, the old labrador, waddled up to him, tail wagging, tongue lolling. Clipping on the lead, Richard quietly shut the door behind him. He couldn't bear any more of the conversation.

He walked Wilkie across the fields until the dog, fat and bow-legged, began to tire, then let him plod his way back again at his own pace. Pushing open the cottage's heavy wooden door, he let Wilkie run in ahead of him. The dog was still panting and Richard caught the fishy smell of his breath. Rick jumped down from the window-sill and knelt on the shaggy rug to cuddle

Wilkie, not minding the smell or the fact that one of the dog's eyes was clouded over.

'All right?' his father said, and went off to make more tea.

Richard's phone buzzed faintly in his pocket. He took it out and looked at it.

'Jo,' he said vaguely, into the air.

His father came out of the kitchen with two mugs of tea. 'What's that?' he said, pointing at Richard's phone. 'I don't like all these messages. Why can't people talk to each other if they need to? Who did you say it was from?'

'Jo.'

'What, that funny sister-in-law of yours?' He tapped his forehead and winked at Rick.

'My sister-in-law, yes.'

'You don't want to go messing with her; you've got enough to cope with without that.'

Richard clutched the phone in his pocket and stared at his father.

'Well, is she all right? You know, not doing anything daft?'

Richard said neutrally, clenching his hand tighter round the phone, 'I'd better ring her. Talk to her, like you said... So what you been up to, Ricks?'

Rick muttered something about Grandad making chips. Then he said, 'You won't ask Jo to come and see us, will you?'

'I don't think she'd come.' Richard was sure of that.

Upstairs in the spare room, Richard stepped over Rick's inflatable mattress with its earthquake of duvet and toys. Perched on the edge of the bed he read Jo's text again:

It wasn't you. There were hands that did things. I saw them. Can I speak to you?

He took a deep breath. It was easy to think Jo was losing the plot, but he wasn't sure. He knew that, unlike Jo, Kate had seemed to enjoy sex – but often in a slightly frantic, desperate way, as though it was something she needed to get to the end of. 'Calm down,' he'd sometimes said to her, 'Just relax a bit.' There

56

had been times when, as they started to make love, her body had stiffened and she too had pushed him away. She hadn't known why any more than he had, but it had reminded him momentarily of the way Jo had shrunk from being touched. Must be a family trait, he'd thought, something to do with their mother. He'd believed then that that was all it was.

He hesitated with his thumb over the button, feeling out of his depth. He remembered Jo bending over that notebook of hers, how she'd avoided shaking his hand. What did you say to someone who might have been sexually abused, or thought they might have been, even if it was just a delusion? *Sexually abused.* Until now the phrase had meant to him creepy paedophiles molesting someone's children – he prayed never his. Could it be here now, in his family? Unthinkable, but he was thinking it. The hands, Jo had said. Did that imply it wasn't only her but Kate as well? No, he couldn't read so much into it. Brave, capable, driven Kate – she'd been all right. As for poor Jo, did that explain why she'd become 'poor Jo'? Despite her obvious suffering she wasn't just a poor creature, he could see that. Glimmers of her spirit showed through.

She answered almost at once, as if she'd been waiting for his call.

'Jo?'

'I didn't think you'd ring. Not, like, straight away.'

'Why wouldn't I? It sounds awful. Remembering – or thinking you remember – something like that.'

'You don't believe me?' The pitch of her voice had risen.

'I don't know, Jo. I've never...'

'You think it's my illness. That's what Emmeline would say.'

'Who's Emmeline?'

'She was... Just a friend.'

He didn't know what to say. 'Listen, Jo. I'm really glad you felt you could tell me about it. Really glad. I meant it when I said I'm your friend.' He felt himself floundering. 'But... I mean, I don't want to tell you what you should do' – he guessed people often did – 'but don't you think it might be a good idea to, you know, talk to someone about it?'

'I'm talking to you,' she said stiffly. 'I thought you said you were glad.'

'Well, yes, but don't you think... Wouldn't it be better to talk to someone... professional?'

'Yeah, sure. Get more medication. Be told to go to the fucking drop-in. Get a lecture on how to manage my symptoms. Damian is OK, pretty much, but I don't tell him everything.'

'I meant a... you know, a therapist or counsellor or something.' Maybe Damian was her counsellor. She didn't explain who people were; she must think he knew already.

'I tried that. Mother sent me to one. The woman just sat there where I couldn't see her and never said anything. It was even worse than Mother.'

'Well, then... maybe a... a psychiatrist.' He had only a hazy idea of what psychiatrists did but thought it included talking to people. 'Perhaps you see one already?'

She snorted. 'You don't know Dr Greenland.'

'Sorry. I don't understand about these things.'

'No. People like you don't. Jans was lucky she could forget; it meant she could be normal.'

'You mean she...? You mean it happened to her – if it happened, that is?'

'We were in the same room. It wasn't just me.'

He swallowed, feeling hot. She sounded so sure. It was bad enough that Kate was dead, without this... fabrication, if that was what it was.

'I want to go,' Jo said. 'This isn't helping. I thought talking to you would help.'

'I'm sorry.' Richard felt completely useless. 'I've never known anybody who... Not that I knew of, anyway. Maybe you're not really sure it happened, just upset? Maybe... Look, I've got to go to London again soon. We could meet. Perhaps then it would be easier to talk.'

He heard her hesitate. Then, to his surprise, she said, 'If you like.' She paused again. 'Only you don't really believe me, do you?'

'Well, I... I just don't know, Jo.'

'You won't tell anyone I said it? Like, any of them?'

'Who?' For a moment he thought she was imagining some sort of conspiracy.

'The mental health people,' she said flatly. 'Who else? It's none of their fucking business.'

'Isn't it? I don't know anything about that either. Wouldn't it be better for them to know?'

'Shit. You really don't get it. I don't know if I do want to see you.' She cut off the phone and Richard sat hunched up, staring at the wall. He'd helped his father hang the paper years ago – beige, textured to look like linen. His hands remembered the feel of it as he smoothed it against the plaster. He shouldn't have been so equivocal with her. She'd wanted him to believe her and he hadn't known what to say. And how could he tell this wasn't just her illness? His body ached with shame at his own inadequacy. He might well have lost all her trust, just as they were beginning to get to know each other again. Even if it was a delusion, perhaps he should have gone along with it. He couldn't be sure it was a delusion, though; that was the awful thing. He sat there for a long time with his chin in his hand, staring at the wall, then put the phone down on the bed beside him and lay back.

As he sat up again, the image of his old friend V came to him: the denuded head, the robes more suitable for the forests of Asia than urban Scotland, the clean, peaceful, unworldly face, the round brown eyes made larger and more staring by the absence of eyebrows. He was sure V would have something wise to say. As a Buddhist monk that was his job. He'd been a social worker before taking the robes and wasn't naïve about that sort of thing.

He picked up his phone again but didn't text V. It amused him that though the monks were supposed to own nothing but their robes and begging bowl, they always seemed to have the latest technology. People kept giving them things; it was considered meritorious. As he eased himself off the bed he found his legs shaking slightly with the shock. Had Kate, his Kate, suffered at the hands of some monster and never told him? If she had, he could only blame himself for not knowing, not taking more care of her. Was that why she'd died? Could some long-ago trauma have caused it or contributed to it? He didn't know if that was possible; the doctors had just said it was one of those things. Then there was Jo. He hated the way his father joked about her, slyly including Rick, as though mad or having-been-mad people didn't deserve respect.

He padded down the thick stone stairs, taking care not to bump his head on the beam that overhung the turn. The smell of frying engulfed him as he neared the bottom – his father was making chips for Rick. Richard was hungry but would have preferred to sneak up to his room with a sandwich and his own thoughts.

'Dad,' Rick called as soon as Richard's feet came into view. 'Dad, the chips are ready. Grandad's been waiting for you. Where have you *been*?' He sounded like an exasperated parent.

Richard looked at him with a new unease. Rick was still pale and peaky, his face thinner than Richard liked to see it. There was no question that he was grieving – they both were – but now Richard wondered if there was something else, something Rick couldn't speak about. Once you started thinking about abuse, you began to see it everywhere. 'Don't be silly,' Kate would have said, knowing what a worrier he was. Whatever had happened to her, if it had, she hadn't let it spoil her life, or theirs together. Only her death had done that.

'What's the matter, Dad?' Rick turned his head quizzically towards his father. 'Why are you staring at me? Do I look mad like Jo?'

Richard felt fury rise inside him. 'Jo is *not* mad,' he said through clenched teeth. 'Don't speak about her like that. There are things you don't understand.'

'OK.' Rick reddened and lowered his head, but then caught his grandfather's eye and gave a shamefaced grin.

'Enough of that,' Richard's father said, his accent becoming more obdurately Yorkshire. 'We all know there's some folks as aren't quite normal, and there's no harm in saying so. Anyhow, the chips have got cold. I'll have to fry them up again.' He sighed pointedly.

Richard had to keep eating to stop himself shouting at his father, who was pretending to steal chips from Rick's plate while Rick fended him off with the sauce bottle. They were laughing together in a way Richard didn't recall from his own childhood. His father, as he remembered him, would have told him off for misbehaving at table. You don't know anything, he wanted to say to him. You've no idea what people have been through. We're never sure how near any of us are to madness. How near might he be, now? Swallowing down a too-large mouthful with a gulp of water, he thought again of V. Somehow the monks always managed to look calm, whatever was going on inside.

Jo

She'd managed to tell Richard about it, and that it had been both of them, but she wasn't sure he'd believed her. She knew she'd remembered something horrible, though, and now a voice was saying, *You mustn't see more. It'll make you bad. You'll have to kill yourself.* She kept hanging on to what Damian had told her: say you can't listen right now, tell it you don't believe it, drown it out with music, just don't let it take you over. But it tried so hard to make her believe it.

This voice was like the one she knew best – *his* voice – but it was more seductive. *Come on,* it said, *no need to be frightened.* And then it hissed, *Shut up! You mustn't tell anyone, ever.* When it came she could feel a hand round her throat. It didn't hold her tight but she know it could.

She felt her heart pounding. Hard to believe it wasn't happening now. She nearly screamed 'Get off me' but shoved a fist in her mouth instead. When people in the drop-in had talked about flashbacks she hadn't understood what they meant. Now she didn't know how to stop seeing and feeling these things. It had all started coming back since Kate's death, and the memories seemed to be happening right now. She did need to tell someone. Perhaps if she saw Richard again... only he hadn't really known what to say. Damian would be concerned, but then he'd have to tell the rest of the team. That meant Dr Greenland, and no surprises from him: more medication, take up running, go to the activity groups at the drop-in. Jewellery making was on offer at the moment; she didn't much like jewellery.

She rolled another cigarette and lit it from the smouldering end of the previous one. She'd been trying not to smoke – she'd tell Damian that – but then it had all got too much. As her heartbeat slowed again she looked round the room. Junk mail was scattered over the grey cord carpet and the gas fire that didn't work properly was fluffy with dust. She could picture Emmeline's frown when she saw it. You'll feel better if you take more control, Emmeline would say, and would then take control for her. The dustpan and brush stood in the corner where Emmeline had put them. Jo longed to be enfolded in Emmeline's arms, wrapped in the warmth of her big firm body, lulled into not thinking or feeling anything. Emmeline and Kirsty were away in Nottingham, where Emmeline came from, caring for Emmeline's alcoholic mother. Emmeline had been born a carer.

Jo had been trying to forget that her mother expected a visit. She'd stopped wanting to be anywhere near Mother long before Jans died. Jo hated calling her Mother - the word had sharp edges that still cut. She and Kate had longed to have a Mum or Mummy who baked cakes and had fun with them. Mother had called her own parents Mother and Father and had never seen why her children shouldn't do the same – she had never enjoyed closeness. Even now she preferred to write to Jo rather than speak. 'I would hope that in the circumstances you might see fit to visit your mother,' she'd written after the funeral, excelling herself in barbed formality. She'd used the paper with the embossed letterhead, as though Jo wouldn't have known the address. Jo hadn't replied; going to the house would remind her too much of Jans. But Mother expected her to do the right thing and already the demand was tugging at her guilt-strings. She felt the familiar pull in her solar plexus, just as she did when Damian had expected her to do something and she hadn't done it. She'd have to write back as soon as she could find a decent sheet of paper – she wasn't going to tear one out of her notebook. Mother wouldn't come to see her; she'd never liked London and on her one brief visit had been disgusted with the flat.

Jo resented having to think of Mother now, when it was Jans who was important. Mother had written, 'I am sure you understand how much I miss Jancis' – she'd never accepted the change of name either. She wouldn't mention Jo missing her in case that aggravated the illness; she'd always played down their relationship with each other.

Jo jumped up and went into the bedroom. Without seeing or smelling the unmade bed she picked up from the rickety bedside cabinet the only photo she'd kept, the one of her and Jans under the apple tree in Oxford. The dust on the glass made the two of them look foggy and distant, sending that time farther into the past. She knew Jans had kept that picture too: despite her marriage and Jo's isolation they had never given up on each other. Not even now, Jo whispered to her. You deserve the truth. She took the photo back with her into the living-room and stood it on the table so that she could glance at it while she was writing. It fell over first time. She apologised to Jans and placed it more carefully. Keeping it in sight, she curled up again in the armchair and found the place in her journal. She sat thinking, not yet ready to write.

Perhaps it was all coming back now because Jans needed her to remember. She could say that to Jans, but not to anyone else in case it sounded mad. They'd been put in that room together, having been moved from their cots into real beds, side by side. Jo's was on the left, Jans's on the right. They'd both had the same duvet covers with Paddington Bear on them – surely Mother wouldn't have bought them? They hadn't been allowed much TV, but somehow Mother thought Paddington wouldn't do them any harm.

They'd both worn the same clothes then. Jans had had a blue butterfly in her hair and Jo a yellow one. Jo could see it all at a distance, as though watching both of them through a mist. They'd talked in bed at nights, sometimes in words, sometimes just in thoughts. She was doing it now, sending messages just as they'd always done. It didn't matter who said what; it belonged to both of them. Mother would to come up and tell them to be quiet, shushing them with her finger on her lips, and then sometimes, after she'd gone, the door would open terribly slowly and both of them would lie there pretending to be asleep. Jo couldn't remember clearly after that, except that they'd both had to hide. Jans had hid so well that Jo always hoped she'd dodge what was coming.

She stared towards the picture, not seeing it. Her body had started to twitch and shake with fear. For a moment she heard someone breathing and sensed the heat of a big body. Her sister was there but no one could help her. The unseen person had an unfamiliar bitter smell. *Don't see,* the voice said. She jumped. *Don't look, don't see. If you know, you'll have to die; I'll make you.*

Her body stiffened in the chair, arms rigid by her sides. She clamped her lips together so that she wouldn't scream out. The voice stopped and then she felt something on her body, pressing on her, pulling down her pyjama trousers. There was more; she knew there was more. She couldn't stop herself retching and ran into the bathroom, her own hand over her mouth.

Propping her arms on the sides of the washbasin she bent over and retched again, but she wasn't sick. She saw only blackness, a terrible empty dark as though the whole world had been wiped out. As though she'd died too. She turned the cold tap full on and splashed her face again and again. The voice was laughing at her, remote, mocking, waiting for things to get worse.

She stood up slowly and wiped the water from her face. From far away she heard a new voice – maybe a woman, maybe an angel. *The poor thing*, it said. It was almost crying. *The poor little kid. She shouldn't have had to go through that.* Then immediately the other voice again: *You're bad, you know you are. It happened because you're bad. That's why you're being punished.* She was shuddering with huge dry sobs and her legs were shaking so much she could hardly walk. All she could think was that she had to have a cigarette. A cigarette first and then coffee, and then she'd find a blade. The thought of cutting, draining the pain out of herself, began to calm her; if she punished herself it might make the voice leave her alone. She needed to talk to someone. She didn't know if Richard would be a safe person but there wasn't anyone else.

Richard

'It's good to see you,' Richard said to V, reassured by his friend's calm face.

'Good to see you too.' V paused, looking at him. 'How are you doing? Such a huge loss.'

'Yes.' What else could he say? 'I really wanted to talk to you about...'

V had come to stay in Edinburgh with two other monks who, like him, had moved out of the monastery; he arrived with a rucksack on his back and a covered alms bowl on a stand, looking like a drum, held under one arm. As they walked up the slope from the station he smiled at the people they passed, seeming not to think about his odd appearance, while Richard grinned awkwardly beside him, suddenly aware that he was taller than his friend.

Richard drove them over to the Meadows. It wasn't raining and both of them preferred to talk while walking. He was glad the clocks were still on summer time as that meant an hour longer before V had to be fed. The monks weren't allowed to eat after noon, except puzzling things like cheese and chocolate. All those crazy rules, Richard thought, glancing down at V's stubbly head as he got out of the car. Were they any more crazy, though, than the unspoken rules that ordinary people lived by? His rule, for instance, that you had to carry on as usual and pretend you were coping, even when you weren't. V stood unmoving as Richard locked the car, quietly watching him as though about to say something.

They set off through an avenue of lime trees. The branches arched over them, benign and protective, drenching them with their bittersweet scent. As Richard and V emerged into the wide green space, mingling with the other walkers, V broke the silence. 'Was there something you wanted to talk to me about?' he said. 'Not just...?'

'No,' he said. 'Not that. It's too hard to talk about.'

V waited.

'It's my... It's Kate's sister. I'm not sure what to do.' That sounded as if she might be attracted to him, or he to her. He wasn't going to go there.

V's face showed no expression.

'It's ...'

V gazed respectfully into Richard's face.

'It seems a bit weird, talking to you about it when you're a monk and everything, but I didn't know who else to speak to. You see, I don't know whether it really happened or not, or if it happened whether it was just Jo – my sister-in-law – or Kate as well.'

''It' being...?'

'I'd never even thought about it before. I knew Jo was funny about – well – being touched, but that might just be Jo.'

'I'm not sure what you mean,' V said neutrally, in what Richard imagined was a social worker voice. 'But if you're talking about touching, are you thinking about abuse?'

Richard nodded. 'I don't know what to think... I know Jo has what you might call a history, but I sort of believe her. It makes a lot of sense – of how she is.' He didn't add, of how Kate was.

'If she's telling you about it, she must trust you.'

'Seemingly, or she did. I'm not sure she does now, I was so clumsy with her. I didn't know what to say; I don't know anything about these things. How can I tell she's not having delusions or something? I told her she should talk to a psychiatrist but that didn't seem to go down very well.'

'No,' V said thoughtfully. 'Did what she said sound as though it might be real?'

'She said something about hands. In a text, not when I spoke to her. Do you think she was remembering? God, how awful if so.'

'She could have been.'

'She said she'd always thought I'd abused her, and now she knew I hadn't.'

Their pace had slowed almost to a stop. V said, 'Just because she has a history, that doesn't mean it's not real. If there was abuse, perhaps that's why she had a breakdown in the first place.'

'I thought so.' Richard felt the ache of shame all over again. How could he have been so crass? 'So… what should I do?' He didn't just feel sorry for Jo, he realised; he cared about her. He remembered her hunched over the café table, her hair and hands so like Kate's it had given him a start. He didn't want her to suffer more than she had to.

V shrugged and shook his head. 'All you can do is listen, for now. Maybe you don't have to think yet about whether you believe her.'

Panic rose in Richard's throat. 'But if…' Oh, surely not. 'If it was Kate as well, then…'

'Yes, that's terribly hard. But in the long run perhaps it's better to know.'

Richard saw Kate in bed that last morning, writhing in pain. What about all the pain she might have had to endure before? 'I'm not sure how I'd deal with it,' he said. 'I can't help Kate but I want to help Jo.'

V said nothing for a moment. Then he asked quietly, 'And what about you? How are you doing?'

'What about me?' Richard shrugged. 'I suppose you think I should say I'm feeling calm and peaceful and everything is just fine.' Until he said it, he hadn't realised how angry he was – with the world, with everyone. It was wrong, what had happened. It was wrong that he, Richard, couldn't do anything about any of it. It was wrong that well-meaning people like V should barge in with their sympathy. He tried to dab at his eyes without V seeing.

'Of course you're not fine,' V said. 'How could you be?'

'All your Buddhist guff about impermanence and equanimity,' he said to V accusingly, 'as though nothing fucking mattered. As though nobody mattered. It's all very well for your lot, floating around all the time on Cloud Nine.' He knew they didn't; V had some very rocky moments.

V drew a breath. When he looked at Richard his eyes were soft. He said, 'I wasn't going to talk about any of that just now. I only wanted to know how you are. As a friend. Shall we walk on a bit?'

Richard hadn't noticed they'd stopped. All around them people seemed to be scurrying across the wide grassy area as though they were compelled to move. The sky was a thick grey-white and the trees were flapping in the wind. Behind them Arthur's Seat and the hill beyond it rose up like the humps of an asymmetrical camel; Richard always had an urge to even them out. He shaded his eyes and stood staring at it as a fierce gust scourged the trees.

V stepped forward, his Birkenstocks flapping against his strong white feet. Though he was shorter than Richard, their strides almost matched. He walked fast but Richard had noticed before that he didn't seem hurried.

Following behind V, Richard caught the word compassion. He associated it with pictures of unwanted dogs or famine victims, but something about the way V talked made him think of Rick and then again of Jo, her bitten nails and frayed cuffs and that look she had as if she expected people to hurt her. Was it compassion he felt for her?

He stopped and rubbed his eyes hard. 'Tree pollen,' he said. 'Rick's allergic to it too.'

He walked on quickly. Ahead of him V was saying something about compassion for himself.

'I'm not the one that needs compassion,' Richard cut in before V had finished speaking. 'What about Kate, for God's sake? What about Jo? What about my son? Compassion for yourself is self-indulgent.' He couldn't stop coughing and thought he was going to choke.

'Is it?' V brushed a stray leaf off the top of his head and turned to Richard, who frowned at him.

'It's self-pitying and it doesn't help you get over things. I'm not going to feel sorry for myself.' He stiffened his face and stared at the long expanse of grass. The rigid effort stopped him taking in any more than the patch directly in front of his feet. He fixed on it with such concentration that he could see every flower of clover, every dandelion and plantain leaf.

After a long silence, by which time they'd nearly reached the far edge of the park, V began, 'The Buddha—'

'You know I'm not a Buddhist, Mark.' Richard wasn't going to call him by his monk name. 'Please don't come the teacher with me.'

V smiled. 'Sorry. It's a habit.'

Richard smiled too, and looked at his watch. 'Anyway, stuff the compassion; it's time we got you something to eat. Can't have you missing your mealtime.'

V hitched the free end of his robe over his shoulder and nodded politely. Richard strode on ahead of him, leading him towards the wholesome vegetarian café where he and Kate had often ended up. Thank goodness the damn begging bowl had been left in the car.

As they sat at the thick oak table, sipping their tea and waiting for the food to arrive – for V Richard had ordered soup, a main course and a dessert – V took a small oblong of ochre cloth from his shoulder bag and laid it down carefully. 'So you can offer the food,' he said. 'Otherwise I can't eat it. You have to touch all the dishes.'

'Oh, for God's sake,' Richard said. 'Surely the Buddha up there in the sky won't notice if you don't do it by the book for one day.'

The solemnity was broken and they laughed together; they'd relaxed into being friends again.

'What Buddha is that, then?' V's smile was wide and showed his gums; his teeth were uneven, with long, pointed canines which stood out in his eyebrowless face.

The seating occupied a large upstairs space with polished floorboards and wooden chairs and tables, in a room that smelt of cooked cheese and garlic and herbal tea. It was nearly full; none of the people tucking into stoneware bowls of soup or salad had given V's robes a second glance. All sodding Buddhists, probably, Richard thought, and wanted to laugh again. He and Kate had sometimes eaten there, sharing a concealed smile at the untidy, earnest people who weren't as different from themselves as they pretended to believe. He glanced at V, who was drinking his tea with slow enjoyment.

Once the food had arrived and been duly offered, V asked that they ate in silence. Before he picked up his spoon he sat with eyes closed – presumably saying grace, if that was what they called it. He didn't ask Richard to join in. He ate his food – all of it – with a concentration that Richard couldn't help finding rather beautiful. When Richard tried to do likewise he dropped spinach leaves or forked in too much frittata and chewed awkwardly. In the high-ceilinged room the clank of cutlery on plates and the echoing flow of voices crashed into his eardrums. V's meal seemed to go on for a very long time.

When he had at last finished his apple crumble, V laid down his spoon, put his hands together and gave Richard a little bow. Richard found himself bowing back. Then V said, 'All I meant about compassion was that you're being hard on yourself. You can't *make* yourself get over it.'

'I know,' Richard said, watching the pepper mill intently as he pushed it about between the empty plates. 'But if you knew what it was like, you'd do anything not to feel it. I keep telling myself it hasn't really happened and it'll just go away again. Pathetic, I know. Anyway, never mind about being kind to me; I want to do the best I can for Jo.' He was surprised how much it mattered.

V said gently, 'I do mind about being kind to you. You matter too. If you care about Jo, you'll find a way, I'm sure.'

They both stood up. Richard reached awkwardly across the table and clasped V's shoulder. V was a good friend and somehow, Richard wasn't sure how, what he'd said had helped. Now all he wanted was to go home and phone Jo.

Jo

As she was leaving the flat she found another text from Richard: Sorry. I didn't understand. Let's talk again. Meet in London?
She texted back: When you coming? At mother's now till Sun. Not sure can stand it. Text don't phone.

In the end Mother had sent her an open return from Waterloo to Axminster, dated today – Thursday. Jo usually missed trains, especially for visits to Mother. It had taken her till mid-afternoon to sort out the few things she needed and pack them in her bigger rucksack, toy with the washing-up and finally run some more water on it, drink all the coffee she needed, and write at least a little before the notebook too went into the rucksack.

She and Jans had both known Mother was a cold person, even though Mother had been nicer to Jans. Jo often felt that when Mother saw her, it was as though they'd never met before. She hates it that I'm not normal, and that I'm not you, she said to Jans as though she could do something about it. She might not have said it if her sister had still been alive. When Kate had started to go wild in her teens, Mother's view had been that it was just a phase. There was a lot she never knew about the parties, the sex and the drugs; she hadn't wanted to know. She had seen, without much sympathy, that Jo was unhappy but it hadn't seemed to occur to her that Jans might be too. Jans had been lucky that at art college she'd found what she wanted to do. Jo still hadn't.

Jans had taken her to parties sometimes. She'd felt she embarrassed her sister, though Jans had never said so. People always liked Jans better – she was more like them, laughing, sleeping around, pretending not to care. Jo remembered being introduced to people and not knowing what to say; they'd offer her a cigarette, smile and walk away. She hadn't much liked going out and had mostly stayed in her room, working and thinking about philosophy. Smoking and cutting, burning matches right down till they hurt her fingers. Mother had made it clear she thought Jo was odd but had never bothered to find out what she was doing. Being a don's daughter, she had liked it when Jo did well at school, though of course had expected her to do better.

It wasn't till later, in the bad time after Jo came out of hospital, that Mother had paid a lot of money for her to go to a therapist. The therapist turned out to be cold and distant, like Mother, and Mother had been annoyed that it didn't put her right. Depression with psychotic features, they'd called it in the hospital, and it had proved to Mother that Jo wasn't normal. Since then she had always felt Mother looked at her as if she were something that shouldn't be there. Mother had said more than once that she had never wanted twins, and Jo knew she was the one Mother would have dispensed with. She'd always thought it was her fault; she'd taken it for granted that Jans was better than her.

She knew, though, that she had to go and see Mother. She'd always used to wish Jans could go for her. If she didn't go Mother would be angry, and even if they hated each other she was still the only mother Jo had. Now, of course, Jo was the only daughter Mother had. At least the train would keep stopping, so that past Basingstoke it gave the illusion that it was never going to get there. Basingstoke made Jo think of trying to stoke a fire when it had gone out; she felt liked that with Mother.

She would have to ring and let Mother know what time she was arriving. Mother would be waiting for her in the car and would look disappointed when she saw her. To Jo, Mother's Dorset house was like a stage set: all fake, the same as the smile she put on for her WI people. It was terrible to say such things about one's mother but she whispered them to Jans. She knew Jans understood.

Getting all the way to Waterloo would be bad enough, never mind going down to Dorset. Mother knew how hard it was for her. She'd have to get three buses but the Tube would be worse: being crowded together with all those people and not being able to get away. Not being able to smoke, though Damian would say that was good for her. She knew he looked out for her. Damian was a good person, even though it was his job.

She hadn't managed to write anything. Her hand was shaking with nervousness and she had the sinking feeling in her stomach that always preceded her visits to Mother. By the time Mother picked her up a deep grey fog would have enveloped her, an emanation of Mother's dislike and her own sense of being trapped. Without thinking she took out her tobacco and papers and quickly, clumsily, rolled a cigarette. Holding it in her mouth unlit, she shrugged on her rucksack and stood facing her front door. It was several minutes before she could pull down the handle and step out into the no-man's-land of the staircase. She locked the door behind her, dropping her keys. When she picked them up, she was ready to unlock it again. Instead, pulling the wet cigarette from her lower lip, she clomped down the stairs and stood by Eric Gaines's door. He was out – it was always ajar when he was home – but for once she would have welcomed his ramblings. Now there was nothing but the front door between her and the world. *Coward*, one of the voices said, not the terrible one. *Can't face your own mother*. She locked the door behind her and strode towards the bus stop.

'I do think you might have got here earlier,' Mother said, greeting Jo at the station car park with a perfunctory hug. She smelt of lavender water, which revolted Jo. 'I don't understand what kept you.'

Jo saw the thin dusting of beige powder on her mother's face and noticed how her white hair had yellowed. It made her seem more ordinary, less indomitable, but there was little welcome in the tight pink smile. Jo said nothing in reply and nibbled what was left of a fingernail, feeling exactly as she had when she was thirteen. She stood by the car door, rucksack over one shoulder, staring without interest at the other cars as they drove away.

'Would you like to get in?' Mother said impatiently.

Jo opened the door and slid into the car, perching the rucksack on her lap. She still had nothing to say. The voices hadn't bothered her much on the train but they were starting up now: *You're stupid. No wonder she doesn't like you. You're stupid.*

Mother started the car, her face set in purposeful silence. The village was some way out of Axminster, towards the Dorset coast. Mother had never enjoyed driving on main roads and took them through narrow lanes, muttering crossly if she had to reverse to let another car through. Jo was still adjusting to the difference from London, the greenness of the hedges laced with white cow-parsley and deep pink campion, the sounds and smells of grazing animals, the glimpses of grassy hillsides. It was peaceful, but with only Mother there she felt how lonely it was. Loneliness in London was surrounded by people; here there was just space. As the road opened out she could look for miles over hills patterned with the darker green of hedgerows and woods. It would have been good to stay here and not have to bother about anyone, but there was Mother sitting beside her. The sea wasn't far away – on one of her good days she'd been to Lyme Regis – but Mother didn't care for it. Jo had never understood why Mother had moved here when Oxford seemed to be in her bones, but she had decided and wouldn't go back.

Jo hunched into herself as Mother parked the car in the drive. The house was modern, painted pale cream outside like most of them in the little cul-de-sac. The garden was well-kept but sparse; Jo thought the plants looked afraid to grow. As Mother opened the door, Jo smelt Earl Grey tea and a discreet lilac air freshener – since when had Mother bothered about such things? It was nothing like their big bleak Oxford house and to Jo it had always felt unnatural. The living room carpet was thick and silver-grey, the curtains were striped in grey and cream – all inherited from the previous owner – there was a china cabinet filled with a floral tea set that Mother used to despise. Jo sat down on a small chair, her rucksack still on her lap. In their new setting, pieces of furniture she remembered from Oxford – a small mahogany table, a couple of faded armchairs, an undistinguished writing desk – looked like antiques. Perched there, she felt like a piece of cheap tat among all the good taste. In the chilly summer evening the room felt cold, but she'd expected that.

Mother had gone straight into the kitchen to make tea – she didn't offer coffee – and put the ready meals in the microwave. The roar of the kettle and the whirring of the microwave barely disguised the house's unfriendly silence. She came back with two mugs on a tray and a plate of Rich Tea biscuits, the kind they gave you in the drop-in when the nicer ones had run out. Jo couldn't see why they needed biscuits when they were about to have a meal, but Mother must have thought it was appropriate.

'So, Joanna,' Mother said in a social voice as she handed her a flowered china mug, examining her with those light blue eyes that told you nothing. There was milk in the tea, which Jo couldn't stand. 'And how are things in London?'

Jo shrugged. 'OK. I don't have milk in my tea. I thought you knew.'

Mother's face contracted in annoyance. She took the mug away and came back a few moments later with a plain grey one filled with strong black tea. Jo looked at it and put it down on a cane-legged table in front of her, then started drinking it to distract herself.

'I was sorry you didn't see fit to join us at the funeral,' Mother said with a furious smile. She never let things go.

Jo gave her a cold stare and said, 'I couldn't. You didn't understand. I just couldn't. Jans would have understood.' She did understand.

'Letting the family down? I don't think so.'

'How do you know? She was my twin.' Jo was already on the edge of outraged tears.

'Jancis would not have done such a thing. She would have supported me.'

Jo looked down, picking at the skin round her thumbnails. Just like you supported us when those awful things happened, she wanted to say. Just like you supported me when they put me in that hospital. She chewed the inside of her lower lip, not quite drawing blood.

'And how is your illness? What does the doctor say?'

'Keep taking the tablets. That's all he's interested in.' Jo piled on the cynicism. 'If I'm lucky I might get injections instead.'

'But you are still working in that... that voluntary job? You are still going to the centre?'

'Mm. Still doing what they tell me.'

The timer pinged and Mother got up to fetch the meals. Her legs, which had always been slim, looked shrunken under a dark blue skirt that was too big for her. She was eighty-four, after all; Jo and Jans had been an unexpected late addition. Their half-brother Paul, twenty years older, had been in Australia for most of Jo's life and was barely a memory. His photo was there on the dark wood sideboard – another Oxford relic – beside one of Jans aged about sixteen. The picture was hazy, the face blurred by sunlight. Mother had also had the picture of both of them under the apple tree, but that seemed to have disappeared. Jo didn't remember ever having seen a photo of her father.

The door opened and there was a smell of garlic and tomato. Mother had left the meals – some sort of pasta, which Jo had once told her she liked – in the plastic dishes and, using the oven glove, placed one in front of her on a thick rush mat.

'Can I have a fork?' Jo asked. She wasn't hungry.

Mother put out her own meal and then, taking her time, handed Jo a fork from the tray. As they started eating she said, 'I seem to remember you liked this. You were always fussy about food.'

As though Jans wasn't. They'd both disliked similar things, refused sweetcorn and celery and softboiled eggs and picked the raisins out of their cake, when they got cake.

'It's all right,' Jo said, eating it. It had come from the sort of shop she didn't go to – Waitrose or Marks and Spencer's – but it wasn't as good as the pasta you got at the drop-in on Wednesdays.

Mother glanced at her. 'You look as though you don't eat much. Don't they make sure you care for yourself?' Her tone lay somewhere between concern and contempt.

Jo didn't reply. It was demeaning that 'they' should have to make sure she did anything. Damian didn't make it seem demeaning, but seeing herself through her mother's eyes she felt like someone incapable of doing the simplest thing for herself.

They ate on in silence. *Don't say anything*, one of the voices said, a less familiar one. *Mustn't say anything. She'll break you in pieces if you do.* And then the new one: T*he poor little things, they were all alone. Now one of them's gone.* Jo put down her fork and covered her eyes with her hands. Surely no one could bear so much sadness.

'Are you feeling ill?' Mother asked. 'Have you taken your medication?'

Jo nodded. People always thought you needed medication. She wished Emmeline could engulf her in her big warm arms. Mother had met Emmeline once and hadn't liked her – probably because she looked like a dyke. She'd never told Mother about their relationship; perhaps she hadn't needed to.

She took her hands from her face and picked up her fork again as Mother tidily finished her meal. The ache inside her left no room for food but she carried on trying so that Mother didn't start again. When she couldn't manage any more, she put her fork down and tried not to look at her mother.

For a moment she thought she saw the hands again. She did her best to control the shaking but knocked her mug on to the carpet. Thank goodness it was empty. As she picked it up the voice – the worst one – laughed at her and said, *Look how useless you are. No wonder you were...* It tailed off into an obscene mumble more menacing than proper words.

'Be careful!' Mother called out too late. 'Tea will stain the carpet.'

'It hasn't,' Jo said, but as she looked down at the carpet, for a moment – just for a moment – there was a glistening patch of blood. It shocked her: a long time since she'd seen anything that wasn't there. The voice laughed again but said nothing. She knew she shouldn't have come.

'I'm going upstairs,' she said. 'I've got to...' The blood on the carpet had told her she needed to cut. Sitting here with Mother's icy stare on her felt so bad she had to find some escape. How could she ever have thought she would be able to stay until Sunday? She'd go home tomorrow, whatever Mother might think.

Mother said nothing. Whether or not she knew what Jo was going to do, she didn't stop her. In the background the voice said over and over, *Serves you right*.

After a while, when Jo had felt the relief that came with the pain in her arm, Mother called up the stairs, 'Are you all right, Joanna?' She sounded as though she was concerned, which Jo found hard to believe. She couldn't trust the concern, but when she came down she could see Mother had been waiting for her.

She knew she couldn't stay. When Mother had seemed icy cold, that was bad enough. To feel she might actually care, underneath that bland pale front, would be intolerable.

Marian

It was disheartening that Joanna was being so difficult – for no good reason, so far as she could see. Whether she was in London or here in Dorset, it seemed the symptoms of the illness were liable to erupt. Marian had hoped Jo might be able to manage them better while she was here: she had every comfort and Marian had made an effort to choose food she liked.

It had been disappointing that the psychoanalysis, which she had paid for, had fizzled out so soon after it started. She did think Joanna could have tried harder with it, especially as Dr Rasen had come with an impressive list of qualifications, not least a First from St Hilda's, Marian's old college. Joanna had complained that the woman had hardly said anything and had sat hidden behind the couch where she couldn't see her, but Marian had read up enough to know this was how it worked. She thought Joanna could have done more to accept the treatment on its own terms, but she had to admit it hadn't done her much noticeable good.

When Joanna had knocked her tea mug on the carpet – thank goodness it was empty – and sat staring at the floor, Marian had felt shame, revulsion, and a kind of pity that set her teeth on edge. Jancis had been through a wild patch in her teens, but she had got over it and had a career and a family. She had always been less troubled than Joanna, less inward-looking, easier to like. Not knowing how to help Joanna irritated Marian and gave her a sense of having failed as a mother – though she firmly believed that people were responsible for themselves and it did no good to over-protect them. Or to talk about the bad things that might have happened: one had to put those aside and carry on. She had always taken pride in doing so.

Joanna had fled upstairs to her room and stayed there doing God knows what. Marian had forbidden her to smoke in the house, but she knew Joanna would sometimes lean out of the open window with her cigarette, perhaps not realising that the smell of those disgusting hand-rolled objects would drift back into the room, making it unpleasant for other guests who might stay there. It was unlikely there would be other guests, but it was the principle. Too often Joanna seemed unable to think of anyone but herself.

Despite her irritation, Marian had found herself feeling concerned for Joanna, to the extent that she called up the stairs to her. She had thought for a moment of going up and knocking on the door, but had felt reluctant. It would have been an invasion of privacy. Still more, she had no idea what she might find or whether she could deal with it. She knew, and usually preferred not to know, that Joanna sometimes cut herself deliberately, and she had never been good at coping with the sight of blood. When the children were small she had just about managed to bathe their grazed knees and put plasters on them, but she had taught them to do it for themselves as soon as they were able. If Joanna were cutting herself, Marian hoped very much that the blood would not stain the bedding or the carpet.

When Joanna came down, looking – Marian couldn't help seeing – pale and shaken, and not smelling of smoke, Marian asked again if she was all right.

Joanna shook her head and made an 'Uh' sound that could have meant anything. For someone who manifestly had intelligence, she could be surprisingly inarticulate.

'Would you like a cup of tea, Joanna? As you know, I don't have coffee.'

Joanna made the 'Uh' sound again but it seemed to be accompanied by a nod.

As her daughter dragged her feet into the sitting room, her socked toes making trails across the pile of the carpet – she had had to take off those unprepossessing boots – Marian escaped to the kitchen. She remembered not to put milk in Joanna's mug of tea and made it strong, to help her pull herself together. She made herself a small cup of Earl Grey, feeling she too needed fortifying.

They drank their tea in awkward silence. Marian didn't know what to say, afraid of beginning a conversation that would take them both into troubled waters. Looking at Joanna over her teacup she said,

'I'm concerned about you, Joanna. Are you sure you're taking your medication?'

Joanna sighed wearily. 'Yeah, yeah. Can't you see it's not all about medication?"

'That may possibly be so, but it is the main treatment for the illness you have.'

She thought she heard Joanna mutter, 'It's not just an illness. It's something that happened.'

'What was that? I hope you're not saying you know better than the doctors. That would be very unwise.'

Joanna glared at her – like a sulky teenager, Marian thought.

'It's my life,' she said. 'They don't know what it's like to be me. Nor do you.'

'How is that relevant to your treatment, knowing what it's like for you?' How could they possibly know what it was like to be Joanna – or anyone else, come to that?

Joanna looked despairing, which seemed to Marian overdramatic. One had to face the facts and deal with them. Thank goodness Jancis had never had these problems. Jancis had never disappointed her in the ways Joanna did.

'Your sister—' she began.

'Is dead,' Joanna said bluntly. 'You've just got me now. If you don't like me, I may as well go home.'

'That's up to you, of course,' Marian said, not unwilling, if she were honest, for Joanna to leave. 'I had hoped we might be able to remember Jancis together. You're not the only one who has lost her.'

Joanna took time drinking her tea, then said, so quietly Marian could barely hear her, 'I'm your daughter too.'

'Yes, you are, and we'd get on much better if you behaved more reasonably, illness or no illness.'

"I'm going tomorrow morning,' Joanna said, putting down her mug of tea on the carpet, which made Marian wince. She ran upstairs and – still like a teenager – slammed the door.

Marian finished her tea and tried to relax, but found herself wondering what had gone wrong. Surely Joanna could see that her mother would want what was best for her, especially with her condition. She had let them all down at the funeral and now, it seemed, she was letting Jancis down. Marian couldn't see what good it would do for Joanna to go straight back to that squalid flat in London and that peculiar Emmeline person – she chose not to think what their relationship might be. If Joanna could only behave in a more civilised manner, she and her daughter might have a proper conversation. Despite its unlikelihood, Marian had hoped for that. She found it hard to envisage a rapport between people that was not a meeting of minds, and Joanna's constant giving way to emotion was frustrating. But, like it or not, Joanna was now her only daughter. In some way – she was hard put to say what – that mattered.

Richard

He had heard the phone buzz and guessed the text was from Jo. He hadn't looked at it straight away but now, sitting in the kitchen with a mug of coffee in front of him in the dead hour before Rick came home from school, he knew it was hers:

Going home tomorrow. Awful. When you coming to London?

Helpless though he felt, he wanted her to depend on him. He'd try to save her, if he could, from the grim misery of the life he imagined she led. Clinging to those wrecked spars of hope might stop him going under. And he'd be doing it for Kate. Whatever Jo was going through, perhaps in some sense she was going through it for her sister too. He and she seemed to be in it together.

His work was at a stage where he could easily arrange a meeting in London, so long as Fran could come up. It would be good to see his sister again, a transfusion of normality into his life.

'You're sure you don't mind?' he said as Fran dropped her bag with a thump on the hall floor. Like him, she was bad at travelling light. She'd come up at less than a weeks' notice, bless her, and remembered to bring the bread Rick always asked for.

She shook her head. 'You know I wouldn't come if I did.'

'Rick likes you, you know that.' He could say it freely as Rick was at Robbie's.

Fran smiled and pointed to a carrier bag beside her weekend holdall. She always brought Rick presents, books she thought he'd like or games they could play together that weren't too childish. She didn't insist he played them, either.

'Yes,' she said. 'We get on all right, him and me. He'll miss you, though.'

Richard coughed and went to put the kettle on. He couldn't say how guilty he felt, being let off the hook of their shared grief even for a day or two.

'So you're going to see – what's her name, Jo? – while you're down there,' Fran said neutrally when they were drinking their tea. Her job had made her good at not judging.

'Yes.'

'Of course I don't know her much. I saw her at your wedding but I probably haven't seen her since then. She seemed a troubled soul.' Fran said it kindly; she was used to dealing with troubled souls.

'You could say that. Anyway, she's Kate's sister – well, twin – so I sort of feel…'

She nodded sympathetically. 'Yes. Naturally you'd want to look after her.'

He didn't need to tell Fran the rest. He didn't have the words for it: what seemed to have happened to Jo and Kate was so far outside his family's experience. He watched Fran dunking a Hobnob in her tea, completely at home. 'It's strange,' he said, 'how like Kate she is, and how unlike.' He and Fran had never expected to be alike but kept catching ways in which they were.

'It's good to share memories with someone so close to Kate.'

'I'll take your case up to your room,' he said, not knowing how to get Jo's prickly reality across. It was good, but it certainly wasn't easy. He wanted to protect Jo from the kindness even of well-meaning people like Fran.

She smiled again as she thanked him, as though he were the one doing all the favours.

Jo's latest text had said: Can u come here? More private. Hope u won't mind the mess. He pictured a dingy room awash with unopened mail, ashtrays with butt-ends spilling out like maggots, mugs scummy with old tea, Jo drowning in chaos and neglect.

Sure, he texted back. Be good to see you there. He risked saying Take care, knowing she might not like it.

He was getting to London the day before his meeting – less than five hours on the fast train – and planned to see her in the afternoon. If she'd let him, which he doubted, he'd take her out for a meal after they'd talked. He was sure she didn't eat properly. Kate had sometimes been funny about eating too, pushing her plate away when it was still almost full as though she didn't have the right to be fed. That mother of theirs, he thought again, remembering how the top flight of stairs in that chilly house had only had bare boards and how sparse and uninteresting the meals he'd eaten there had been: a badly baked potato, a small lump of cheese, lettuce without dressing. Kate had loved to cook but Jo still seemed to carry the house's dreariness, its lack of sensual pleasure.

He packed a few things in his case – the one he'd brought back the box of ashes in – and wondered if to Jo his usual clothes would look intimidatingly smart. He hadn't thought about that last time. He decided on a navy T-shirt rather than a shirt under his light jacket, and a pair of chinos that had seen better days – clothes he felt at ease in. As he arranged his things in the case – Kate had teased him for being so precise about it – he felt, more than saw, a piece of soft fabric bundled in one corner. One of Kate's scarves – not the one the box had been wrapped in. He must have picked it up with that one without noticing. It felt strange, not like him, to have been so careless.

The scarf had a splotched design in black, brown and white, dark but not sombre. Kate had made it when she'd been experimenting with fabric paints. He hadn't thought he could part with anything she'd made but knew he had to give it to Jo. There'd be other things, he realised, that she would want to have, but for now this would be enough. The colours were right for her; it would go with the leather jacket he seemed to remember she'd had. He pulled it out and folded it properly, leaving it on top so he wouldn't forget. Jo might be shocked, appalled – it wasn't hard to picture her running out of the room in horror – or she might be touched, pleased he'd thought of her. There was so much he didn't know about her.

Jo

She was used to the dull ache low down in the belly. It always went on for days before there was anything to show for it, but now she could feel the real cramp. Once it came it was a relief, the mess of blood flowing out of her, pink and watery at first, then dark and clotted. The pain felt good: it had an identifiable cause and would come to an end – at least until next time. It was real, ordinary blood, not the terrible more-than-blood she had seen at Mother's. It felt cleansing, like the cutting.

At least she was back now, at home in the flat as much as she ever was anywhere, hunched up in the armchair, cuddling an old hot-water bottle wrapped in a holey jumper that Emmeline was always trying to get her to throw away. The blood on the carpet had scared her; Mother's trying to be nice had scared her too and led to the inevitable argument. They only had each other now, she thought, and they didn't seem to want each other. A picture of one of the baby monkeys in Harlow's experiment flashed into her mind, the one left with the wire mother, whose hunched-up body and haunted face spoke of devastation beyond hope. Of course it wasn't like that with Mother, but being with her felt more like wire than soft cloth. Without thinking, Jo shoved her thumb into her mouth and sucked it for comfort.

She hadn't been alone back then: she and Jans had had each other. Always, even when they weren't together. Even now Jans was there with her. She reached out her hand and thought she could feel Jans's, always warmer than hers. They'd often done that in their separate places while Jans was alive, and each had known the other was doing it. She felt an ache that wasn't like the ache in the belly. That stayed in one place and could be soothed with a hot-water bottle; this started in her chest but seemed to spread everywhere and settle deep in her solar plexus. It was dark and it contained a single word: No. No, it couldn't be true. Jans must still be there. She felt like a torn half-sheet of paper, its other half thrown away. Her thumb went back into her mouth and she left it there until she felt able to get her notebook.

She wasn't going to write about the physical pain; it was too obvious, too ordinary. Her mind went to the sideboard in Mother's sitting-room: how there was no picture of Father there. He was a black space in her memory, an obliterated phrase in a redacted document.

It was strange how Mother had never talked about Father. Jo didn't remember a single word about him except when Mother had told them he'd gone away. But that wasn't until later, when they were old enough to ask. Before that all they knew was that he wasn't there. Now it seemed as though everything about him had been sealed away in a freezer marked DO NOT OPEN. They hadn't asked; somehow they'd known not to. They'd just made up stories about him. He was an explorer who'd discovered something that made him famous, only it was very secret. He was a spy who'd had to go and live in hiding a far-off country. He was a naval captain who had to stay with his ship but would come back covered in medals. He would come back, of course, and would recognise them at once and take them in his arms, even though he could have had no idea what they looked like.

As they got older the stories changed. He was in prison for murdering someone, or for some huge fraud; he'd gone off to South America with an exotic dancer and couldn't come back, or else he was dead and perhaps had died so shamefully Mother didn't want to tell them about it. Sometimes Jo had had a sense of him, a sort of feeling that was warm and close, but now she wondered about it. Jans had said she'd never felt it, but Jo knew that wasn't true. They'd never been able to hide what they felt from each other.

They'd stopped talking about it as they got older and realised he never would come back. She thought Jans had stopped first. There was a dead look on Mother's face if ever they mentioned him, so perhaps he really had died. But Mother's face often had that look and maybe it hadn't been to do with him at all.

Jo had often thought their father might have been the one who did those things to them. Not that it could have been; he would already have left by that time. But supposing it had been?

She wouldn't dare say it to anyone in case they thought it was her illness; even thinking of it felt like an illness. And it did seem to be someone else, someone who came and went in the night. The two flashbacks – if that was what they were – had terrified her. The voices terrified her too. Jans had never wanted to know about them because they scared her.

It surprised her that the other voice had been there, even for a moment, even at Mother's. *The poor baby*, it had said. *She couldn't help it. It's so sad.* It had made her want to cry and nestle in its arms, only there were no arms. She wished she and Jans could put their arms round each other.

Now wasn't the time for writing. The bad voice kept coming; it haunted and taunted her but was somehow less troubling, as though the other voice had wrapped a blanket round her. Inside the blanket it still hurt that Jans wasn't there, and the memories didn't go away.

Clutching the hot-water bottle to her front, she got up and took a look round the room. She'd almost forgotten she'd asked Richard to come. Tomorrow, it must be. She'd better do something about tidying up, so that he didn't get too much of a shock. Apart from Emmeline and occasionally Kirsty, and Damian who was paid to come, nobody ever saw the inside of the flat. Even Eric Gaines didn't get beyond her front door, though he was always angling to come in and park himself in Emmeline's chair. Richard was different. He wasn't coming to do good to her or because he wanted something; she'd asked him to come.

Standing on a tattered rug striped like ice cream in pink, green and chocolate, in front of a gas fire so ancient its wooden surround was falling off, she saw the mess and clutter as Richard might see it. He might not disapprove the way Emmeline did, but she couldn't think he'd like it. She picked up the two ashtrays – white plastic pub ones scarred with burns – and emptied them into the overflowing bin. It had been a while since she'd smoked much but she'd got used to seeing them there. She'd thought about taking out the rubbish for days and made herself do it now:

it felt oddly shaming to be coming down the stairs with such a full bag. Having stuffed it into the already full wheelie bin outside, she dragged herself back up the stairs.

Clutching the hot-water bottle again, she started picking up the junk mail scattered on the floor and putting it in piles in the corner. Tidying the flat felt like using a part of her brain she had forgotten about; it tired her and she had to keep stopping to rest. As she chucked the white envelopes on to the unsteady piles, their plastic windows crackling as they fell, she could see how awful the carpet was – a moth-eaten shaggy brown dusted with ash. When she'd done as much tidying as she could, she gathered up all the mugs with scummy or mouldy dregs in them and dumped them in the sink. Emmeline had been round not long ago so there wasn't too much washing-up.

Still bent over with the cramp, she went across the road to the nearer of the two supermarkets to buy fresh milk. The bottle she had in the fridge had been there so long that the contents had clotted into a solid lump above watery whey. It had looked disgusting; the smell was disgusting when she opened it and tried to shake out the sour curd. It must have been there since Emmeline had brought it the time before last. In the supermarket the reek of singed fat as they butchered the meat made her want to gag. One of the brothers (she imagined they were brothers) was chopping at a pathetic carcass with a huge cleaver that cut deep into the board, shocking her each time with its sound.

Turning her head away, she hurried to the tea and coffee shelves. The coffee she'd been using was almost finished and the granules in the other jar were a sticky mass. She didn't usually think of tea, but perhaps he might like it rather than coffee. And biscuits; they would show she was being nice to him. Not Rich Tea, like Mother had. Emmeline sometimes brought Hobnobs and they were better. On her way to the checkout she noticed rows of air fresheners and thought she'd better get one of those as well. She sniffed a few to make sure they didn't smell like Mother's house and found one that was bearable. If you breathed it in in the right way, it almost smelt like roses.

When she came out, carrying the things she'd bought in a blue plastic bag, it was raining again. It seemed to have been raining an awful lot, especially since Jans died. Climate change had worried her for a long time, but that was another thing she dared not talk about to Dr Greenland or even Damian. They would only say it was part of her illness, that she mustn't get more depressed and thinking about such things would affect her mental health. But how could you pretend it wasn't happening? It never used to rain like this. She hoped Richard might understand but she couldn't be sure.

She meant to do more tidying but instead refilled her hot-water bottle and flopped into the armchair. Richard was coming at around teatime tomorrow, so she'd have a bit of time. Did she really want to see him, or had she asked him because she felt she ought to?

'You've tidied up,' Damian said approvingly the next morning.

She'd forgotten the appointment and was in the middle of heaving open the sash window that did open to get rid of the smoke. She'd had a couple of cigarettes and thrown the stubs into the garden below, which wasn't a proper garden but earth and a few weeds, overshadowed by the plane tree in the street outside. She'd sprayed some air freshener and the room was scented now with artificial roses.

'Fresh air too.' He smiled. He had a nice smile, big and warm and guileless. When she'd first known him he'd had long thick locks, which had made him look more human, less professional. Not that he wasn't human now, with shorter hair that brought his face more into focus. Jo knew from the women at the drop-in that not all the CPNs were as friendly as he was.

'My… brother-in-law is coming,' she said, feeling awkward about it.

'Your sister's…?'

'Yes. He's coming to London.'

'You're sure you want to see him?'

'Yes. He's OK.' That was as far as she could go.

'Great. It's good for you to see people. And hopefully he's someone you can talk to. A support. Maybe you can support him too.'

'Maybe.' She'd never thought she could support anyone, apart from Jans. She looked round the room, waiting for Damian to go so that she could prepare herself for seeing Richard. He took his time, though. He had to do all the stuff about medication and how she was coping with the bereavement, and she had to let him.

After he'd gone, she stood in the kitchen staring at the mugs she still hadn't washed up. There was a blob of congealed milk in the sink that hadn't dissolved when she ran the tap on it. Instead of walking out again, she managed to wash up the mugs, clear the sink and find a cloth to wipe over the cooker. The new milk was in the fridge and the packet of Hobnobs was ready on the worktop.

It didn't surprise her when the voice came again: *You stupid cow. What are you letting him in for? You'll regret it. You'll regret it. If you say anything to him, I'll kill you. I'll kill you.* She hated its new habit of repeating itself, becoming more insistent when she tried not to listen. 'Shut up!' she said aloud. 'Leave me alone!'

She rarely talked to it and it felt strange to think that her own voice might be as strong as its – his. It went on battering her, again and again, till all she could do was throw herself on to the bed and lie there with a pillow over her ears. And then, finally, the other voice, the angel, came: *The poor little child*, it said. *Leave her alone.* The other voice didn't stop, but it grew fainter as she remembered the blanket around her. 'Thank you,' she said to the new voice, and hoped it heard.

Richard

He couldn't help feeling anxious as the Tube lurched up the Piccadilly Line. Manor House, Turnpike Lane, Wood Green – all places that he couldn't picture as real but that sounded surprisingly rural. At Bounds Green there would be the shock of the traffic as he stepped out into the street, and then the house was just up the road – he checked on his phone. He put the phone back in his pocket and waited, perched on the edge of his seat.

The woman's voice that had tirelessly announced every station finally came up with Bounds Green. There was no 'Alight here for...' – the place didn't seem to have very much. Why 'alight', he wondered; it sounded as if the train had caught fire. One of those awkward transport words, like 'board'. The fact that he was playing with words showed him how nervous he was. Kate had taught him to do it and made him laugh with it. Now it wasn't funny: it reminded him her laughter had gone. He had few memories of Jo laughing.

Rising up on the escalator into the fluorescent light, he remembered the scarf. It was in his briefcase, which he hadn't intended to bring but hadn't wanted to leave in his poky B & B room. The B & B was at the King's Cross end of Bloomsbury, in a street that couldn't make up its mind whether it was smart or seedy; somehow he distrusted it. Though he was casually dressed – he was glad he'd chosen the T-shirt – the briefcase might give Jo the wrong impression. He didn't want to look like one of those mental health people she seemed to dread so much, but there was nothing he could do now. As he walked along the road the trees dripped on him. It was raining again; it always seemed to be raining. Somehow it felt fitting for seeing Jo.

He was looking out for house numbers but most of them seemed to be either hidden or non-existent. He soon realised he'd gone too far. Turning back, he looked more carefully at the houses themselves; Bounds Green wasn't as bad as he'd thought. Most of them were Victorian and well-kept, with cars parked on paved forecourts. One, half-hidden behind a plane tree, seemed to have resisted being smartened up. He guessed that might be it and peered beyond the tree to see if there was a number. It was surprisingly clear: large curved black figures that were broken off at the edges. He checked on his phone, but he was sure this was it. The front garden had gateposts but no gate. It had some paving; two large wheelie bins stood on dark, practically bare earth with nothing but a few dandelions and thistles. It seemed so forlorn he had the urge to fill it with flowering shrubs. The plane tree obscured the window of the flat upstairs, which must surely be dark inside. He looked up at it, guessing it was Jo's. The paint on the window frames was flaking and the windows looked as though they hadn't been cleaned for years.

He made his way along the half-submerged crazy paving and stood staring at the chipped blue paint on the front door. To the right of the door were two bells. The lower one had a stuck-on label with GAINES in blotchy felt pen; the one above it had a slip of card in the plastic holder printed with the name FRIEDLAND. For a moment he thought this couldn't be Jo, then he realised it was the manufacturer's label. He'd been caught like that once before: people were meant to take the label out and write their own name on the other side. It didn't surprise him that she hadn't; he didn't imagine she'd welcome visitors.

He stood there for a while and was about to ring again, when the heavy door opened just enough for him to see Jo looking warily out at him.

'Hi, Jo,' he said, with an unintended note of false heartiness.

'Oh, it is you.' She glanced away and didn't open the door any wider. She looked rumpled, as though she'd been taken by surprise. He didn't think he was too early.

For a moment he stood wondering whether she was going to invite him in. Then, just as he was about to ask, she seemed to come back from wherever she'd been and stepped aside for him to pass.

He had to stop himself offering her a hug and made do with the best smile he had. She looked up at him with a flicker of surprise, then gave him a grin that lifted the corners of her mouth.

It was so unexpected and so much like Kate that it shot straight to his heart. She turned and started walking up the stairs, leaving him to follow. He couldn't help noticing the hallway; it was so much what he'd expected and hoped not to find: grey-blue cord carpet curled up at the edges, showing its cracked black backing; white-painted woodchip on the walls flaking and peeling at the joins, a smell of dust and damp, faint whiffs of smoke and stale urine coming from the ground-floor flat. He felt sad for Jo before he even reached her door. She had already gone inside but had left it ajar. He knocked softly and pushed the door open into a small, dark hallway cluttered with carrier bags and piles of unopened envelopes.

She was standing just inside what must be the living room, nibbling a fingernail. 'Do you want to come in?'

'If it's OK?' He wasn't sure; the shell of privacy surrounding her was almost tangible.

She nodded. 'Yeah. I wanted to talk to you.' She pushed back a strand of hair that had fallen over her face and Richard saw again the ghost of a grin. She was forty, just as Kate had been, coming up to forty-one, but she seemed as young as when he'd first known her – barely out of her teens. When the grin petered out she gazed at him intently, her eyes naked, as if she didn't have a grown-up face to put on. They could have been Kate's eyes, except that Kate's were never so anguished, always faintly guarded. He looked down, noticing the worn brown carpet was cleaner than he'd expected. Perhaps she'd made an effort on his behalf. There was an old carpet sweeper in a corner, behind a cathode ray TV that must have stopped working years ago.

He took in the rest of the room. The coffee table was ringed and stained, the heaps of letters and papers looked as though they'd been shuffled together in haste, the gas fire in the old pink-tiled fireplace was of a kind he remembered from his childhood, with a wood surround that had begun to disintegrate. None of it surprised him, all of it depressed him. Jo shouldn't have to live like this, but he guessed she wouldn't thank anyone for trying to make it different.

'Do you want coffee?' she asked anxiously. 'I bought some milk.'

'If it's no trouble.'

She winced, and he realised that could have meant he thought she wasn't capable. God, how sensitive did he have to be? He was treading among all the pieces of a damaged life.

He tried again. 'Thanks. That would be great.' She disappeared before he'd finished saying it.

While she was out of the room – he tried not to picture what her kitchen was like – he pulled the folded scarf out of his briefcase and held it to his face. It was soft, slightly crepey, and still smelt of Kate's perfume. He was tempted to hold on to it but he wanted Jo to have it. He laid it across his knees, not trusting the table would be clean.

She came back carrying two mugs with adverts for a local building firm on the side, trails of half-dissolved coffee running down over the coloured lettering. As she put them down on the table, he saw her hand was shaking.

'Just a minute,' she said, slipping away again. This time she brought in a full bottle of milk and an unopened packet of Hobnobs.

He smiled at her, seeing the effort she'd made.

When he'd opened the packet of biscuits and offered her one, he said, 'I've got something for you.'

She looked startled. Perhaps people didn't normally give her things.

'You may not have seen this.' He picked it up and handed it to her clumsily. 'Kate made it – the first one of this kind. I thought you might like it – your sort of colours. Of course, you'll have other things later on, when I... I can't manage it yet.'

She was wearing a mouse-brown jumper that had felted in the wash. The scarf toned with it perfectly. Instead of putting it on, she handled it with great care and lifted it to her face as he had done. Clutching it tight, she rocked slowly backwards and forwards. Richard ached to comfort her; it would be like comforting himself. After an unbearably long time she held the scarf away from her, studying it.

'I wouldn't have known it was hers,' she said. 'She didn't go for those colours, not like me; she always wanted bright things. We hated having to dress the same.'

'It suits you. Goes with your jumper. And your eyes.'

'Does it? I don't look at myself much.'

That made him look at her. Under the untidy hair her face had the same elvish quality as Kate's – more so as she was thinner. She hadn't minded letting him see her cry, but for the first time he glimpsed something other than her fragility: a steely determination to be herself. It wasn't quite the same as Kate; it seemed more uncompromising.

'You wanted to talk to me, Jo,' he said gently.

'Yes.' She tossed her hair back and started biting a nail.

'Was it about…?'

'Yes. I wanted to say I'm sorry. It wasn't about you, any of it. I just thought it was. Now I've started having these… flashbacks. I must have been very little – we must have been.'

'So it was Kate as well, as far as you remember?' He hated having to ask it.

She nodded, and didn't pull him up for not calling Kate Jans. 'It was both of us. Usually her first.'

He winced.

'I always sort of knew about it, but somehow she managed to forget. It feels like I'm doing the remembering for her, even though there's only me left. Now…'

'Has something been happening now?'

'I'm sure it's his voice.'

Had she said she heard voices? It seemed possible.

'I can't see the face. Sometimes there's a feel of someone…' She put her hands over her own face and bent forward but then sat up, looking at him again with a sort of urgency.

'That's sounds horrible.' He wanted to say more but didn't know what. Vague though it was, it made him feel sick. She'd mentioned something about hands before but didn't now. 'Are you sure you want to talk about it?'

She nodded.

'Sorry – I don't know if this is the right question to ask – I mean, do you know who it was?' He didn't dare use the words 'abuse' or 'abuser' in case they were too much for her.

This time she shook her head, baffled. 'It could have been Father, I suppose, only I don't think it was. The person I saw... he wasn't dark, he had ginger hair. Mother said once or twice that Kate and I were dark like our father. That was about the only thing she ever said to us about him, and she said it as though she didn't like it. But then she didn't like us very much, especially me.'

Richard could picture her mother's look of distaste only too well. It had crossed his mind that it might have been the father; so often it was.

'Does it bother you, not knowing?'

She screwed up her face, as if thinking. 'I'd like to think it wasn't him, but I don't know who else it could have been.'

'I hope it's OK for you, telling me about it,' he said tentatively, already feeling out of his depth.

'It's good telling someone who doesn't go on about my mental health. You just treat me as though I was a person.'

He couldn't help smiling. 'You are a person. And you're Kate's sister –

'Jans,' she broke in quickly. She still clung on to the old name. Then she said sheepishly, 'Kate to you.'

'I need to know about it for her sake too,' he said, no longer smiling. 'Something about her I never understood.' He saw her face fall, as though she was used to being discounted. 'And I care about you, Jo. I'm not just saying it.'

'I don't suppose so. People don't usually.'

'I do. Did you want to tell me more?'

'Not really. I just wanted you to know. And to say I'm sorry. I do know – most of the time – when things aren't real.'

'I understand. And I do believe you. It was hard to take in, that's all. I had no idea.' It was still hard to take in. He looked at his watch. 'Listen, would you like to come and have something to eat with me? It's a bit early, but we could go out soon.'

Her look of panic surprised him.

'I'm on benefits,' she said. 'I can't…'

'My treat. We won't go anywhere expensive, if that makes you feel better.'

'Nowhere expensive round here anyway.' She gave him a wry grin and looked down at the floor.

They found a small, empty Indian restaurant with purple carpets and a smell of incense and ingrained curry. He'd suggested Chinese but she'd worried it might not be properly vegetarian. She found it too much to choose from all the different dishes, so he ordered a selection of vegetables and hoped she'd like some of them. The food might not be as good as his and Kate's special Indian in Newington, but when it came she tucked into everything, tearing off strips of naan and dipping them in the sauces. The starched white tablecloth was soon spotted with red and yellow. It gave him pleasure to see her eat with such gusto; he guessed she didn't bother to make proper meals for herself. He was drinking Cobra but she'd said she couldn't with the medication and anyway she didn't like beer.

Even without alcohol she seemed more relaxed, more like the Jo he'd sometimes glimpsed in the Oxford days, before she retreated from him. He didn't want to ask too many questions, but slowly he began to form a picture of her life: the charity shop, the drop-in where she met other women who had mental health issues (don't we all? he thought, but he knew what she meant), someone called Damian who was a CPN, whatever that was, and Emmeline, whom she didn't seem to like very much but who must be some sort of friend or carer. He said little about himself. What could he say that wasn't to do with Kate, or with Rick who seemed irrelevant to her?

Laying down her spoon and fork, she asked him, seemingly out of the blue, 'Do you think she was happy? She was always better at being happy than me.'

Such a painful, loving question. Somehow he knew it wasn't about him. She looked at him intently, her chin tilted up, really wanting to know – a look that was so like Kate it startled him; he'd begun to see Jo more as someone in her own right. But there it was again, the likeness, and it wouldn't go away. As well as feeling the pain of it he found it comforting, as though for that moment Kate's death had become less real.

'Was she happy? I like to think so. She had her demons, though. And now I'm beginning to realise what they were.'

She nodded. For a moment they shared an intent silence, then Jo said, 'I know you're a good person. I can see it now.'

Richard found himself touching her hand – lightly, gently, drawing away again as soon as he'd made contact. She didn't seem to mind. 'And you're a good person, Jo. Don't let anyone tell you otherwise. You matter.'

She let the tears fall without stopping them; they mingled with the smears of sauce on her plate.

'You mustn't say that,' she said. 'They won't like it.'

'Who are 'they'?'

She shook her head and sniffed. He found a clean tissue in his pocket and offered it to her. She took it and used it but didn't thank him. The shell of privacy had enclosed her; he knew better than to ask again.

Jo

She was glad Richard was walking back with her to the house. She liked being with him; he listened to her. He was a nice man. That made two nice men she knew: him and Damian. Two men she didn't have to be afraid of. And it was good to talk to someone privately. she didn't often have conversations that weren't in the shop or the drop-in. She felt more like a normal person again; she hadn't thought she could remember how.

At the front door he smiled at her and she found herself smiling back. She felt him edge closer but didn't move.

'Goodbye, then,' she said. 'Thank you for....'

'You're very welcome. I'm glad you talked to me.' He seemed to mean it.

He was reaching to hug her; she felt her body tighten.

'Bye.' She swallowed the word and turned away, fumbling her key into the lock.

Curled up in the armchair, she relived their conversations. Had she really talked so much? All the things she'd said, especially about flashbacks and how it couldn't have been Father. She was shaking now at the thought of it. If she told Dr Greenland he'd probably think it was all a hallucination, but she was almost certain this was real. It wasn't mad to think it; Richard didn't think she was mad. 'I'm not mad,' she said out loud, then looked round the room in case the voices had heard her. They'd been quiet while she was with him, but the evening was always the worst time.

It wasn't the voices that came. It was *his* enormous body bearing down on her, his bitter male smell, the harsh bristles on his face. *Shut up,* he was saying. *Shut up. I'll kill you.* His huge hand now across her mouth, her trying to bite it, the blend of sweat and saliva. His pinkish-white skin, his wide pale lips marked with fine ridges. She couldn't see his eyes. When she tried to look into them, her own eyes closed as though a black curtain had come down. Her heart was pounding so hard the sound seemed to reverberate from outside her body.

For a long time his face kept coming back. When he left her – she knew it wouldn't be for long – the voices started again, especially *that* one. It wasn't quite the same as his voice but she knew it was him: the harsh, relentless tone, the things it said, over and over again. *You know you'll have to die. You're so bad you don't deserve to live. You must never, never tell anyone our secret.* It kept repeating *never, never.*

She couldn't stop herself screaming 'No!' but muffled it in a cushion. She nearly bit into the dark red nylon, despite the dirt and the dusty smell. When his voice stopped, other voices started, ones she knew and ones she didn't. Sometimes the voices were jumbled together, like people talking in a crowd. Sometimes one would push itself forward, not his voice but saying the kinds of things that his voice said. *How can you go on living? You don't deserve to live.* She was assaulted by them, buffeted as if by a strong wind; never knowing when another one would come.

'No!' she cried out again and again, as loudly as she dared. Some part of her knew that if she was too loud they'd take her to hospital again. She rocked backwards and forwards, her hands over her ears, willing them to stop, willing herself not to do what they said. No matter how terrible they were, she didn't believe them the way she used to. Damian had helped her with that. She held him in her mind, kind and warm and smiling, and her breathing began to slow. Then the other voice came; she thought it had deserted her. *The poor child*, it said. *The poor baby. What a terrible thing. Not her fault.* It was soon gone but she could feel it holding her as though an angel had its wings around her.

The flat was in darkness and she had no idea what time it was. Wiping her hands over her face, moving cautiously so as not to disturb the voices, she stood up and felt her way towards the light switch. It was clear what she needed to do now. However untidy the flat was, she always knew where to find a blade. She kept a stash of packets in the bathroom cabinet, hoping that if anyone noticed them they would just think she was zealous about shaving her legs. Some sense of self-preservation – perhaps it was the new voice – made her get a clean blade and a packet of plasters; the thought of taking care of herself brought unexpected tears.

It was a deeper cut than she'd intended. The pain felt clear, straightforward: she knew what it was and how to feel it. She let the blood run for a little while, watching it leak out of her and weep slowly down her arm, letting out some of the terrible things inside her. When it had run for a while she soaked a wodge of toilet paper in cold water and mopped it away; it was still oozing but beginning to slow. When she'd looked at it enough she put a plaster over it. It didn't reach the whole length of the cut and the ends stuck to the wound, but it was the best she could do. She prodded the covered area to reawaken the pain, then went to get coffee and a cigarette. She was shaking so much she could hardly pick up the cup.

The bitter tastes of smoke and coffee began to calm her. She'd switched on a small table lamp and the semi-dark was comforting. There was no clock in the sitting-room but it felt late. Too tired to sit upright, she half-lay in the armchair. When the cigarette was finished, she didn't light another one but picked up her coffee and dragged herself into the bedroom. Taking off her boots and her jacket but not much else, she curled up on the crumpled sheet and pulled the duvet over her.

As soon as she lay down, the voices started again. She shoved her head under the pillow and told them to go away. It felt like a war of attrition and she was running out of strength. Then *he* came back, only this time it was different. She saw his shape move towards Jans's bed and lean over it. The beds were close together, so close that when he bent towards Jans she caught the smell of peppermint on his breath, mingled with something sour and sickly. He didn't always smell like that. She heard Jans struggling to say 'No' and then her voice being muffled. Then Jo was under the warm, dark bedclothes, cuddling her furry rabbit, trying not to see or hear. The dark in bed now felt the same as the dark back then: not safe, never knowing if or when things would happen. She curled up tighter and another voice boomed in her ear. It sounded like a woman: *If you'd saved her she wouldn't be dead. You should have died, not her.* Then him again: *Why don't you just die now? So much easier. Go on, die. Go on, die....* It repeated the last phrase again and again, as though it wouldn't take no for an answer. The voice echoed in her head as she thrashed about, trying to get away.

Why not die? It *would* be easier. She didn't much like her life, anyway. She could get a blade and cut, deeper and harder, till not just the pain but life itself poured out of her. But then the other voice came, the angel one. *You were so little. You couldn't help it. She hid too. She couldn't save you.* She felt the arms around her; as they held her, her body was shaken by huge sobs. She burrowed under the duvet, trying to stop them, but they went on until she was too exhausted for more. She turned and lay on her back, neither awake nor asleep, her mind quiet.

She hadn't drawn the curtains and the grey morning light seeped in through her closed eyelids, waking her to remembrance of last night. Opening her eyes, she turned on her side to face the window.

At that moment *he* came back. It was so real it could have been happening now. His smell, the heat of him, the feel of his fingers as they covered her mouth, his voice – his ugly, grating voice. *Shut up! Shut up! If you make a noise I'll kill you.* Not so much his face this time, the part of it she'd seen, but the sense of him looming over her, and Jans in the other bed, hiding. Then the voice again: *If you remember, it means you're bad. Go on, die.*

'No,' she half screamed. 'No! No!' She knew the voice was there, even though it had gone quiet, and went silent as though the hand was still over her mouth. She lay rigid, hardly breathing, still feeling she was pinned to the bed. Other voices came: *Look at you. You're so fucked up you're a waste of space. Just look at you.* Mother was there too, from when she was young. *Behave yourself, Joanna. There's nothing to make a fuss about now. Just be quiet like Jancis.* Of course Jans was quiet: she was dead. A voice, not Mother's, said: *She's dead because you didn't look after her. It's your fault.*

'No!' She wanted to scream again but managed to stop herself. 'It's not my fault. It's Mother's fault.' Why had she said that? She couldn't remember what Mother had done, where she'd been. She hadn't been there; she hadn't known and probably hadn't cared, about Jo or even about Jans. The awful quiet: it was all kept so quiet. Had it really happened? Jo started to feel she couldn't tell what was real from what wasn't. It felt real, but how was she to know? The voice said, *You don't know anything. You're not right in the head. They won't believe you.*

Batting it away, she got up and went to the bathroom. Her arm was hurting from last night's cut and she saw it had been bleeding. Blood was oozing under the dressing she put on, long trails that left round splotches on the dirty grey flooring. She watched them as though they were nothing to do with her, but then she realised cutting last night hadn't made her feel better. It was awful; an awful mess. Maybe she should give in to the voice and just end it. Then she wouldn't hear it any more. No more Kate, no more her. So much the better.

Then she heard Damian. A memory of him saying, one afternoon when he'd dropped in unexpectedly, 'If you ever think you might – you know – do anything, you can always give me a call. Doesn't matter what time it is. I'd rather that than...' He'd said it as though he meant it. Of course he and the team might get into trouble if she did anything, but it hadn't sounded like that. It sounded more as though he cared. She could call him, even though she never had. She'd always waited till he came and sometimes wished he wouldn't come.

She wrapped a towel round her bleeding arm. The pain nearly made her cry, but it was better to cry for that than for her mangled life. She couldn't remember where she'd put her phone or if it had run out of battery. Looking for it was too much effort, but when she sat down in the armchair, she felt something hard beside her. Pulling the phone out, she saw it had just enough battery to make a call. There was a text from Richard, but she ignored it and brought up Damian's number. The phone told her the time was 8.04; she hoped it wasn't too early.

'Jo,' Damian sounded surprised and a bit flustered. 'Is everything OK? I don't start work till nine.'

'I know. Sorry. Can you come? I need to talk to you. '

'What's happened? You haven't...?'

'No, but I cut myself. It's bleeding.'

'How badly?'

She felt the dark red patches on the towel. There didn't seem to be any fresh blood. 'Not too bad. Maybe stopping now. I want... I have to tell you about things. It's all too much, what happened.' She couldn't keep her voice steady but held the phone away from her so that he wouldn't notice.

She heard him take a deep breath. He said, in the calm, deliberate way that meant he took her seriously, 'OK, Jo. I know you don't usually ring me. I'll look in on my way to work. Just hang on, I won't be long.'

She came downstairs to open the door, holding the towel round her arm. It was pale blue and the bloodstains on it had begun to darken. Her clothes were crumpled from having been slept in. Damian looked less focused than usual, as though he hadn't quite got into work gear. He had his briefcase with the shoulder strap and carried a white paper bag in his other hand.

'Hi, Jo,' he said. 'How you doing?'

She looked at him, turned and ran straight upstairs. She could hear him plodding more slowly behind her in his thick-soled trainers.

She was used to letting him into the flat, but this time it was different. It felt as though he was really coming in. He sat down in the bigger chair, the one Emmeline sat in, put the briefcase down beside him and stretched out his legs. He was still holding the paper bag. She stood grasping the back of the other chair; she couldn't bear to sit down.

'Did you have that coffee?' he said, offering her the bag. 'I thought you might need one of these.'

She stared at the two croissants in the bag. Surely he wasn't supposed to do things like that. He was behaving like a person, not a professional. Still holding the towel round her arm, she took one of the croissants and munched it, standing up. She hadn't known how hungry she was.

When she'd finished he said, 'Better look at this arm first of all, make sure it's all right. I am a nurse.'

She hadn't realised psychiatric nurses were proper nurses too. She sat down in the chair and let him unwrap the towel. The dressing she'd put on was soaked with blood, like a sanitary pad on a heavy day, and her arm throbbed. He lifted the dressing very gently and looked at the cut. She could see him trying not to wince.

'You might need that seeing to,' he said. 'Have you got a clean dressing?'

She fetched it from the bathroom, not wanting him to see the state of the place, but he asked about antiseptic.

'Shall I get it?' he said. 'I can put the kettle on at the same time, if you'd like.' She didn't think he wasn't supposed to do that either but she didn't much mind. He wasn't like Emmeline, coming in and taking over. She didn't even mind him seeing the dirty kitchen. He knew where the bathroom was; he'd used it once or twice. The kitchen was opposite the bathroom, so he'd have seen that too. Perhaps he'd just dress her arm and make coffee, and then go. When he came back she'd say sorry, it was all a mistake. Maybe thinking she could talk about it was a mistake. But then the voices, which had been quiet since he arrived, started up. *You think he's going to help you? He'll get you locked up in hospital. Where you deserve to be.* Then a child's voice that sounded like Jans's, chanting again and again: *Good girls don't tell, good girls don't tell, good girls don't tell...*

By the time he came back with an old tube of Germolene and a mug of coffee, she was huddled in the chair with her fist in her mouth, pushing away the terrible voice that was now saying: *Last chance. You'll have to die. Hurry up and do it.*

'So, Jo,' he said, when they'd dealt with the dressing. 'What's all this about, then? Looks like you're not in a good state.'

She opened her mouth and no words came. Then she started to tell him. 'First of all there were hands,' she said.

Jo

'So you were seeing hands,' Damian said carefully, the way he would if Jo had said she could see spiders crawling all over him.

Usually that would have stopped her saying more, that and him asking about her medication – which he hadn't done yet. But now something made her say, 'No. Not *seeing* like that. It was more like...' The voices were threatening to break through again. '...like remembering.' She held her hands tight over her face so it wouldn't happen again. It felt like hiding under the duvet with her eyes shut.

'You mean like flashbacks? You haven't mentioned those before.'

'No.' She didn't want to say the voices had told her not to. 'It's all started coming back more since Jans – my sister – died.' She curled up tighter in the chair with her arms over her head. She was shaking again and tried not to let him see. 'He did things to us. In bed. We were only little.'

'Who was he? Do you know?'

She shook her head. 'No. I don't know but I sort of feel I should. He was horrible. I can't... It's all getting too much now. That's why I cut.'

'I can see it's too much. Are you thinking about...? Do you feel you might make an attempt? You know I have to ask you.'

'I don't know. The voices tell me to. Sometimes it seems like the easiest thing. It's all so awful, the voices and now the flashbacks.'

'Have you actively been making plans?'

She shook her head. 'It's not like that. They could just push me too far, and then...'

She uncurled for a moment and stared at him in fear. 'Will you have to tell Dr Greenland? Will I get sectioned? I don't want to go to hospital again.'

He thought for a moment. 'I will have to tell Dr Greenland, but I don't think you'll have to go to hospital. Leave it with me.'

'What do you mean?'

'There are other possibilities. Maybe you won't have to be sectioned right now.'

She shook her head, not believing him. 'Don't you have to do what Dr Greenland says?'

'Leave it with me,' he said again. 'I'll phone you as soon as I can. Just make sure you keep that phone switched on. You may not believe it, but I'm on your side.'

She couldn't remember anyone having said that to her. She and Jans had been on each other's side, deep down, but they'd never spoken about it.

'It's OK, Jo,' she could hear him saying once the pain was less. 'It's OK. Just take it easy.' Emmeline was always telling her to take it easy, but when he said it, it didn't feel patronising.

She wanted to thank him but the words wouldn't come. He'd have to go now, she knew, and talk to Dr Greenland and the team. When he stood up he put the bag with the second croissant beside her on the chair.

'I won't tell Dr Greenland about that,' he said, and grinned at her in a way that made her think he might like her.

After Damian had gone she went back to bed; the safest place. The voices could still get her but she could muffle them with the duvet. They'd gone quiet for the moment but she knew they'd be back. Her arm felt sore under the dressing Damian had put on. She wished now she hadn't cut it so hard, but in that desperate moment she hadn't realised what she was doing. She swallowed down her medication with a scalding gulp from the mug of coffee she'd just made. The tablets would dull the voices and make them less insistent. She'd found the phone charger under a cushion on the other armchair and now it was plugged in near the bedside table, the phone next to her in the bed. It felt like having Damian and his smile there beside her, keeping her safe. The bag with the croissant in it was beside her too. She took big bites of the sweet buttery bread, savouring the luxury of it.

She licked her fingers and lifted the last flakes from the paper. When she'd finished, she glanced at her phone. It was still telling her she had a message from Richard. Not sure if she wanted to, she opened it. Good to see you, it said. Hope you're OK. Let me know if there's anything I can do. Will be in touch. R. There was nothing she could say. She wanted to tell him how terrible it was, how the flashbacks and the voices had got worse after she'd seen him. *Don't you dare tell him*, one of the voices said. *He'll turn against you. You don't know what he'll do to you.* Perhaps she should tell Richard to leave her alone. Maybe seeing him hadn't done her any good; he'd been kind and it hadn't helped. She put the phone back beside her and turned on to her side.

As she curled up she heard the other voice soothing her, saying, *Take care now. Wrap yourself up. Go to sleep.* Just as she was letting herself drift off, the face came, clearer now. She saw the flared shape of the nose, the pink skin with its open pores, the blue eyes with thick lids and gingery lashes. She smelt the breath, the sickening peppermint-alcohol fumes; she felt it hot on her face. He loomed over her, enormous, his eyes boring into her, hard and cold with blue-tinged whites. She had no idea who he was but the face was familiar. It couldn't be Father, she knew that. Shuddering uncontrollably, she curled up tighter, her arms over her head to keep him out. She was freezing cold; her whole skin quivered with animal fear.

When the image began to fade she wrapped the duvet tightly round her and huddled into herself, biting her nails for comfort. When was Damian going to ring? Surely he wouldn't forget her. Maybe it would be Dr Greenland instead, telling her she'd have to go into hospital. As a voluntary patient, she hoped, but even then she knew she'd be sectioned if she tried to leave.

She felt the phone buzz beside her. Damian, at last. Of course she'd have to go to hospital. What else could she do? Even knowing it, she answered.

'Hi, Jo. How you doing? You hanging on in there?'

'Still alive,' she mumbled.

'That's good. Listen, I need to talk to you about possibilities.'

'Possibilities? You mean hospital? I hate that ward.'

'Hang on. I didn't say hospital. There's two things. One is you could stay there at home and have the crisis team come in. You might know Bridget; she used to be a CPN. They'd help you stay safe. Or ...'

Or hospital. People wandering about the corridors all day or lying on their beds and staring into space. People packed into the smoking room, chain-smoking till the smoke in there was so thick you could hardly breathe. People crying, shouting, groaning. OTs running groups where nobody said anything. The supposedly cheerful yellow of the walls. The nurses sitting in their office, busy with their paperwork, emerging now and then to make sure nothing untoward was happening.

'Jo? You still there?'

'Mm.'

'Jo, I said there's another possibility. Not hospital.'

'No?' She didn't believe him.

'No, something else. We've been incredibly lucky.'

'Yeah?'

'We can get you a place at a crisis house. It's quite small – twelve people – and it's all women. They understand about trauma and abuse.'

He was calling it trauma now, not just 'your illness.'

Damian went on, 'You're very lucky they can take you straight away. They want to take you,' he added. 'You're the sort of person they can help.'

She was glad he couldn't see her doubled up in bed. The pain again, the pain of people being kind. She was sure they wouldn't want her when they saw her.

'So, Jo,' Damian was saying. 'I'll be round in about an hour to take you there. Can you pack a few things, or get someone to pack them for you and bring them along later?'

That would mean Emmeline. She didn't want Emmeline to know she was having an 'episode'. 'OK,' she said noncommittally.

'I'll see you soon, then,' he said. 'And Jo...'

'Yeah?'

'Just keep hanging on. OK?'

Packing things felt much too hard; even getting out of bed seemed beyond her. Perhaps she'd stay there and not bother. If he wanted to send the crisis team, let him. She pushed herself upright, found the old T-shirt and torn leggings she usually wore in bed and stuffed them into her rucksack. From the bathroom she took a box of blades and a packet of plasters, just in case, her medication – they'd be bound to ask if she was taking it – her toothbrush, a nearly empty tube of toothpaste and a half-full box of tampons. She threw it all into the rucksack with her tobacco and papers. Then she remembered the scarf, which she'd left on the sitting room table. She had to have something of Jans. Instead of stuffing it into the rucksack, she made an attempt to fold it and pushed it well in so it wouldn't fall out. Leaving the rucksack half-shut, she curled up in bed again to wait for Damian.

As she lay down, her knee touched against something small and solid. She fished it out from the crumpled bedding, recognising the furry feel of it. Squidge, the toy rabbit that she'd had since the time when she and Jans... maybe even before that. Jans had had one the same, called Squdge. Squdge was green with a white face and front; Squidge had once been light tan and white, though he was darker now and stained with coffee. She'd always slept with him under the duvet and even now he was a comfort, when she remembered to find him. He had the same reassuring softness as the new voice. She stroked the little toy and held him close to her face, smelling his familiar bed-smell.

She was in her bed next to Jans's, curled up under the duvet with her thumb in her mouth and her cheek resting on Squidge. Her eyes were closed to keep everything dark but she knew the bedside lamp was on. She heard Jans's bed creak, shufflings and mutterings and *him* breathing hard, each breath an attack on Jans. Then: *Shut up! Shut up! Not a word.* She heard Jans give a tiny whimper and then the black curtain came down.

Waves of terror shuddered through Jo's body, far worse than before. She shoved her fist into her mouth to stop herself screaming and forced her eyes open. For a moment she didn't recognise where she was. The grimy cream-coloured walls and cracked lampshade meant nothing to her, then slowly she began to realise it wasn't happening now. Her heartbeat was still hammering through her body and when she tried to get out of bed her legs felt soft, like spaghetti. She sat on the edge of the bed, clutching Squidge, her feet hardly resting on the floor. If Damian came now, she wouldn't be able to get downstairs to open the door. Her coffee had gone cold but she drank it anyway. It tasted flat and disgustingly bitter, but it was real.

When the bell rang she was still shaking. She put her feet to the floor and found her legs just about held her up. She picked up the rucksack and hitched it on to her shoulder, even though it wasn't properly closed. Slowly, clutching at walls and furniture, she made her way through the flat. At the top of the stairs she paused. Going down and opening the door would mean being taken into a world where people would know about what had happened to her and Jans. Clinging on to the wooden banister rail, she manoeuvred herself to the bottom.

When she opened the front door, Damian was looking across the garden as though he'd expected to wait a long time.

'Hi, Jo,' he said, and smiled a smile that made her feel safer. 'You ready to go now?'

She nodded and pulled the door shut behind her. She didn't stop to think about her keys.

Richard

On the train back to Edinburgh, jammed in a window seat beside a perky orange-haired young woman with a large laptop that nudged into his space and a phone that was forever pinging, he tried to work from the notes he'd made at this morning's meeting. He could hardly remember anything about it, his mind still full of yesterday's time with Jo. The train was so packed that he couldn't move seats, though he longed to be to sitting on the right-hand side, where he'd be able to see Newcastle and the huge white arches of the Tyne bridge, and then relax into the expanse of grass and sky on the way up to Berwick. There was a way to go yet. On this side, if he was lucky, he might glimpse the Angel of the North, embracing the landscape with its huge flightless wings. He and Kate had sometimes played Angel of the North with Rick at the top of Arthur's Seat, spreading their arms as though they were flying, Rick giggling and swooping about, then standing stiff like a statue till one of them tickled him. Kate had looked so free up there, laughing with her head thrown back, arms stretched wide to the sky, hair blowing over her face. Remembering her like that he laughed with joy, just for a moment until it hurt again.

He'd taken it for granted that they would go on playing the game till Rick grew out of it. He couldn't do it on his own, even if Rick wanted. Rick always been a serious boy but he shared Kate's capacity for moments of exuberance, Richard following after them like the tail of a kite. The pale, buttoned-up child Rick was now seemed like a different person. Richard wondered guiltily how much his inability to express his own grief was affecting his son. His father had no truck with emotional display and his mother had always tried to make things better. From both of them he'd learned to stifle his feelings inside himself. He thought something of their mother had rubbed off on Fran, though he was probably underestimating her. Unlike their mother she wasn't trying to make it better, just helping when she could. He thought of her slightly crooked smile that showed her uneven teeth – she didn't like them but they were part of her kind look – and the way she squinted up at him through her glasses. But when he thought of her being there in the house, it still felt as though she had supplanted Kate.

Thinking of Kate made him think of Jo: the naked suffering in her eyes, the way she'd held the scarf to her face and confided her grief to it, how much she'd enjoyed the Indian meal. What did he feel for her? Fondness? Affection? It was more than feeling sorry for her, more than their shared loss; it was almost the kind of tenderness he'd sometimes felt towards Kate, only Kate had laughed it off or pushed it away. 'You don't have to make such a fuss of me,' she'd often said. 'I'm all right' - even when she patently wasn't. In his mind he stretched out his hand to let Jo know he was there. He'd sent her a quick text but didn't suppose she'd reply. He wouldn't follow it up: he didn't want her to feel he was breathing down her neck.

He tried to settle to work but found his eyes closing and his head dropping forward. He was climbing up a mountain with Kate, who was Jo, and when they got to the top she put on a huge pair of wings. She tried to fly off but crashed to the ground and lay there, crooked and groaning, the way Kate had lain in bed that last morning. He tried to make her sit up but she kept saying, 'Don't touch me. It's your fault.' In the dream he felt a huge guilt that he had harmed both her and Jo.

He woke with a jolt to find they'd pulled into York. The platform was dimly lit and the pale, grimy brickwork looked cold. People were scurrying away from the train or queuing to get on. The orange-haired young woman had gone and he enjoyed the luxury of spreading his cramped limbs, until a man in a grey suit leaned over him, lifting a suitcase into the luggage rack.

'Anyone sitting here?'

He had to say no. He shuffled back into his own seat and resigned himself to the discomfort, knowing there would be no Kate to laugh about it with him at the end. He dreaded opening the front door: seeing her coats hung up with the immutability of an exhibit in a museum, while the house met him with its subtle odour of change.

The man beside him was thin and seemed take up less space than the young woman. He talked on his phone almost non-stop in the sort of hard-edged business voice that always made Richard feel tense. He gave up trying to work and imagined the feel of Kate sitting there beside him, poised between the cream plastic surround and the orange-red upholstery of the seat. People always said a dead person could appear to you as though they were there. He'd kept trying to conjure her up but never could. Once or twice she had appeared quite naturally, standing there in the kitchen or beside her drawing board, smiled at him and vanished again. The other times he'd seen her he'd known she was simply a memory; however real it was. He turned to her, now, facing the window, and felt, rather than saw, her presence there. He needed to know what she'd say about Rick. It felt cruel to remind her of leaving her son, but who else could he ask? Right now Fran didn't count.

Kate would have put her hand on his arm and told him not to worry. Just be natural, she'd say, smiling at him in a way he was sure no one else ever would. You're so uptight. Relax. She'd lean her head against his shoulder, nudge him or tickle him to make him laugh. But they had talked seriously too. Sometimes when she'd been tense he'd tried to soothe her. She'd seemed full of angles then, almost like Jo. For a moment the two sisters merged together in his mind and he wasn't sure which of them he was comforting. He hoped Jo was all right – as all right as she could be.

Fran was there at the door as soon as he turned the key. So was Rick, which surprised him. He'd stood for several minutes before opening the door, his bunch of keys in his hand, staring down the quiet suburban street at the solid brick semis and bungalows. Arthur's Seat loomed behind them, dwarfing them so that they looked like the row of miniature houses that had stood beside the track of his boyhood model railway. He still had it but hadn't got it out for a long time: maybe it was something for him and Rick to do together. Boys' toys, people said, but Kate had loved it too and had made a little rural scene, with a river and trees and sheep on a hillside, that fitted between the stations.

Fran's warm hug touched him more than he expected; it was good to have a sister. He thought of Jo without one.

'Hi, Dad,' Rick said, joining in the hug.

When Richard stepped back, he saw not the peaky changeling child he'd grown used to but someone more like the boy he'd known. Rick's face looked less gaunt; the dark rings round his eyes had almost gone. He was still pale – he always was – but the skin below his cheekbones had a faint pink under the surface. He wasn't smiling but his face looked less drawn.

'Good to see you, Rick. How's it going?'

'OK.'

Richard knew not to expect more.

Fran said, 'Rick was beating me at chess.'

Richard smiled. Fran was a hopeless chess player, though she would keep trying.

'I slaughtered her,' Rick said, grinning. 'She's even worse than you.'

For a moment they all laughed; Richard felt he'd only just remembered how to. He saw Rick struggling to keep his smile, his face momentarily a clown's face until he righted it again. Richard held out his arms and felt Rick move willingly into them. His own body relaxed in response and for the first time since Kate's death he felt tears come gently. It wasn't until Rick drew away from him that he noticed Fran wasn't there. It touched him that she'd slipped out and left them together.

Rick gave another sad, wonky smile and said, looking at him quizzically, 'I thought you didn't want me to see you cry, Dad.'

'I didn't want me to see me cry,' Richard said. 'It's hard for both of us.'

Rick nodded. 'It's OK if you cry,' he said, in that way he had of sounding like the grown-up. 'I still keep thinking Mum is going to come back, like she hasn't really gone. But then I sort of know she isn't, and there's a kind of hole where she used to be. That's what Fran said.'

'You've been talking to Fran?'

'Yeah. She's cool.'

'Is she?' It was hard to picture his dumpy, dishevelled sister as cool.

'She asked me about things but she said I didn't have to tell her. That's cool.'

What Fran had done sounded so simple. But then she wasn't struggling with her own loss. He thought of the awkward non-talk he'd had with Rick at his father's. It didn't come easily to him to talk about things – not with Rick, not with his friend V, not even with Fran. But perhaps words weren't what mattered most. At best, he and Rick seemed to get through to each other without them.

Fran was waiting in the sitting room, watching the news with the sound turned down low. When Richard came in she switched it off and looked up at him.

'Don't let me stop you watching,' he said, hoping she might leave him to his own thoughts.

'That's OK. It was just something depressing about Brexit. You're lucky, being in Scotland.'

'Mm. You talked to Rick, then?'

'He talked to me – a bit. You don't mind?'

'Course not. You're better at that sort of thing than I am. He likes you, I said.'

Fran smiled. He could see her trying not to look too pleased.

Rick had started building a Lego crane on the sitting-room floor. Richard knelt down on the Persian rug to look at it and had an almost irresistible urge to put together the little bricks scattered around it. The way they clicked into place would be mindlessly satisfying, to the point where he could stop thinking about anything else. He contented himself with picking up one of the little people and sitting it on a brick.

'How was Jo?' Fran asked.

Richard looked up. Fran's face had the concerned expression he'd pictured before he saw it. Her hair had grown longer, he noticed. The way it fluffed out round her head and the shape of her eyes, big and wide open behind her round glasses, reminded him of a rag doll.

'Well, you know. She's dealing with a lot. She's got spirit, though. I wish she had something better than a dismal flat in a nowhere sort of place.' He wanted to give Jo some of the simple good things in his own life – a garden, chairs you could lounge back in, a cosy kitchen where you could sit and drink a cup of tea. He wasn't sure any of them would mean much to her.

'Good you could make time to see her, then. She must have liked that.'

Richard shrugged. 'Hard to tell. I took her out for a meal. I don't think she eats properly.'

Fran looked sympathetic. 'Poor love. Difficult enough being on your own even without all her problems.'

Richard wondered if Fran minded being on her own. She hadn't said and he hadn't asked: they had a keen sense of each other's privacy. Her short marriage, to a man whose name Richard could never remember, had been such a disaster he'd always imagined she fought shy of trying again. Perhaps she was lonely.

It hit him belatedly that Fran had also been talking about him. Looking up at her, he saw her redden. She took off her glasses and busily wiped them on the front of her T-shirt.

'I didn't mean...' she said awkwardly. 'Oh, I'm so sorry, Richard. Tact is never my strong point.'

'No. Lucky I'm a bit slow on the uptake.'

They both laughed, trying to make it better for each other. Richard stood up to get them both a glass of wine. As he did so, he felt his phone buzz in his pocket. Jo had texted: Going to crisis house. All got too much. Shouldn't have seen you.

The last sentence hit him like a punch in the stomach. He'd been enjoying the warm feeling that their meeting had done her good, hoping they'd meet again. When his breath calmed he asked Fran what a crisis house was, fudging it by saying it was for a friend of his. He was sure she'd guess who it was.

Jo

She sat in the car, nibbling her nails down beyond the tender skin, hardly noticing as they took the familiar route up past the bus terminus at the top of Muswell Hill then steeply down towards Crouch End clock tower and the quirky little shops around it. The voices were coming and going but the noise of the engine was masking them. She had no idea where the place was and didn't ask. Once she was there it wouldn't matter anyway. As Damian drove down Crouch Hill towards Stroud Green, he half turned to her – making sure, she thought, she wasn't rolling a cigarette or perhaps secretly cutting.

'You OK, Jo?' he asked. 'Not far now.'

She nodded, sucking a finger that was beginning to hurt. Jans had always winced at her bumpy fingertips and truncated nails. Jo could feel her there in the car beside her and told her silently, I'm doing this for you as well. You know that. She had a familiar sense of Jans being close by, not touching but near enough to sense each other's bodies. They'd been able to feel one another sometimes even when they were in different cities. She hugged her rucksack close to her, to feel less alone.

They reached Mount Pleasant Crescent. The jingle of the name had always amused Jo; it was the kind of thing she and Kate had laughed at together. Damian stopped the car in a small road off the crescent, in front of a pair of tall Victorian semis with grey brick walls and pointed gables. Her senses had woken up: she noticed one of the houses had a larger front door, painted orange-red to match the decorative brickwork around it, and plants in large pots at the sides of the steps. The voice started up again. *Don't go in there*, it said. *You'll die if you go in there. I'll kill you.* It laughed, a fat, breathy, complacent laugh that shivered down her back.

Damian opened the car door for her and looked in. 'You ready, Jo?'

Her stomach dropped as though she was about to face an exam or, worse, a case review where everyone said they didn't think she was well enough to be let out of hospital. She imagined a panel of people in the house asking her questions, then telling her it was a mistake and sending her to the hospital instead.

Damian reached out his hand for her rucksack but she clasped it closer to her. When she stood up, her legs were so shaky she tottered against him. He held her arm until she was steady.

'Come on, then,' he said. 'You'll be all right.' He rang the entryphone and a woman's voice answered. Jo couldn't make out what she was saying.

'Joanna Brookfield,' he said.

The door buzzed and Damian signalled for Jo to go in.

Clutching her rucksack in front of her with one hand, she grasped the door with the other; its edge was rounded with many coats of paint. She had to push hard against the hydraulic door-closer to get it open. The hallway, with its blue heavy-duty carpet and faint smell of air freshener, felt like a doctors' surgery. Off to the left was a room with the same carpet, where a woman with straggly dyed-blonde hair and a persistent frown sat behind a small desk. She looked up at Jo over her computer screen.

'Hello, Joanna,' she said. 'I'm Stacey.'

'Jo,' Jo muttered. She heard the door creak and felt Damian standing behind her.

'Do take a seat.' The chairs weren't standard waiting-room issue but flowery armchairs arranged round a low table. She and Damian sat opposite each other, leaving spare chairs between them.

'I'll get you some tea,' the woman said. 'Eleanor will be down in a minute.'

'Can I have coffee? Black?' Jo said. Perhaps they thought coffee wasn't good for you.

'Of course.'

Eleanor turned out to be one of the psychiatrists, though to Jo she didn't seem like one. She was small, with bobbed dark brown hair and round dark-framed glasses which seemed to dwarf her face. She was wearing trousers and a red-and-blue flowered top and held out a small plump hand with painted nails. Jo stared at the hand and realised she was supposed to shake it. She reached out her own, suddenly ashamed that her nails were so bitten. *Don't trust her*, a voice said. *She doesn't like you.*

Eleanor sat down between Jo and Damian and turned towards Jo, asking questions about how she was feeling. Jo tried to listen to her and not the voices but kept moving her head to shake them off.

'So it's all got too much?' Eleanor said. 'Your CPN has told me a bit about how you are but I want to hear it from you. If you can.'

Jo meant to say something, but a great wave was rising up from her chest into her throat and spurting out of her eyes. Her body heaved again and again; it felt more like being sick. Eleanor put a hand on her arm and sat quiet while Jo bent over, her hands covering her face.

'It's OK, Jo,' she said. 'You don't have to tell me right now.'

Jo moved her hands down her face and peered up at Eleanor. Despite what the voice had said, she thought Eleanor was all right. She was neither smiling nor grim, just calmly waiting as though she wanted to hear.

Jo propped her chin on her hands and stared down at her jeans. Being looked at felt too much. 'It keeps coming back,' she said.

'What does?'

'Someone. He did things to us, both of us. I couldn't protect her.' She felt the wave rising again.

'Someone... You don't know who?'

'No. We were very little.'

'You've never remembered him before?' She seemed ready to believe it was a memory, not just a symptom.

'Not like that. I always knew something had happened. She managed to forget.'

'And she is?'

'My sister. She's died.' Another wave came and she covered her face again. 'We were twins,' she said through her fingers.

'I'm so sorry. That must be awful. I can imagine; I'm a twin.'

Jo sat up in surprise. Psychiatrists weren't supposed to tell you things about themselves: you were the one that had the illness. She nodded.

'And it was after she died that... you started seeing him?'

Jo nodded.

'And voices?' Eleanor sounded matter-of-fact about it.

Jo said nothing. *Don't tell her*, one of the voices said. *You'll be sectioned.*

'It's OK,' Eleanor said. 'All sorts of people hear voices. Did they start before then?'

Jo nodded again. 'When I went to hospital. A long time ago.'

'And they trouble you a lot? More now?'

'They won't leave me alone. They don't like it if I remember. He tells me I'll have to die.'

'He's the man who...?'

'Horrible. On and on. Making me listen to him.' Jo couldn't believe she was telling Eleanor all this, showing her how ill she was, but something told her it was all right. She'd be given so much medication she wouldn't be able to think straight.

'You think you might do something to yourself, because he tells you to?'

'Yes.'

'We'll keep you safe here. There'll always be staff around, and people will pop in to make sure you're OK.'

'You're going to let me stay here? I won't have to go to hospital?'

'Of course you can stay here. For a week, for definite, and for a month if you need to.'

Jo had almost forgotten about Damian, but he was still sitting there, leaning back in the armchair with one long leg crossed over the other, nodding at her if she happened to glance his way. Eleanor turned to him.

'I'm afraid I'm going to have to ask you …?'

'Damian.'

'…Damian, to leave now. We're an all-women house and men aren't normally allowed in. But I'm glad you came with Jo.'

Damian stood up easily and gave Jo a little wave. 'You'll be all right. I'll see you when you get back.' He grinned at her as he went out.

'No men?' Jo asked. She'd wondered if Richard might want to come and see her. If there were no men, she could tell him he couldn't.

'No. Most of the women who come here feel safer not having men around.'

They're trying to get rid of me, the voice said. *I'm not going.*

She was sitting on the bed in a little white-painted room that looked out over a long lawn with dark trees at the far end. Damian had told her she was lucky to be there. She'd never thought of herself as lucky. To her, Jans was the one who'd had the luck, until it turned against her. This was certainly better than being in hospital. There was a bed with a striped cotton bedspread, a table and chair, a small wardrobe and a washbasin. It was a bit like a student room. There was a flowered chintz armchair too, its arms worn down to the white stuffing as though a lot of hands had clutched it for comfort. The room felt quiet and clean and smelt faintly of roses. On one wall was a large photograph of a river with crinkled patches of light, green where trees were reflected in the water. On the wall above the table another photograph, framed in shiny metal, showed a small bay surrounded by rocks. The picture was so bright it felt like an intrusion: the vivid sky, the gleam of water against pale sand, the deep blue sea glittering in the sun. A memory came of her and Jans running into the waves in a little tucked-away cove with steep steps leading down to it. They were in shorts; their legs were brown. They were happy. The memory stopped as though a shutter had fallen and a jeering voice said, *You think you can be happy? Never.* She wanted to cut but she'd been told it wasn't encouraged. She'd be helped to stop, they'd said. The wound on her arm had been dressed; she could feel the tight bandage when she bent her elbow.

Eleanor had said someone would pop in 'on a regular basis' and she was bracing herself for the next visit, hoping they wouldn't catch her doing something they didn't think she should be doing. After she'd spoken to Eleanor there had been a long agreement process where she'd been told in detail what would happen and which people would be there to support her. She couldn't remember it all but they had printed out a document for her, with a photo of the house on the front. At the back were pictures of the staff, smiling, with their first names underneath. In between was a list of all the things that had been agreed. It was Stacey who had taken her through the agreement process. Jo had a vague impression of someone tall with big breasts, wearing a long, floppy cardigan. She'd noticed that when Stacey wrote she clutched the pen in her fist, as though she wasn't used to writing. Let me do it, the once-academic part of Jo had wanted to say.

Now she was here, her mind was as blank as the wall in front of her. She felt nothing at all, not even the discomfort of being in an unfamiliar place. The voices sounded muffled, far away. When she glanced down at her hands they had a rubbery look, as if they weren't quite real and didn't belong to her. Nor did the jeans, worn white at the knees, with thin legs inside them. She recognised the square-shaped jut of the kneecaps under the fabric but couldn't feel they were hers. This body sitting on the bed seemed almost inanimate, a thing someone had put there. She was looking at it from a distance, drifting away from it, until she found herself gazing down from a corner of the ceiling. In a detached way she noticed how messy the hair looked.

Then it changed. She saw a bed with a Paddington Bear duvet shoved back in a heap. An upside-down bear face with a red hat stared out from the tangle, pointing her towards a scene that for a moment she couldn't make sense of. A ginger-haired man in a blue shirt was lying on his front and wriggling about. Under his hands was what might have been a doll, it lay so still: a tiny dark-haired child, her face frozen blank. When Jo saw her, a judder of terror brought her back to her body. She covered her eyes with her hands and lay shuddering.

Someone knocked lightly on the door. She felt as if electricity had jolted her body. Involuntarily she screamed.

'It's OK, Jo,' a woman said. 'Just seeing if you're all right.'

Jo didn't move or open her eyes. With the edges of her skin, she felt the woman come closer. She sensed a hand hovering just above her arm and twitched away.

'It's OK,' the woman said again. 'Easy does it.' Her voice was low and soothing and had a slight lilt.

Jo tried to open her eyes but her eyelids fluttered down again, protecting her with dark. It was terrible, having someone see her like this, but she hoped they wouldn't go away.

'I'm Bethan,' the woman said. 'I'll be coming in to see you quite often. Looks like you've been having a bad time. Do you want to tell me about it?'

Jo shook her head.

'All right, then. Would you like me to stay with you for a bit?'

Jo nodded and felt herself coming back into her body. Hardly opening her eyes, she saw Bethan settle in the armchair. A warm face, frowning a little with concern; honey-blonde hair with dark roots; navy trousers and deep pink Crocs.

'You're safe here,' Bethan said. 'And whatever it is isn't happening now. Just breathe and remember that. Shall I get you a cup of tea?'

Jo didn't think she could move her face enough to talk but managed to say, 'Coffee, black, no sugar.' Then she muttered, 'Please.'

'OK. I'll be right back.'

When Bethan brought the coffee she took Jo's hand and talked to her softly. It didn't matter much what she said – something about a group meeting and did she feel able to go to it and would she like someone to sit with her at supper. It was a real human voice and it kept the other voices at bay. The way Bethan spoke reminded Jo a little of the new voice that had come but had more rise and fall to it. She could be Welsh.

After a while, when Jo was sitting up and drinking her coffee, Bethan said, 'You've hardly got any of your things here. Do you want somebody to go and get some more clothes for you? There's someone ...' She leafed through the agreement. 'Emmeline Forrest? You said she's got your keys.'

'Did I?' Jo couldn't remember what they'd asked her or what she'd replied. 'Well, she could bring some stuff. Would she have to come in and see me?'

'Not if you don't want her to. She could drop the things off.'

It surprised Jo that they weren't going to make her see Emmeline. With Emmeline she always felt she had no choice.

'OK.'

'Anyone else you'd like a visit from? Your mum, perhaps?'

Jo stiffened.

Bethan shrugged. 'Up to you.'

'Would Richard come?' She was surprised she'd said it. She hadn't thought she wanted to see him.

'Who's Richard?'

'My brother-in-law. He's in Scotland.'

Jo turned her head away. She heard Bethan draw a careful breath.

'Well,' Bethan said, 'this is a women-only house. Having a man here might upset the other guests. If you stay the full month and you're well enough near the end, perhaps you could meet him outside. There's a nice coffee shop down the road. See how it goes.'

Guests. Jo liked the word. The hospital would never call people guests. It sounded almost like a hotel, except nobody would be here if they could manage not to be.

In a moment of silence she heard one of the voices again. *They won't keep you for a month. They'll chuck you out.* Another one said, *You won't last a month. You'll kill yourself.* Jo shook her head to get rid of them, hoping Bethan wouldn't notice.

'Having trouble?' Bethan asked. 'Just tell them to leave you alone. Otherwise they'll have me to contend with.' She put her hands on her hips and laughed in a way that made Jo feel better.

'Coming down to supper, then?' Bethan said. 'I'll sit with you, if you like. They make very good soup here and the bread's homemade.'

Jo thought it was probably a joke.

Richard

His first thought, when Fran explained to him about the crisis house, was that seeing him must have made Jo worse. Perhaps he should have realised it wouldn't be good for her, even though he'd wanted to; perhaps he should have stopped her talking about those things. Kate had always told him how careful she had to be with Jo. He'd sensed that same protectiveness when Jo talked about Kate, even though Jo hadn't been in a position to do much for her. The sisters hadn't seen each other often in the last few years, with Kate in Paris and then Edinburgh and Jo stuck in London, but he knew Kate had often sent Jo cards and messages. She'd gone to see her a couple of times in the psychiatric ward but felt suffocated by the atmosphere, the pain and confusion and purposelessness. The sisters had often spoken on the phone, though, Kate usually waiting till he and Rick were out. Sometimes he'd come back and found her in tears after an argument that seemed to have torn both of them to shreds; sometimes she'd be sitting, head bowed under the weight of Jo's misery; sometimes she'd been surprisingly light-hearted, bubbling with childhood jokes he'd never quite been let in on.

He told Fran he needed to get something from upstairs and shut himself in the bedroom. Perhaps he shouldn't text Jo when she'd said he'd made her worse, but it felt wrong not to. Hope you're OK, he thumbed on the screen. Of course she wasn't OK. She wouldn't be in that place if she was. He looked at the text and added 'there', to make it sound less worried. How long are you staying? – as if it were a holiday. He was tempted to add that he'd be in London and could come and see her, but it seemed that was the last thing she wanted. His wanting to see her was becoming a longing, his hopes of a next meeting now broken scraps. It wasn't just because of Kate that he wanted to see her. Something about Jo, and the grief they shared, had found its way through the barrier he'd put around himself.

He wanted to say 'Take care' or 'Look after yourself', but the point was that she was being looked after. He had no idea where this crisis house was or what it was like. His images of it alternated between a mini-hospital with squeaky floors and a smell of disinfectant, and a cosy guesthouse with chintz armchairs. He hoped it was the latter; Jo could do with a bit of comfort. That and some decent food would make a big difference, it seemed to him, never mind anything else. Being in that flat by herself with all those terrible memories couldn't be good for her.

His finger hovered for a long time over the 'Send' arrow. When he'd convinced himself to click it he sat back on the bed. He'd let the room get untidy – bed not made, clothes piled up on the unused side, dirty socks and underpants dropped on the floor. Kate had always hung things up, shaking out the creases, and he'd learnt to do the same – he could see how far he'd lapsed. The lack of order depressed him, but without Kate there he didn't see the point of clearing up. He hadn't moved anything of hers – not her photos, not her scarves and jewellery on the dressing table, not even the mascara and eyeshadow she'd used when she wanted to smarten up, which were no good for anything now. He bent over to smell them and their faint, familiar perfume teased him into thinking she might be hovering there. The only change he'd made in the room was that the black box now sat on the shelf in the corner behind the bed, less shiny in the shadow but always there at the edge of his vision. He'd opened the wardrobe just the other day and caught sight of it inside, still carefully wrapped in its scarf; its loneliness – her loneliness – had squeezed at his heart. From being a reminder of her absence it had imperceptibly become *her*, all he had left of her. How could he have left her neglected like that? 'I'm so sorry, my love,' he'd said, placing her on the shelf, asking her if she minded, speaking to her all the while.

He was talking to her now, silently, wondering what he should do about Jo, hearing her voice, real or imagined, say there was nothing to do except be kind and wait. Kate hadn't always been kind, to Jo or to him. Once she'd laid into him with devastating force because he'd forgotten to take his wet shoes off and once, only once, she'd shouted maniacally at Rick when he knocked over a glass of orange juice. Afterwards she'd been crushed with remorse, just as she was after her arguments with Jo. 'I don't know where that came from,' she'd said, and meant it. He hadn't always been kind to her either. That morning when she'd woken up feeling so ill, he'd groaned and tried to get back to sleep again, before he realised how serious it was. He'd thought she was exaggerating and wanted to block it out, to tell her to put up and shut up. Thank goodness he hadn't. He pressed his hand over his eyes to stop himself remembering how heartless he'd been.

It was terrible not to have found the right place for her. He kept asking her about it, hoping she'd somehow let him know, but there was only a blank. He couldn't picture a place at all. All he could see was himself and Jo close together, maybe arm-in-arm, walking down a path to a stretch of quiet water that could be anywhere. They couldn't do it yet. First of all, Jo must get better – he was sure she could, at least partly – and then she must want to see him again, if she did. Then he must feel ready release Kate to the water. It felt more impossible now than it had at the beginning.

'Richard,' Fran called up the stairs. 'Supper's ready.'

He touched the box lightly, letting Kate know he'd be back soon.

Round the kitchen table the three of them made a makeshift family. Fran had tidied everything. The previous lot of washing-up was stacked on the draining board, the papers were in a neat pile on the dresser, the floor had been swept. Rick was eating the shepherd's pie Fran had made, even though it was vegetarian. There was a calm in the room, almost a normality. There they were, quietly eating their supper, as though the ragged hole torn by Kate's absence had been hemmed round its edges. For now, while Fran was sitting and eating with them, pausing to look at him and Rick between forkfuls of pie and nodding thoughtfully when she did, he felt soothed.

'Dad,' Rick said in a voice muffled by mashed potato, 'Did you go and see Jo?'

Richard started. 'Yes. Do you mind?'

Rick shrugged. 'No, not really. Only she's not going to come back here, is she?'

'No, son. Why would she?'

'I don't know. Just that you seem to like her. And she's sort of like Mum.'

'They were twins. But I wouldn't... She can't come here, anyway. She has to be in London.'

'It's all right, Dad.' Rick gave him a cheeky mock-grown-up smile. It was good to see that smile again, even briefly. 'I just wouldn't want her to come instead of Fran.'

As if she could. Jo could barely look after herself, never mind anyone else. It would have been easy to text her again, holding out a hand to her even if she didn't want it.

He noticed Rick needed a haircut, then felt his own hair and realised he did too. How could he remember these things without Kate reminding him? He felt a rush of gratitude as he looked at Rick, for the way his soft brown hair flopped down over his face, the bony sharpness of his knuckles as he held his fork, the fact that he was eating and surviving. Rick glanced up from his plate and held his father's gaze, and for the first time since Kate's death Richard thought, just for a moment: It's all right; we'll come through it somehow. He noticed Fran watching them both, eyes slightly averted so as not to seem intrusive, with a kind of wondering sympathy.

Jo

She didn't know how she'd managed to end up at Chestnut Tree - that was what the house was called. She'd never been in a place where people were so kind. She didn't believe in angels, but now she wondered if the new voice might really be one. Was it mad to think that? They hadn't treated her as though she was mad; they'd tried to understand about the abuse. That was what they kept calling it, as though it wasn't just an illness but something bad that had happened to her – to her and Jans. Most of the women in the house had flashbacks and some heard voices or cut themselves, but they were still treated like regular people. Bethan and the other staff touched and hugged Jo sometimes, but it didn't feel swamping like Emmeline. When all the guests sat in the group, people said how awful things were for them and nobody told them it was just their illness.

She had no idea what day it was or how long she'd been here. The days of the week didn't mean anything: there was no inside or outside, just things bombarding her – the voices and sometimes *him*. She kept smelling him and couldn't wash the smell away. Today was the first day she'd even thought of writing. Eleanor had told her she didn't have to go home yet but could stay for the month, so it must be a week already. Jans had been with her all the time and Jo had told her she was doing this for both of them. Bethan had said, 'You've just lost your sister. No wonder it's been overwhelming.' She'd tried to explain about them being twins, but Bethan didn't understand the way Eleanor did.

She didn't have the energy to write much, and it wasn't just the medication. She was exhausted by the voices' relentlessness, the moments of memory coming at her as if they were happening now, the waves of grief and terror alternating with numbness. She'd been seeing the hands but couldn't frame the worst of it: a whole hand gripping her, the fingers ... No, that was too much.

Right now, she was resting on a plateau of calm. She lay back on the bed, looking at the photograph on the wall that reminded her of good times with Jans. She'd made herself some coffee in the little kitchen near her room and sipped it instead of gulping it down. She tasted its bitterness as if this were the first time she'd drunk black coffee. In their teens she and Kate had often sat drinking coffee on the bed in one of their rooms – by then they each had their own – talking about everything except how unhappy they were. Sometimes they lay close together under the crumpled duvet on a rucked-up sheet that smelt of their bodies – they had almost the same smell, sweet and slightly musty. Back then they'd both been untidy. Jans's room was a whirl of art materials, makeup, posters for everything from Heinz baked beans to a Gustav Klimt exhibition. Jo's room had had toppling piles of books, clothes scattered on the floor and unemptied ashtrays. They had curled up in each other's clutter like mice in a nest, not minding it. Jo could sense Jans's body beside her on the bed now. They both seemed very little. Sometimes, after *he*'d come in, they'd slept together in one bed, their tight circle keeping him out until the next time the door creaked open.

A slow wave mounted from deep in her chest. No, not again; there couldn't be more. It took her over until she could hear nothing but the sound of her own pain. Before long there was a knock at the door. When she looked round she saw Leisha, her other key worker, come in softly and stand by the bed. She didn't feel as much at ease with Leisha as Bethan. Leisha seemed a bit like Emmeline, big and caring in a way that might engulf her, even though Leisha's quiet, low voice was nothing like Emmeline's and she had an earthy laugh that made Jo laugh with her. The feel of Leisha's body when she put an arm round Jo and her warm hands weren't like Emmeline either.

'Just dropping by,' Leisha said. 'Making sure you're OK... What's upsetting you, honey?'

Jo stared at her.

'Do you need a hug?'

Jo shook her head. A hug was the last thing she wanted; her whole body felt like a suit of armour.

'OK. Take it easy.' Leisha moved towards the armchair.

Jo wished people wouldn't keep saying that.

'You want me to stay with you?'

Jo shook her head again, hard enough, she hoped, to send Leisha away.

'OK. But you know where I am, don't you?'

Don't trust her, one of the voices said, a female one. *You can't trust any of them. She might...* Jo hated it when they mumbled.

She heard the door close quietly and shuddered with relief, but then Leisha's leaving felt like a cold draught. Because of *his* intrusions the staff did their best to come and go as quietly as possible, apart from a woman in an overall who'd barged in carrying a grinning vacuum cleaner that bore the name Henry, and cheerfully started terrorising the carpet. 'Just making it nice for you, darling,' she'd said, flattening out the duvet and tweaking the bedspread straight. Jo had sat frozen in the armchair, flinching as the cleaner approached the table with her journal on it. 'Could you leave that?' she'd managed to say just as the cleaner was about to descend on it with a duster. The cleaner – whose name wasn't written on her – had simply picked up Henry and left. Jo wasn't used to having her wishes respected.

At some point Emmeline had appeared with clean clothes and even tobacco and papers – Bethan or Leisha must have had a word with her. When they'd asked Jo if she wanted to see her, she hadn't been able to say no. Emmeline was so sure she had a right to be there, that as a carer she'd be wanted and needed.

She'd asked Jo how she was doing and then said, shaking her head, 'So it wasn't a good idea to see him, after all.'

'Who?' For a moment Jo couldn't think who she meant. Not Damian, surely?

'Your brother-in-law.' Emmeline was trying to sound neutral but gave the word an undertaste of dislike. 'You knew it wasn't going to be helpful.'

'He's called Richard.' Jo didn't say he'd texted her and, in some way, she'd been glad of it.

Emmeline gave her a quizzical look. 'It was disturbing to you. It was after you saw him that your mental health deteriorated.'

Jo wished Emmeline wouldn't talk in nurse jargon. Most of the nurses here didn't speak like that; they were interested in how you felt.

'I hope you're not going to go on seeing him,' Emmeline said. 'You need to look after yourself. Remember you're vulnerable.'

As if she needed to be reminded. Jo sat rigid; her hands clutched in tight fists. How dare Emmeline interfere? Emmeline would say it was the illness that was making Jo angry; she'd never see it had anything to do with her. No doubt she'd talk to the staff about it.

'Stop interfering.' Jo said through clenched teeth. 'It's up to me whether I see him or not. It's my life. I don't need you to tell me what to do.'

Emmeline stared at her. 'I'm only looking after you. I know he's abused you. You told me.'

'He hasn't. I said I'd made a mistake. I'd like you to go now.'

Emmeline's face stretched with surprise. 'It's not a good idea to push away people who are helping you,' she said stiffly. 'I hope you haven't been doing that with the staff.'

'No. And anyway it's nothing to do with you. I had to name you as my next of kin but I don't want you to be my carer.'

'No? Well, I wouldn't make that kind of decision in a hurry. You're not well right now. And anyway, who else have you got?'

'I may not be well but I'm still me. I know what I don't want.'

'OK. If you say so. But you need to think about what you're doing. I've always had your best interests at heart.'

Jo felt a hot, insistent buzz rise up into her mouth. Leave me alone, you bossy, patronising cow, she wanted to say, but was too afraid. 'I'd like you to go now,' she said again. 'I don't want to talk to you any more.'

Emmeline took her time. She raised herself out of the armchair, exuding hurt benevolence, and made a slow exit, looking back at Jo. She was bound to go and talk to the staff but Jo felt Bethan and Leisha might be on her side. They talked a lot about patients' rights.

She lay back on the bed. For the first time she'd told Emmeline to go away and meant it. A female voice started nagging: *You were rude to her. You shouldn't have done that. Why aren't you grateful?*

She couldn't remember now when it was that she'd seen Emmeline. The days had muddled together like squashed sandwiches and she only knew what time it was when people reminded her about meetings or meals. She didn't know what the time was now, but a smell of vegetables cooking for soup was drifting up to her room, meaning it might soon be suppertime. All this food: there seemed to be so many meals. At home she'd just grab an apple or a piece of cheese when she noticed she was hungry – or not, if she couldn't be bothered. Here, the meals almost seemed to be part of the treatment.

The guests were expected to go down to the dining room if they could; eating in your room wasn't encouraged. Tonight she decided not to wait for Bethan to take her down; she'd go on her own and hide in a corner where people wouldn't talk to her. Several women had come and gone during her stay – most of them wrapped so tightly in their own agonies that greetings were irrelevant – but she'd begun to recognise a few from the daily group. At the beginning she'd hardly looked at any of them. One older woman, with long grey locks and a couple of missing teeth, seemed to be someone she could like. The woman, whose name she believed was Margaret, had been raped and neglected as a child; she'd had two abusive husbands and one of her children had been taken into care. Many of the women in the drop-in told similar stories, but in the group Margaret didn't just recite it in a mechanical, much-repeated way; she seemed to feel it, and Jo felt it too.

The dining room was on the ground floor, behind the reception area. As she walked in, Jo was dazzled by light from the tall windows that overlooked the garden. It cast leaf-patterned shadows on the small round tables with their checked plastic tablecloths. Jo chose a table near the windows, in the shade of the long dark-blue curtains. Margaret wasn't there. The few women who had appeared sat separately, engrossed in their soup, not looking at anyone. Jo hated having to go up to the servery to get her meals; it reminded her of school dinners and the way the dinner ladies had looked at each other and sniggered when she took her food. She held out her tray and felt the weight of a thick white bowl of tomato soup and a matching plate with a hunk of wholemeal bread. The cook serving her said, 'Here you are, dear,' and gave her a smile that wasn't a snigger. She looked Indian, small and slight with fine black hair and big, searching brown eyes. Her name badge said she was called Mala. Jo tried to smile back but couldn't make herself. She turned away to get cheese from a side table.

As Jo went to sit down, Margaret came in. Jo bent over her bowl of soup but Margaret shuffled unevenly towards her table. One of Margaret's husbands had left her partly paralysed after he'd knocked her head against a wall. Her left leg was stiff and her permanently curled left hand rested against it. Once Margaret had sat down, Mala brought her tray to her. Jo tried not to notice how awkward Margaret was at buttering her bread with one hand but couldn't ignore her when she said, 'Can you help me?' One of the voices, the one that sounded like Mother, whispered: *You can't do anything for her. You're no good to anyone.*

Jo nodded and took the knife. The butter was hard and the bread crumbly but Margaret thanked her. Jo was used to being on the receiving end of help; she wasn't used to being thanked for what she did. They both ate in silence – there was an understanding that you didn't have to talk – but she didn't mind Margaret being there. Perhaps Margaret didn't mind her either.

When Margaret put her spoon down and said, 'I was sitting in the garden. I like the trees,' Jo realised, as though a window had opened, that since she'd been in the house she had been living entirely in an inside world: voices, memories, people who came to her in her room, the bigger room where they sat in the group every day trying to make sense of what had happened to them. She had been outside to smoke on the back patio but had fled indoors again as soon as she finished her cigarette.

Margaret said, 'It's quiet out there. The trees don't talk.'

Jo glanced out of the window at the semicircle of trees surrounding the large lawn. They weren't the same as the plane trees that grew in her road and shed jigsaw pieces of bark; these reminded her of north Oxford. From somewhere in her memory it came to her that they were horse-chestnuts, like the ones in the Woodstock and Banbury Roads. Like the one that had stood outside their house. At one time she and Jans had made a point of touching their tree before they went into the house. She couldn't remember how it had started, but they'd had to do it. They'd believed it protected them, from what they never said. When they moved into separate bedrooms, hers had overlooked the neglected garden but Jans's had had a view of the tree. She wanted to go outside now and touch one of the trees, but it wouldn't be the same on her own.

'Could you…?' Margaret said, holding out the jar of jam.

Jo took the jar, opened it and spread jam on the remains of Margaret's bread. The voice that was like Mother's said, *Made a mess of that, didn't you?*

Margaret smiled at her, the pale yellow of her teeth standing out against the dark gaps. 'You're very kind,' she said.

Jo shook her head. She and Jans had done things for each other naturally, without thinking. She wasn't sure if she had ever in her life been kind, the way some people were. Being told she was felt wrong.

'I'm going now,' she said, trying to smile.

'See you tomorrow.' Margaret waved, the bread and jam still in her hand.

That night the terror came again. Jo lay curled up, her hands covering her eyes, her whole body shaking, her heart hammering so hard it seemed to be jumping out of her chest. At first there were no voices, no images. Then *his* face was looming above her. She was sure she knew him. Then a name: Paul. Was that the right one? She couldn't think who Paul was. *You little bitch*, the voice said. *If you scream I'll kill you.* She stifled her scream and reached for the panic button.

Marian

When the phone rang, Marian expected it to be someone about the WI. Compost making, was it, or a slide show of travels in Ladakh? She was on the committee, so she should know. But the woman said she was calling from Chestnut Tree, a 'crisis house', whatever that was, because Jo had asked to see her. She was one of Jo's key workers, she said.

'You mean *Joanna* wants to see me.' Marian said. 'Are you sure? She usually seems rather reluctant.'

The woman, called Leisha – strange sort of name – said yes, Jo wanted to talk to her urgently.

'You do realise I live in Dorset?' Marian said. 'I don't go up to London unless I have to.' She couldn't help feeling Joanna was being tiresome. If she had something to say, why couldn't she have said it when she was here in the house?

'I understand that, Mrs Brookfield,' this Leisha person said, 'and if you're not able to get here I'm sure Jo will too. Only there are things she really wants to talk to you about.'

'Are there? I don't suppose you can tell me what they are?'

'I'm afraid not. We have to respect her confidentiality. '

'Well, if you say she wants to see me… What is this crisis house?'

'It's for women who are going through a mental health crisis.'

'Yes, she's had a few of those. You mean it's a hospital? I hope she hasn't been sectioned again.'

'She hasn't, and it's not a hospital. I can send you a link to our website.'

'I don't use the internet,' Marian said. 'I don't see the need for it.'

'OK.' There was a pause. Marian wondered what would come next.

Leisha said, 'If you can get here, Mrs Brookfield, it might make a real difference to Jo's recovery.'

'I shall need to think about it, especially at my age.'

'It would really be helpful if you could.'

Marian thought of the long train journey, stopping at station after station, and then the wearisomeness of travelling across London. She had never heard of Stroud Green but supposed it must be somewhere in the outer suburbs. London taxis were so expensive and the Tube was a nightmare, especially as these days most young people wouldn't give up their seats for an older person. She would need to stay overnight and that would mean asking her friend Barbara, who lived in East Finchley – probably miles away from Stroud Green. She and Barbara had known each other since schooldays but their friendship had never had much substance. Marian would not willingly talk to Barbara about Jancis's death or Joanna's difficulties, so that left the WI and the shortcomings of the local council. They usually ended up watching television while Barbara eulogised her late husband, dead these ten years, and complained about the difficulty of finding a good gardener – she worried about her roses. Barbara had no children but had had a succession of small, fat dogs. The latest, called Sherwin for some obscure reason, was a Tibetan temple dog with a face like a moustached Northern comedian and an alarming yelp. Marian had never liked the idea of having an animal in the house; it seemed unhygienic. She had allowed the twins a goldfish or two, but nothing that licked or sniffed or defecated noticeably.

Going to London would be too much, but even as she complained about it she was getting ready. Joanna was her daughter, after all, and the urgency of the call bothered her. She found it hard to tolerate Joanna's distress – she and her own sister had got short shrift for their unhappiness from their father, who had considered academic work the panacea for all psychological ills – but somehow the decision to see her daughter made itself.

She rang the crisis house and told the woman who answered, who seemed to be called Tracey or Stacey – one of those names – that she would be coming to see Joanna Brookfield tomorrow.

'Who?' the woman said. Marian supposed she was not very intelligent. 'Oh, you mean Jo.'

'My daughter, Joanna.'

'Yes. We'll let her know you're coming. I think it was Leisha who rang you?'

'I believe it was.'

'It's great that you can come. I hope the journey won't be too difficult for you.'

'I'm sure I can manage it, thank you. I expect to be there in the early afternoon.'

Thank goodness Barbara could put her up, and seemed delighted at the prospect of company. East Finchley was not entirely impossible from Stroud Green, though not entirely convenient. That was the trouble with London: getting to places even a short distance apart could mean an elaborate sequence of changes on Tube and bus. As she packed her overnight case – clean skirt and blouse laid as flat as possible along the bottom, underwear and tights at the side, spare cardigan on top, *Little Dorrit* in the pocket to stave off boredom in the train – she kept wondering why Joanna should want to see her, now or at all. Joanna had never turned to her when she was in difficulty and she had never been the kind of mother who fussed and fretted over her children. If their father had been there, it might have been different; she might have been different too. She had done what was required for the twins and seen that they had a good education; beyond that they had had to make what they could of their lives. It was a pity Joanna had been so unwilling – unable, Marian was inclined to say – to think of anyone except herself. She found herself feeling impatient again.

She left the case open by the foot of the bed and, having made a final cup of tea, was ready for an early night and an equally early start next morning. Thank goodness her legs, eyes and ears all worked well enough, even if not quite so well as they used to, but being in London would be an annoyance. The noise, the traffic, the endless rows of shops and houses, too many people shouting and smoking in the street, spitting chewing-gum on the pavement and jostling each other on and off the buses.

As she pulled the sheet and blankets over her – she had never seen the point of duvets – the thought came that perhaps Joanna's wanting to see her had something to do with things she never spoke about and tried not to think of: Desmond leaving – the twins were so young they couldn't possibly remember him – and something else that had bothered her from time to time. She had seen Paul coming out of the twins' room one night looking awkward and rather red in the face. But that could have meant anything: fun and games, though he had little obvious sense of fun. She had never spoken to him about it but the doubt had lingered. Something had seemed not quite right, something she wouldn't want to believe of her own son. As her father would have said, 'people like us' didn't do those things. Paul had left for Australia not long after, but then he had always intended to go when his company had a vacancy. The girls had still been small and were not likely to remember him any more than they remembered their father. People didn't think so much about such behaviour back then, probably quite rightly. It seemed to her far too much fuss was made now about the damage it did. Surely it was better just to get on with life, the way she and her siblings had, and not keep complaining about what was no more than conjecture.

For some reason she found it hard to sleep. She always kept *Pride and Prejudice* on the bedside table but tonight it failed to engage her. She had to admit she was worried about Joanna: not just the state she was in – that had been managed before – but what she might have to say.

It was early afternoon by the time she arrived at the house in Stroud Green. She prided herself on having taken the Tube all the way to Finsbury Park and only resorting to a taxi from there. People had been kinder than she expected, giving her directions and helping her with her case on the escalator. To her surprise she had been offered a seat on both trains – first by a tall young man with an accent she had never heard before and then by a woman who was probably in her fifties at least. It was a surprise too that the outside of the house looked smart and welcoming: pots of geraniums on the front steps, a newly painted front door – though what had possessed them to choose such a vulgar colour she couldn't imagine.

The woman who had let her in had been welcoming and had brought her a mug of tea. In the village, or even in local towns like Axminster and Bridport, it was rare to see someone with a dark skin, and the woman's appearance had taken her by surprise: tall, broad-shouldered, wearing tight jeans and a bright baggy top, her hair a mass of tiny plaits. She had – Marian had to admit – a smile that looked genuinely warm. This, it seemed, was Leisha.

Leisha had shown her into a smallish room with three bucket-like armchairs and a round coffee table. On the wall was a framed photograph of a bluebell wood. Marian sipped her tea, wondering how long she would have to wait – she was used to Joanna keeping her waiting. Leisha hadn't enlightened her as to why Joanna had wanted to see her. She couldn't understand the fuss these people made about confidentiality: surely she had a right to know. She was Joanna's mother, whatever that meant to either of them. When you came down to it, neither of them had anyone else to turn to.

Joanna came in looking as though she had just got out of bed. Strands of hair stuck out, escaped from their clip, and her sweater, the old matted brown one that Marian wished she would throw away, was rucked up over a black T-shirt. Joanna pulled it down as Leisha gently laid a hand on her shoulder, guiding her into the room. Her eyelids were puffy and she seemed to be finding it hard to focus, but her face was less gaunt. At least they seemed to feed them here.

'Joanna,' Marian said. She found herself feeling sorry for her daughter, with less of the impatience and irritation that turned sympathy into cold pity. She stepped forward and, unusually, kissed Joanna nearly on the cheek, smelling cigarette smoke in her hair. 'You wanted to talk to me?'

She and Joanna sat down in the narrow armchairs while Leisha stood looking intently at Joanna.

'I'll just be next door, Jo,' she said, moving slowly out of the room, glancing back at Marian in a way she found disconcerting. It was almost as if the woman thought she wasn't safe to be left with her daughter.

Joanna nodded at her mother, sniffed, and wiped her nose with the back of her hand. There was a box of tissues on the table and Marian pushed it towards her.

'Yes.' Joanna had no time for preliminaries. 'Someone called Paul. Who was he?'

'Paul? Your half-brother? He went to Australia when you and Jancis were very small. I don't suppose you would remember him.' Marian sat up straighter in the constricting chair, her body tense.

'Of course – Paul.' Joanna's face cleared, as though something had fallen into place. 'He had ginger hair? I do remember him. I've been remembering the things he did. That's why I'm here.'

'You've had another episode of your illness. Presumably that's why you're here.' Marian didn't believe Joanna could remember what had happened then, if indeed anything had. It was just the once that she had seen Paul coming out of the room with that strange face, and it wouldn't be right to draw conclusions. Jancis and Joanna were his sisters – his half-sisters, at least.

'What are you imagining he did? He used to bring you and Jancis sweets and little toys. It was very kind of him.' She had tried to make them say 'Thank you' but they had always shied away from him.

'He wasn't being kind,' Joanna said, looking down at her wretchedly bitten nails. 'Didn't you know what he was doing?' She raised her head and held her gaze on Marian, till Marian had to turn away. It felt like an inquisition.

'I had no grounds for knowing. I should have thought that in any case you would have been too young to realise what was happening – supposing it did happen. Too young for it to mean anything. Are you saying this happened to Jancis too?'

Joanna looked stricken. Her eyes filled and she blinked hard, staring at the wall beyond Marian. She nodded slowly. 'It was both of us. One and then the other each time. You must have known. You were our mother.'

'I didn't know, Joanna. I wondered, once, what he might be up to, but he was – is – my son. You can't expect me to have accused him of...' It was too horrible to name. Of course he wouldn't really have done it; it must be Joanna's disordered mind.

'But what about us?' Joanna was sobbing now, big ugly sobs that seemed to be fighting to come out. 'It was worse because we were so little, not less bad. Jans was better at forgetting it than I was, but it harmed her too.'

'I should prefer not to talk about Jancis. She was very different from you.'

'We were in the same room,' Joanna said, her voice surprisingly steady. 'It happened to both of us. You never cared enough to find out.'

Marian sat up even straighter but said nothing. She wanted to believe all this was no more than Joanna's illness, but it was less incredible than she would have liked. Paul had been secretive about everything he did and she had made a point of not prying. He was like James, his father, a visiting mathematician from Princeton, who hadn't told her he was married until he was about to leave Oxford, nor that he already had four children. It was the only time in her life she had let herself be carried away, by a man with a froglike face and little obvious attractiveness, and he hadn't even kept in touch with her. Jancis and Joanna had been more like their father, especially Jancis: more excitable, less hidden – at least when they were children. Marian had kept a distance from them too; it had seemed right not to be involved in their loves and hates. Now she was confronted with a daughter to whom she had never much warmed, who was implying that she had been negligent.

'I did the best I could, Joanna.' It was what people always said and, in this case, it seemed to be true.

Joanna said nothing. She had always had a disconcerting stare, as though she saw more than she was meant to.

'I'm sorry,' Marian said. 'I don't think we can go any further with this. Even if it were true, I don't imagine it would be the main cause of your illness. As I understand it, that's caused by some genetic fault, which fortunately didn't seem to have affected Jancis in the same way.'

Joanna's face was unmistakably contorted with pain. Clearly she was suffering, whatever the reason.

'I didn't think you'd understand,' she said. 'You never have.'

Marian felt herself soften. In her irritation and disapproval, she had never seen the pain so clearly before.

'I am sorry this is hard for you,' she said. 'I'm glad you're being well looked after here. I can't know what actually happened and what's simply your imagination, but I can see you are troubled.' She struggled to her feet from the confines of the chair and tentatively stretched out her arms towards Joanna. It didn't feel entirely natural but she couldn't think what else to do.

Joanna looked uncertain, then lifted her own arms in Marian's direction. In their awkward not-quite hug Marian couldn't help smelling the smoke on Joanna's clothes and feeling her daughter's bony body as it leaned over her, jerking again with tight sobs. She tried not to be disgusted by the damp patch on her shoulder where Joanna rested her face, and kept hoping the torturous outbreak would end soon. When it did, Joanna stood back, wiping her eyes with her fingers.

'At least you came,' she said, and turned away towards the door. 'I suppose that's something. I couldn't expect you to believe me.'

Marian watched her, not knowing what more to say.

Richard

He hadn't heard from Jo since the text about the crisis house and hardly dared expect to hear from her again. Perhaps, in some way he didn't understand, he really had made her worse. The loss of contact with her lay in his mind beside the much larger loss of Kate, mingling with it and distracting him from thinking about his wife. If he let them blend together, a part of him could almost believe Kate hadn't really died.

It was Paul, her text had said, coming out of the blue some time later, and then: Mother coming. I think she knew. So far as he remembered, Jo had never mentioned anyone called Paul, though she was clearly expecting him to know who he was. As for her mother seeing her, Richard could only hope Jo wouldn't end up in the same state she seemed to have got into after she'd been down to Dorset. It troubled him that she and her mother seemed to hate each other so much. His relationship with his father had always been difficult, but it was nowhere near as bad as this. Everything about Jo felt worrying and perplexing and he'd been spending too much time thinking about her. He didn't know what to say in reply and simply said: Hope you're OK, which didn't require an answer.

From his desk in the office shed he looked out at the neglected garden. In spring and early summer dandelions had taken over the lawn, which he'd left unmown for weeks at a time. White trumpets of bindweed were covering the flower beds and apples that had fallen from the two trees he and Kate had planted lay rotting on the grass. He'd had little energy to do anything about it and the effort of finding a gardener felt too much. It all seemed beyond his control, just as he felt powerless to tidy the papers scattered on his desk or lying in shaggy piles on the floor. Behind him Kate's workspace was as tidy as it had always been, the design on her drawing desk untouched and slowly gathering dust. It would have felt wrong to cover it.

His life had lost its momentum. He was designing websites for companies whose products no one needed or individuals who only wanted to promote themselves. None of them listened to his suggestions about what would look best. He and Kate had shared a love of good design, but in the end what did it matter? What did anything matter beside the reality of death?

Now that the shock and drama were over, his life felt dulled. The world had fewer colours, food had less taste, people seemed more one-dimensional. He had forgotten what it was like to feel interested in anything. He found himself leaving the website he was working on and playing patience again – solitaire, they called it – clicking virtual cards into place on virtual green baize. It was both compulsive and without interest, and left his mind free to run in the same futile grooves. If he'd taken Kate's headache seriously straight away, he could have got her to hospital sooner and those few minutes might have saved her. If he'd known about the abuse, he might have been kinder to her when she pulled away from him. If he'd understood Jo better, perhaps she wouldn't have had this breakdown. As though he could have been responsible for any of those things. Maybe he should see his friend V and get a dose of Buddhism. And maybe he should ask Fran to come and take care of Rick – he seemed to be making such a bad job of it. What mattered to him more than anything was that his son should come through this with as little suffering as possible. Rick was definitely looking more himself again, but the other day his class teacher had rung and asked Richard to come in and have a talk about him.

Oh God, Richard remembered, that was booked for this afternoon, just two weeks into the new term. Was the teacher going to tell him he was failing as a parent, and would he be able to do anything about it? He closed down the solitaire in mid-game, left the computer, making sure he'd saved his work – he was too professional not to – and went to make himself some strong coffee. He wanted to have a glass of wine, but for Rick's sake he was trying hard.

He hadn't minded going to the school for plays or parents' evenings, but crossing the playground towards the low oblong buildings he felt a dread that took him back to his own primary school. The headmaster had thought nothing of hitting the boys – not the girls – with a wooden spoon when they misbehaved. Guiltily, as though he'd done something wrong, he opened the royal blue door and stood in an alcove in the corridor, hoping to avoid the children as they came jostling out. The corridor had sunny yellow walls. One noticeboard was covered with bright imaginary butterflies splodgily painted by the younger children, another had a class's poems about the things they loved – the ones about 'my mum' made Richard's throat catch – a third had a project on endangered species which Rick's class had done. It cheered him to see Rick's careful drawing of a pangolin in the centre of the board.

As the last stragglers wandered through the doorway, a teacher stepped out of a classroom opposite. A nice young man, Richard thought, tall and gangling, with long loose limbs and an air of sincerity. He had wavy auburn hair that needed a trim – Richard fingered the straggly ends of his own hair – and large gold-rimmed glasses. He looked exhausted.

'Mr Johnston? David MacKinnon. Good to see you.' He extended a bony hand. 'I'm Rick's class teacher.' His smile showed large, friendly-looking teeth.

Fortunately, the classroom had two adult-sized chairs. Richard pulled his round to face the teacher, aware of the children's desks and chairs behind him.

David MacKinnon sat calmly waiting. Eventually he said, 'I just wanted to talk to you about how Rick's getting on. He seems to be doing very well, in the circumstances, and I'm sure a lot of that is down to you.'

Richard's body settled into the grey plastic chair. Perhaps this wouldn't be so bad after all.

'As you know,' David MacKinnon continued, in a soft accent that Richard guessed might be from the Western Isles, 'he's quite sensitive. Is he always a bit withdrawn?'

'Not always. He can be fairly quiet, though.'

'I've been wondering…'

Richard flinched slightly.

'You know children don't always talk to their parents, or their teachers for that matter, so we thought maybe some counselling might help. He'd maybe get things off his chest, say what he mightn't say at home. Come out of himself more.'

'I suppose so.' Richard shrugged. 'I don't know if he'd want to do it.' Wasn't it better to leave things alone?

'But you wouldn't object?'

'No, no, if it's for the best. My sister suggested it. She knows about that sort of thing.'

'Your sister. Would that be Fran?'

Richard stiffened a little. 'Well, yes. How did you know?'

'Rick has talked about her. She must be a support to both of you.'

'Oh yes.'

'Emm... I don't want to intrude, but some single parents find a group can help them in the difficult times,' David MacKinnon said tentatively, reaching for a leaflet on his desk. 'Sometimes it's useful to be in contact with other parents who...' He offered the leaflet hopefully.

Richard took it and tried to look grateful. 'I don't really do groups, but thank you for concern. I know you're looking out for Rick.'

David MacKinnon nodded eagerly. 'He's a good wee laddie, and a bright one, as I'm sure you know.'

Richard did know. He nodded back, hoping that would be all. 'Thank you, Mr MacKinnon.'

'David. It's good to talk to you. 'It's Rick's last year with us and we want him to thrive as much as possible.' He gripped Richard's hand warmly. 'And I wish you all the best.'

Outside in the playground Richard said to himself, I'm not a single parent. We were parents together. He stuffed the leaflet into his pocket, knowing he wouldn't read it.

Speaking to Rick felt embarrassing. They were eating the shepherd's pie Fran had left in the freezer and Rick was talking about pangolins. He had pictures of them on his wall.

'The thing is, Dad, that if they die out they can never come back. Never.'

Richard could only sigh and shake his head.

'It's like when a person dies, they don't come back. Only of course there's lots of people, too many. That's a problem, isn't it? So some of them have to die.' He stabbed his fork into his shepherd's pie. 'But if a person dies…'

'Yes. You miss them a lot.'

They held back less now from talking about Kate, but it was still hard. Both of them went on eating quietly. Richard got up to turn the light on; the thick grey cloud outside was a sure sign of rain. The light exposed the kitchen's messiness – the floor that needed cleaning, yesterday's washing-up only half done, plates and glasses not put away, Rick's toys and books filling up the worktops and spare chairs, including the chair that had been Kate's. The other day Richard had noticed the fridge was full of food he hadn't got round to using. Beans on toast were so much easier. Perhaps he did need to do something.

'So, Rick, I spoke to Mr MacKinnon.'

'I know.'

'About counselling. He said you might like to try it. Is that right?'

Rick shrugged and looked away. 'I suppose so.'

'You don't have to, you know.'

'I know. But Fran's not around.'

'You talk to her, then?'

Rick nodded.

'More than me?'

'Well, you're my dad,' Rick shrugged. 'It's different.'

'So long as you want to do it.'

Rick said, 'Any more shepherd's pie? If Fran comes, she can cook things for us. When is she coming again?' If Fran wasn't there, Rick would only eat the few things he habitually ate: fish fingers, baked beans, cheese, no veg except broccoli or tomato, no fruit except oranges, one sort of pasta with one particular pesto. He would only eat potatoes if they were chips and only liked the kind of bread that Fran brought.

'Soon, I hope.' Richard didn't say he might go to London again; it was too uncertain.

Late that night Richard had another text, the longest Jo had sent him:

Mother came. She said she didn't know. It was Paul, her son. It wasn't you that made me worse. You can come next week if you want.

If he wanted – he mustn't let her see how much. He'd have to arrange it straight away.

He had a vague memory that Kate had mentioned an older half-brother a few times in passing. It seemed she'd never really known him. If it was him, they must have been terribly young, little more than toddlers. He remembered Rick at that age, bright and trusting but knowing at once if someone wasn't kind. Kate seemed to have buried the memories better than Jo, and he sensed again that Jo was going through this for her sake too. He was moved by her courage.

So very sorry, he texted back. Would like to come if it's OK. Where and when?

Jo

She felt as though she'd been here always. The time before, even the last day in the flat, was no more than a pale cloud surrounding the vivid planet on which she was now living. Sitting in her room with her journal in front of her, the sun through the window making wedges of light and shadow on the coloured bedspread, she was savouring a moment of quiet. They might only be short but they were getting longer, the times when there were no voices and *he* – Paul, she had to call him – didn't barge his way into her mind, shaking her whole body until she wanted to obliterate herself or else found herself on the ceiling staring down at herself. That had happened once more, and this time she'd rung the bell straight away. Bethan and Leisha had both arrived, panting from having run up the stairs, and stayed with her, each with a hand on her shoulder, till she was back in her body again. She could feel them now, one on either side, telling her it was all right – telling her *she* was all right. It made her want to cry again and again, all this goodness, but it was a kind of crying that wasn't painful. She felt as if something was beginning to heal, even though Dr Greenland said she had an incurable condition.

She lay on the bed, gazing up at the white ceiling, thinking about the group meetings. She'd hated them at first, people's stories of neglect and abuse, hated all the pain that seemed to gather in a pool in the middle of the room, all the anger and bitterness – hers too – that darkened the air. Little by little, without knowing how, she had begun to talk more about herself. Not just the terrible, terrifying abuse but her life before and since the first breakdown, especially how it hurt to be seen all the time as someone who had something wrong with them.

'I don't feel I'm a proper person,' she'd said, and noticed other people nodding. 'I'm somebody who isn't normal, who doesn't know how to live like everybody else. I don't want people to pity me or get irritated with me –' she thought of Mother and Dr Greenland, and her landlord, who never took her complaints seriously – 'I want to be a person like other people.'

'You are a proper person, Jo,' Eleanor had said. 'We take you seriously here. You've been through some terrible things and they've left their mark, but you still matter.'

'Do I?' Jo couldn't look at Eleanor.

'We want to help you feel better about yourself. You and everyone here.'

Jo stared at the carpet. A dark coffee stain just by her right foot seemed desperately important.

'Did you hear that, Jo?'

Jo had nodded, not knowing what to say. Before the pause became excruciating, other women started to speak. It was like being in the drop-in, except that the women in the drop-in had resigned themselves to having their lives circumscribed and had grown comfortable with their limitations. Here everyone was being encouraged to want more and it hurt, as Jo imagined a chick might hurt as it broke out of the egg – a kind of hurting that felt good.

Pressing her head back against the pillows, she saw Eleanor's face vividly in front of her.

'A lot of people hear voices,' Eleanor had said more than once. 'Including people who aren't mentally ill. What matters is how the voices affect you. They don't have to run your life.'

Try telling that to *him,* Jo had thought. Now that she knew who he was, that he was their half-brother, not their father, and that he was safely in Australia, perhaps his power would lessen. Her dread had always been that if it was their father, she could no longer believe in him. It didn't seem that any of the voices belonged to him, though, and she knew somehow that he had cared about her and Jans. She would have liked to remember his voice. Later, when she felt stronger, she'd ask Mother again what had happened to him. The voice that was like Mother's still told her off, but sometimes it was a little less harsh. The new voice, the angel one, had come to sound more like Eleanor. Last night as she was falling asleep she had felt its wings around her again.

Bethan and Leisha had started talking about what would happen when she left. All she knew was that she didn't want to leave. This was a safe place; she hadn't felt safe anywhere before. Not in the cold Oxford house, not in the hospital and not in her sad, messy flat. Next week, they'd said, and asked if she'd like to start going out for walks with them. Just round the block, maybe. Just to see the outside world. It scared her, but then she'd texted Richard to say he could come and meet her in the coffee shop on the corner. Bethan or Leisha would take her there beforehand to make sure she could manage it. It would be good to see him and good to see Damian too, though he would have do all the professional things when she saw him.

In the meantime, there were the trees. From the bed she could see two of them through the window, their clusters of leaves waving like open hands in the soft wind, small spiked conkers dimly visible against them. Her tree was the one she couldn't see from the window, in the far corner of the garden. She'd been to visit it every day since she'd talked to Margaret. She looked at the clock, which she'd only just realised had been there on the wall all the time. Just time to go down to the tree before lunch.

Getting downstairs and out of the house took effort, like making a journey to a different city. She never knew who she might pass on the way and was shy of meeting Eleanor. As she opened the metal door beside the kitchen and went down the iron steps to the patio, she thought she heard someone behind her. She turned round and saw Margaret, hair washed, in a clean smock top and trousers, looking more like someone in the outside world.

'I'm glad I saw you,' Margaret said. 'I'm going home this afternoon.' There were tears in her eyes. 'Fingers crossed I'll be all right.'

Jo didn't say any of the reassuring things people said, like 'I'm sure you will' or 'Look after yourself'. They didn't know, any of them, whether they would be all right, or that they could look after themselves. She said, 'I'll be going next week. It's hard.'

Margaret nodded. 'I've often noticed you there with your tree. They can be friends, trees.'

For a moment Jo felt outraged to have been seen. When she was with the tree it was private to her. Then she realised that nothing here was private. People were living through their separate agonies but around them were Eleanor, the key workers, the office staff, the cooks, the cleaners, everyone who kept the place going. And they – the guests – weren't entirely cocooned from one another. Sometimes, if only for an instant, someone cared. Possibly Margaret had.

'Mm,' Jo said, hoping Margaret would say goodbye and go.

'I'd best be getting ready, then,' Margaret said, as if hearing her thoughts. 'I'm being picked up soon.'

'Good luck,' Jo said. It felt a feeble thing to say.

'Maybe we'll keep in touch.' Margaret looked at her hopefully, but neither of them offered a phone number.

Margaret shuffled away. Jo loped across the lawn and stood under the tree, looking up through the handprints of leaves patterning the light grey sky. She and Jans had always done that, sitting under the apple tree; she loved the way the light shone through the leaves, making them look almost transparent, thin as tissue paper. Checking behind her that no-one was looking, she reached out one hand and then the other and rested them on the rough bark. The tree never minded; it seemed to welcome her. It was calm and slow and not easily shifted – all the things she found it impossible to be. When she touched it, she sensed it was talking to her. It was safe, just as the tree in Oxford had been safe; she felt its leaves sheltering her like the angel's wings. It was good to stay there for a while before she had to struggle again with being a person.

When she went to her room after lunch, she found a card on her bed. The envelope was so white it hurt her eyes. *Don't open it,* a voice said. *It'll harm you.* She picked it up, turned it over and saw Mother's small, scratchy writing – thin blue pen, as always. *You mustn't open it.* She tore the envelope jaggedly across the top with a blunt fingertip and saw her hand was shaking. The fear was coming back, rising in an unsteady line from the pit of her stomach into her throat: fear of Mother's cold words, what she might say, what she wouldn't say. The front of the card had a painting of a vase of flowers, the kind sold as suitable for any occasion.

Dear Joanna, the card said. *After our meeting the other day I should like to say how sorry I am that you find yourself ill again. I do hope you will make a good recovery and will look after yourself as best you can. I am also sorry if what you believe about your half-brother Paul should turn out to have substance. I have no way of knowing, of course, but it is regrettable if you and poor Jancis suffered something so unpleasant and unnecessary. As you know, I have not heard from Paul for a number of years, and I am now not sure that I wish to do so. He is still my son but I cannot accept such behaviour and perhaps need to understand its consequences.*

Affectionately
Mother

Jo read the card several times. For all Mother's distance and formality, she was actually saying that she might believe her – and that she was sorry it had happened. More sorry on behalf of 'poor Jancis', of course, but then poor Jancis was dead. Mother never sent love – her family never had – but 'affectionately' was better than kind regards with little kindness in them. The monkey with the wire mother came into Jo's mind again, but it was as though the wire mother had extended a small cloth-covered hand. She fished inside the bed for Squidge and cuddled him to her. He at least had always believed her. *So she's gone over to your side now*, the voice – Paul's voice – sneered. *Don't you believe it. It won't last.* Jo felt the card in her hand; it was real.

Richard

This time he would be going to London at the weekend. That way Fran wouldn't have to take leave from work and Rick's routine – such as it was – wouldn't be disrupted. There was no excuse of work meetings and no possibility of travel expenses; Jo had asked to see him and that was what mattered. He couldn't keep doing it, of course. It took him away from Rick, it was a big ask for Fran and it was far too expensive. That made him want to see Jo more urgently. He remembered her in the Indian restaurant, tucking into her food, telling him things about her life, and wanted to reach out his hand and say everything would be all right. They had each other. He could feel close to her in the way he'd felt close to Kate.

Oh Kate, he said now to her desk behind him, as he'd said so often to her beloved ashes, as he sometimes said when he walked into the kitchen, Oh Kate, it's not that I'm neglecting you. She's the other half of you; I need her so I can still have you. You understand that, don't you? She did, he was sure, but a small uneasy voice reminded him: Jo isn't Kate; she can't be what Kate was. He needed her because she was different.

He felt trapped, in his blasted office and in his life. The air seemed to cling tightly round him and the mess of papers on the floor looked unbearably stale, as though it had been there for decades. He had got into the habit of hardly going out, even into the garden, letting his thoughts circle in the same repetitive orbit. Even the walk from quiet Mayfield to the bustle of Newington Road had become a major expedition, the short weekly drive to Sainsbury's even more so. This wouldn't do. He'd known for a while that something wasn't right and hoped it wasn't affecting Rick. Was that really why David MacKinnon had wanted to see him: to tell him he should get his act together?

He stood up and went over to the window, making himself look beyond the neglected garden – the bindweed flowers a beautiful fresh white, opulent among the leaves – to Arthur's Seat, which stood out stark in front of a blue sky stippled with cloud. People were walking up, their clothes bright against the grass and sandy paths. How long was it since he'd been there? It was already late August. Kate had died in early April and it was a good few weeks before then that they'd gone up there as a family. He'd been down to Devon, in that futile attempt to find her a place, and there had been the trips to London, but when he was home the house sucked him in like a quagmire. The house, and all of Kate that was in it. He couldn't bear to stay inside any longer.

He'd chosen one of the easier routes but still found himself panting like an old man when it got steep. He'd let himself become horribly unfit, and the wine he was drinking probably didn't help. As he climbed, he felt almost dizzy with the sense of space. The city's buildings were huddled below him, seeming to jostle against each other: the castle hunkered squat and square-shouldered on its crag, the Gothic spire of the Scott Monument standing out dark and thin like a compass needle. Down below, Duddingston Loch was a dazzling mirror for the afternoon sunlight. He revelled in so much green and the sharp-edged rocks that jutted from it; it was all so real. There was a good breeze and the air smelt of late summer sunlight. He stretched out his arms, filling his body with the clouds that floated above him like soft pillows, grey with a white under-edge, the wide-open sweep of land and water, the freedom of sky with no walls around it.

He was still struggling to catch his breath and noticed an ache in his chest, not so painful that he had to stop, but worrying nevertheless. Could this be an angina attack, maybe a full-blown heart attack? His breath seemed to snag in that place, so that each inbreath was a gasp and each outbreath a sigh. It felt so bad he was surprised he could carry on walking. At one point the ache became a sharp pain that seemed to be stabbing into his heart. Finding a ledge of rock, he sat down and bent forward, not knowing what was happening to him. He felt for his phone in his pocket and wondered if he should call 999. His chest was heaving and his breath came faster, aching now in his throat as well as his chest. Then, just as he was fearing the worst, the ache started to dissolve and he found himself weeping more urgently, from deeper inside him, than he ever had in his life. Thank goodness no one was there to see him. He had always thought crying as though one's heart would break was a figure of speech, but this was how it felt. Something in his heart – in the heart of him – was breaking open in a way he didn't understand. Bizarrely, it was good to feel the devastating pain at last instead of keeping it away. After the storm subsided his body felt looser, lighter and, for a while, utterly exhausted. There was warmth in his heart for everything and everyone around him, especially those who meant most to him – Rick and Fran and, yes, Jo. He felt such love for Jo and couldn't let her know because she was too fragile. All he could do was go on caring about her.

He'd looked up Stroud Green – another London place he'd never heard of – and found a not too expensive B & B in Finsbury Park – he couldn't face going back the same night. If he caught an early train the next morning, Fran would still be home in good time for the start of her working week. He wasn't sure he'd ever told her how much he appreciated her coming. Gratitude didn't come easily to him, but he could try. For the second time recently, he thought of V – or Mark, as he still preferred to call him. After the heart attack which wasn't one, he'd remembered V talking about openings of the heart as a part of spiritual practice – not that there seemed to Richard to be anything spiritual in what had happened to him. It would be good to speak to V again, though. Richard could do without the Buddhist stuff, but V talked a lot of sense.

As soon as Fran arrived Rick burst out, 'Hey, guess what? Kelvin and his mum are having to move out of their house—'
'Oh dear,' Fran said, reflexively sympathetic. 'I hope they've got somewhere to live?'

'Well, yeah, but the thing is, they're going to live in a flat and they won't be able to take Livingstone, or not for the time being. Not till they find somewhere else.'

'Who's Livingstone?'

'The dog. He's such a cool dog, and he fetches things and doesn't bark a lot.'

'Right,' Fran said. Richard was putting the kettle on and saw her glance over at him. 'Don't you think you'd better ask your dad, if that's what you're after?'

Rick frowned. 'You know what Dad's like.'

'What am I like?' Richard asked, handing Fran a mug of tea.

'Well...' Rick paused intently. 'You'd probably say no because you don't want things to be different. But a dog wouldn't make things a lot different, would it, Fran?'

Fran laughed. 'I think it would. Someone would have to take him for walks. And you couldn't ignore him if he was here. They need attention.'

The way Rick was co-opting Fran amused Richard. They'd never had a dog because Kate was allergic to them, though he and Fran had grown up with one and his father still had old Wilkie. Rick was right: until now Richard would have hated the idea of bringing anything into the house that Kate wouldn't have had. But a dog wasn't a thing; it was another personality. That might be good for Rick – perhaps just as much good as counselling, which Richard still felt sceptical about.

'Look,' he said to Rick. 'Why don't you and Fran talk about it while I'm away? If it seems a good idea when I get back, we'll see. How's that, eh?'

'OK.' Rick grinned. 'I knew you wouldn't say yes right away.'

When Rick had gone off to his room, Fran sat down at the table and asked Richard, 'So how's it going, then?'

'Not too bad.' She was sitting sideways to the table, legs crossed, chin resting on her hand, looking up at him as he pottered about clearing away the remains of Rick's tea – a plate smeared with baked beans, a half-finished glass of orange juice, a bitten piece of biscuit.

'You look better,' she said.

He thought she didn't look so good. The lines on her face were showing more and her body slumped. 'I feel a bit better – getting out more. I went up to Arthur's Seat the other day.' He wanted to tell her about it but didn't know how.

'You took me up there once. Quite a climb. Rick flew his kite, I remember. Does he still do that?'

Rick shook his head. 'Not now. It's not the same...' Again, the thought: perhaps things being different might be OK. And another thought: too soon yet.

'So he's going to have some counselling?'

'Yes, heaven help him.'

'What's wrong with that?'

'Oh, I don't know.' He hadn't meant to sound peevish. 'It may well be the best thing. But it makes me feel I'm not doing a very good job.'

'Rubbish.' Fran laughed. 'You could even get some counselling yourself.'

'Oh God, no. Don't you start, please. I think I've turned a corner of some sort. Like realising it's better to cry.'

'That's good,' Fran said quietly. She had a sad-dog expression, her eyes bigger and moister than usual.

'What is it, Fran? Is something wrong? I'm not the only one who's allowed to be upset, you know.'

She took a large blue hanky out of her skirt pocket and dabbed her eyes. 'Oh well. It's not like someone's died or anything. It's just...'

Richard sat down and pulled his chair close to hers. It was awkward putting his arm round her but he felt he should. As a family they'd never been big on touching.

She wiped her hanky over her whole face and held it there. 'It's just – well, I was seeing someone and he was very nice. I liked him a lot, really. I met him through a dating website – yes, I thought you'd be surprised.'

He hadn't been able to stop himself giving her a raised-eyebrows look.

'No, we got on well. I thought it was… going somewhere. He's just told me he's found someone else.'

'Oh, Fran, I'm so sorry. I didn't know… I mean I didn't know you'd been trying.'

'Oh yes. I have been, off and on, for quite a while.'

'It's a shame. You deserve someone nice.'

She leant against him and cried quietly into his arm. If only Jo could do that...

'So, there you go,' she said, sitting up and giving him a wry smile. 'Nothing like what you've been through, or poor Jo.'

'Still, it's enough,' he said. 'What a wanker. You're probably well shot of him...' She gave him an uncertain look and he changed the subject. 'The crisis house seems to be helping Jo. She's coming out soon; that's why I'm going to see her.' It was partly why he was going to see her.

'Do give her my best, if she remembers me.'

Richard guessed Jo wouldn't remember people unless they'd had an impact on her.

'Sure. I'm trying to drink less, but I think maybe a glass would do us both good. What do you fancy?'

Once Fran was settled in her room – by now it had definitely become hers – he texted Jo again. Hope you're OK for tomorrow. Look forward to seeing you. He added an 'x' and quickly deleted it.

Richard

The first thing that struck him when she came into the café, blinking a little, glancing round her uncertainly, was how well she looked – or at least how much better. Her face had filled out and there was perceptible colour in her cheeks. Just behind her was a tall, strong-faced woman with hair in intricate plaits, who patted her on the shoulder and slipped away. One of the nurses, he supposed, though she didn't look very nurselike; she looked more like a friend. He was sitting against the wall in the corner, on a seat upholstered in shiny pink plastic, so that when Jo sat opposite him she wouldn't see or be seen by other people. She blundered towards him like a moth towards a light.

'Hi, Jo,' he said. He didn't say, 'How are you?' She could take her time with that.

'Hi,' she said. She seemed bemused, somehow blurred; before, her clarity had always hit him like an arrow.

As she pulled out the chair she said, 'I wish I wasn't having so much medication. It makes things fuzzy. They're going to cut it down soon.'

So that was what it was. 'That's good. You're looking well.'

'Am I?'

'Are you feeling better?' The question felt patronising but he couldn't think how else to put it.

'Mm.' She looked past him, into the corner.

'I'll get the coffees. Black, isn't it? Would you like a cake?'

She nodded.

'OK if I choose?'

She nodded again. He hoped it wasn't all going to be hard going, but she seemed to be coming back from another world – what kind of world, he couldn't imagine.

The café smelt of coffee and stale cake. It wasn't part of a chain but looked as though it was trying to imitate one. The pink seats and light wood tables made it comfortable and unthreatening, at least to him; he couldn't tell how Jo would manage it. Glancing round from the counter he saw her sitting there, still staring into the corner, one hand cupping her chin, the other twisting a strand of hair. It was a flash of Kate, all the more disconcerting because what Jo had just been through was so unlike anything Kate had known. When it was his turn to order, he played safe and chose a chunk of shortbread and a chocolate brownie – he hoped Jo would like one of them. He and Kate had either shared a cake between them or both had half of each; he wanted to do the same with Jo. While he waited for the coffees – his latte with an extra shot, in case needed – he tried to think of an opening that might get the conversation going. Nothing wise or sensitive came to mind.

He bumped the plastic tray down on the table harder than he'd meant to. Jo turned round, startled, and looked at the cakes. 'Which is yours?' she said. 'I like both.'

'Whichever you like.' He was busy transferring everything from the tray to the small table. It felt like a big task: two plates, one glass mug, one thick china cup and saucer, two knives, two teaspoons. When he'd done, he had to find somewhere to put the tray. By that time she was drinking her coffee and seemed almost to have forgotten him.

'Can we have half of each each?' she asked. 'That's what Jans and I used to do, when we didn't have the same one.'

Of course they would have done. He pictured them as teenagers, their heads bent close together over the plate.

When the cakes had been shared out, Richard said, 'So how's it all been? You don't have to talk about the difficult bits if you don't want.' Surely all of it must have been difficult.

Eyes closed, she leaned her forehead into her hand. 'I told you it was Paul,' she said flatly. 'He was supposed to be our brother. He gave us toys, Mother said. Eleanor said it was grooming.'

He didn't ask who Eleanor was. 'And you trusted him?'

'Not after he started... He kept pretending to be nice to us, though.' She shuddered from head to foot. 'And Mother believed him. It was right in front of her face and she didn't see it. Didn't want to.'

He could hardly bear the pain and bitterness in her voice. 'Oh Jo, that's terrible. Both of you, and so little.'

'Our beds were side by side. I couldn't protect her.' She clamped her hand over her mouth. 'Eleanor says that's why I got ill. Mother thinks it's just genes.'

'And Eleanor is…?' He couldn't help asking.

'She runs the group. She's a psychiatrist but she's not like Dr Greenland. She listens to what people say. She says I'm still a person, no matter what I've been through. I wish she'd tell Mother.'

Again he heard the bitterness and pain. Remembering how Marian had been sometimes, with Kate as well as Jo, he felt anger rise in his own throat.

'She was blinkered, your mother,' he said as calmly as he could. 'She couldn't see what she didn't want to believe. Tough on you and Kate.'

Jo looked down at her plate, picked up her half of the chocolate brownie and devoured it without stopping.

'Do they feed you well there?' he asked, thinking of hospital food. It was as good a way as any to lighten the conversation.

'Oh, yes. Proper home-made stuff. All vegetarian. Not like Mother's awful cooking. They even make their own bread sometimes. Eleanor says we deserve good nourishment.'

'You seem to like this Eleanor a lot. Sounds like she's a kind person.'

It was the first time he'd seen Jo blush. It made her look endearingly young.

'She cares about everybody. She wants people to get better.' She looked away and wiped her eyes with a finger. 'She says, don't let *them* run your life.'

'Who are *they*, Jo?' As far as he knew, they could be anybody from the mental health professionals to the CIA.

She looked down at her plate again and muttered, 'The voices.'

He only just caught it. He'd suspected before, back in the days when she'd really lost it, that she might have heard voices, but she'd never quite told him so. He wasn't sure how to respond.

'Are you shocked?' she asked. 'Do you think I'm not normal?'

'I don't know what normal is.' He had to stop himself reaching out for her hand. 'The other day I thought I was having a heart attack, but it was like my heart was breaking – literally. That was pretty weird.'

'Was it about Jans... Kate?'

He nodded, slowly. 'I don't know how you can bear it, when you've got all that other stuff... I mean –' he was getting himself into a hole – 'I mean, it's such a lot to deal with. For anyone.'

She didn't answer straight away but broke a piece off her shortbread and ate it, then broke off another piece and held it between her fingers.

'It's not separate,' she said. 'It's because Jans died that I'm remembering. For her as well as me. I'm still taking care of her. We looked out for each other.'

'I know you did.' He felt a sharp pang of exclusion from their shared world.

'I sort of feel it's got to happen,' she said. 'Even though it's so terrible.' She nibbled a nail for the first time this afternoon; they didn't look as bitten down as usual. 'Like something that's been lurking in a dark hole coming out into the light. Eleanor understands that.'

Eleanor again. The thought occurred to him that perhaps, unlike Kate, Jo was attracted to women. Was that part of the reason she hadn't liked him touching her?

She said, 'Emmeline came to see me. I told her to go away.'

'Your friend?'

'She says she's my carer.'

'You don't have to see her, do you?'

'I haven't got anyone else. Anyway we used to be, you know, together. Not for very long. She bosses me about. Thinks she knows what's best for me. She told me I shouldn't see you.'

'Why not?' Richard didn't like the sound of this Emmeline, though he could see Jo needed her. His hunch about her sexuality seemed to have been right, but people rarely fitted into neat boxes.

Jo looked down at her plate and took another bite of shortbread. Still chewing, she said, 'She thinks you abused me. I've told her you didn't but it doesn't make any difference. She thinks all men are abusers. You can probably guess why...'

Richard shrugged. 'Oh well. You've made up your own mind. I'm very glad you don't see me like that.' She didn't know how glad he was.

'When I realised it wasn't you, for a while I thought it must have been Father. That would have been awful.'

'You didn't really know him, did you?'

'No, and Mother never talked about him. But I think he might have been a nice man.'

So many things that weren't talked about. So many things it felt impossible to talk about. He knew that for himself.

'Can I get you another coffee?' She was drooping, looking as though she'd had enough.

'No, thanks. I think I'll get back to the house.'

Not knowing if she'd mind, he said, 'I'll walk back there with you.'

She stared at him, eyes wide in alarm. 'It's a women-only house. You can't come in. It would upset people.'

'I know. Just to the door?' He wanted to say goodbye to her properly.

'All right. It's not far away. Otherwise Leisha said I could phone her.'

Leisha must be the woman who'd come in with her. Jo hadn't let him have the address of the house – perhaps she'd been told not to.

'It's up to you,' he said.

She caught her bottom lip with her teeth. 'It's OK. It'll be braver with an outside person.'

'I'm glad you trust me.' He couldn't say it had touched his heart – the heart he'd so recently discovered.

She disappeared into the toilet and took so long he was afraid she wasn't coming out. When she re-emerged, the skin round her eyes was swollen and her face looked blotchy. He hoped it wasn't his fault.

'You're sure you're all right?' he asked, not wanting to sound too concerned.

She nodded. 'A bit scared of going outside. All the people.'

'You can hang on to my arm, if you like.' Was that her need, or his? To his surprise she did, as soon as they were out of the door.

'Which way?' he said.

'I think it's round this corner here.'

She looked about from side to side. He could feel the panic in her tight grip on his arm.

'I can't remember,' she said. 'Leisha came with me last time.'

'Do you want to ring her, then?'

She stood still, seemingly frozen. The heavy traffic in Stroud Green Road had slowed to walking pace and he wanted to say to the drivers of the cars, Look, she needs help. Can't you help her? On the opposite side of the road was a large supermarket, its windows covered with garish pictures of vegetables and slogans in what he thought was Turkish. He couldn't see anyone inside. He turned his head and his eye was caught by the street sign for Mount Pleasant Crescent. What a strange name, he thought. Kate would have enjoyed it.

'Not down here, is it?' he said, pointing.

She turned too, and nodded in relief. 'Mount Pleasant Crescent,' she said. 'I remember that. There's a turning further up…'

They walked slowly along a neat row of yellow brick Victorian villas. A nice area, he thought, as the low villas gave way to taller grey brick houses. After a couple of rocky moments when Jo was sure they were going the wrong way, they found the road. She pointed to the geraniums on the steps and said, 'That's it. You'd better go now.' She pulled her arm away as if his had given her an electric shock.

He turned to face her. 'Take care of yourself, Jo,' he said. 'You're doing so well. They seem to be good people here.'

She nodded. 'Damian got me in here. He's a good person too.'

She hadn't mentioned him earlier. Richard was still puzzled as to what he did but it was too late to ask.

She looked down at her feet. The Doc Martens were as scruffy as ever, he noticed with affection.

'Thank you for coming,' she said. 'It was good to see you.'

It would have felt natural to hug her, or at least to give her a brotherly kiss on the cheek. His body ached with the effort of holding back.

'Keep in touch,' he said. 'Let me know how things go.'

She nodded again and turned away towards the house. At the top of the steps she looked back at him. He waved, fluttering his fingers, smiling at her. He didn't know when he'd see her again. She waved back uncertainly, before the closing door took her away from him.

He wandered back the way he'd come, not knowing what to do with himself for the rest of the evening. It was too early to eat and the pubs seemed dispiritingly trendy – not places for sitting quietly with a drink. He decided the best option would be a wander in Finsbury Park followed by a meal at what looked like a cheap but good Indian restaurant. That way he could give himself some space to think. The map on his phone showed a bundle of railway lines alongside the park, but once he was inside the gates he might not notice the noise too much. That was the thing about London parks: even on Hampstead Heath you could hear the traffic.

He headed towards the park gates along a road of substantial Victorian houses like the one where Jo was staying. Some were red or grey brick, some yellow, with white-painted stone surrounds to the doors and gothic-style windows. It looked like the kind of area that had gone downmarket and come up again; unmistakably London, so different from the stone-built houses and 1930s semis in his part of Edinburgh. The panels on the footbridge across the railway lines were painted alternately in shades of blue and terracotta pink. Most of them had scenes on them, not graffiti, though there were patches of graffiti too. A nice area, he thought again.

He found the park unexciting as he approached it in the sunless late afternoon, but at least it was green space. He looked at his watch: 5.45. He'd met Jo at 4.00 and the time they'd spent together was probably less than an hour. He'd come all this way for that and now here he was, by a stagnant boating lake in a park in London when he could have been with Rick in Holyrood Park, which wasn't this sort of park at all but proper countryside. As he walked on, he began to enjoy it more: its wide avenues of trees, the lushness of the municipal flower beds, as he and Kate had called them, even the fact that so many people were out walking their dogs. He knew he'd say yes to that dog Rick wanted.

The park reminded him of his walk with V in the Meadows, when they'd talked about Jo's abuse and he'd been reassured by V's acceptance. What a long way both he and Jo had come since then. A dreadful journey for her and a lost, muddled time for him. However much he needed her as a reminder of Kate, he mustn't let himself go on falling in love with her. She would so easily get hurt. And would he really want to spend his time supporting someone who, however much better she got, was always likely to need help? How could she ever fit into Rick's life? He couldn't see it working. Thinking about it gave him a heavy feeling.

He made a circuit of the park then went to find his Indian meal. The restaurant was vegetarian; maybe he'd have some of the dishes he and Jo had had when he'd taken her to that place in Bounds Green.

Jo

Bethan opened the door; Leisha was going off duty. During her time at the house, Jo had come to prefer Leisha to Bethan. Bethan was kind and caring, like Leisha, but Leisha was funny sometimes too and not afraid to tease her. It was Leisha who had helped her go out to the café – she couldn't believe she'd done it – saying, 'Of course you can do it. You know I'll be there.' Bethan had said, 'If you're sure you're ready…' which had made her feel she couldn't.

It had been hard. She'd told Richard about the voices but hadn't been able to say they'd been speaking to her while she was there. Not enough to spoil the time with him, maybe dulled by the medication, but *that* one had said, *You think you're going to get better. You think you'll be all right with him. You don't know…* and then it had muttered and laughed its tormenting laugh – just for a few moments. She'd had to eat very hard to make it go away, her mouth stuffed with so much chocolate brownie the taste had become unbearable.

She'd been surprised how easily she'd talked to him, even in the café with other people, normal people who might see her as one of those mental cases from that house – she was sure they'd know about it even though it did its best to disguise itself. Eleanor had said no one was normal if you knew what went on in their heads, but as far as she knew Richard didn't hear voices. He certainly hadn't cut himself: there were no scars on his arms. But he had talked about his heart breaking and that had made her feel easier with him.

Something about his smile, his eagerness for her to take his arm – which she'd done because she needed to – made her slightly afraid he might be getting too fond of her. She dreaded that, not just because he was a man; she wasn't sure she'd want a relationship with a woman either. Unless the woman happened to be like Eleanor. She hoped Eleanor didn't realise how she felt but thought she probably did – not much got past her. It felt shaming, like having a crush on a female teacher at school when other girls had moved on to boys, but Eleanor had been wonderful; there was no other word for it. She'd given her the hope – the magnificent, still fragile hope – that she could get better, at least better than she had been; nobody at the house promised more than that.

Bethan opened the door of the interview room, the room where Jo had seen Mother, and sat down in one of the armchairs. The cleaner must have been in: the room smelt overwhelmingly of lilac air-freshener, with an undertone of disinfectant.

'How did it go?' Bethan asked eagerly. Was she expecting Jo to say it had been too much?

'OK,' Jo said. 'It was good to see Richard.'

'Very brave of you to come back here by yourself. We didn't think you'd do that.'

We. That must mean they'd talked about her. 'He walked back with me,' she said. She didn't say she'd taken his arm.

'Oh?' Bethan said, more curiously than Jo liked. 'Was he the man standing just down the road when I opened the door?'

None of your business, Jo wanted to say. She nodded.

'And he's your brother-in-law, your sister's husband?'

Except her sister wasn't there any more – they knew that – so strictly speaking he was Jans's widower. The word sounded old and grey, not like Richard at all. She nodded again and didn't say more, though Bethan was waiting.

'You did really well,' Bethan said, after a pause. 'How was it, being in the café?'

'OK. I'm glad to be back here.' The house felt like her home. 'I don't want to go back to my flat. It isn't home, it's just where I happen to live.'

'Well, I'm very sorry, but you've had as much time here as we can give you. Eleanor is happy with the progress you've made. We've been glad to have you.'

She glowed inside to think Eleanor was happy with her. Had they really been glad?

'Yes, but –' She thought of the drab hall carpet, the smell of Eric Gaines's flat, the washing-up she never managed to finish, the voices and memories that seemed to have soaked into the walls.

Bethan patted her on the arm. 'You know you'll still be able to come here. To the group, every Thursday. And, as Eleanor said, we're going to try and get you some one-to-one sessions.'

'With Eleanor?'

'No, love. She doesn't do that. But we have some good people coming in.'

Jo's heart sank. She was afraid the one-to-one sessions would be like the ones she'd had with Dr Rasen – lying there helpless and talking into empty space. But if Eleanor organised them perhaps they'd be different.

'Don't you worry,' Bethan said. 'We'll support you as much as we can. We don't just drop people.'

Jo shook her head in disbelief. 'Does Damian know?' she asked, hoping he'd be glad too.

'Who? Oh, your CPN. He's coming to pick you up, isn't he?'

'Yes.' That was the only good thing about going home: she'd be seeing Damian.

It was nearly supper time but she went up to her room, hoarding Richard's visit and the good things she'd heard like treasures so precious she hardly dared unwrap them. She picked up her journal but didn't feel ready to write; sometimes things had to settle first. Seeing its battered cover, she felt the ache of loneliness that had made her start writing. Not just the loneliness now, since Jans's death, but the loneliness that had always been there. The cold room at the top of Mother's Oxford house, the tiny bedsit in Dalston where she'd lived while at university, the cubicle in the hospital ward, the drop-in. all the places where she'd been among people and still felt alone. She didn't feel it now; she was welcome here.

When she went down to supper, she noticed someone new sitting in a corner with her key worker. A young woman, improbably tall and thin, whose white face had brown craters under the eyes as though she hadn't slept for months. Either that or she'd been crying non-stop for a very long time. She was dressed in black, with a black scarf wound round her head, and sat staring into space, chewing at her bottom lip instead of the food on her plate. She looked utterly terrified and bewildered. Jo remembered she'd felt the same. The flashbacks still came, the voices hadn't stopped, but now there was more space between them and she seemed to be filling it with more of herself. She didn't know how it had happened, except that the people who worked here had something to do with it.

The soup tonight was carrot, her favourite, and the bread was firm and crusty, not like the soggy stuff she was used to buying, that disintegrated as soon as you put it in your mouth. There was fresh cheese too, and it wasn't oily from being kept in plastic in a too-warm place. She'd miss the food here, not as much as she'd miss the staff, but still quite a lot. It was part of being looked after. She felt like a chick forced out of its shell before it was ready to meet the outside world. As she started eating, a wave of homesickness rose up inside her, homesickness for this house. She wished Jans could have seen it, and whispered to her in her head the way she always used to. She was sure Jans could hear her.

Leisha had helped her pack her rucksack and the bag Emmeline had brought, and had made sure she didn't leave anything behind – not that she had much to leave. Now it was empty of her, the room seemed just a room again, the duvet turned back, the bed made up freshly for the next person. She glanced at the photographs that had reminded her of Jans and wondered if she could get prints of them. She'd never put up a picture in her flat, not even a postcard, but these meant something. She was saying goodbye to the pictures, and to the Jans who had been there with her, when terror rushed in like a wind through her mouth and turned her insides to ice. She sat down on the uncovered sheet, her hands over her face, shaking so hard she knew Leisha would notice. She wasn't seeing anything, wasn't hearing anything; it was a sheer physical sensation, as strong as any she'd had. She felt Leisha sit down on the bed beside her, a firm arm holding her shoulders as she shook and shook.

'Breathe,' Leisha was saying. 'Nice deep breaths, now.'

After a while her body began to remember what it had been taught. The shaking became less violent and she felt less cold inside. She was breathing in air, just air, not the panic that had seemed to fill the room. It was all right, and it wasn't all right because she didn't want to go home.

Leisha helped her downstairs, carrying her bags, and waited with her in reception, keeping a steadying hand on her shoulder, till Damian rang the bell. Then, Jo didn't know how, she was walking towards the door and Leisha was giving her a hug and wishing her well and Damian was carrying her bags to the car and asking her how she was doing.

'Good to see you, Jo,' he said as he opened the car door. 'I've thought about you. You're looking a lot better, even if you've just had a bit of a wobble.'

How did he know that, she wondered. Had Leisha told him? She'd been in a kind of cloud while they waited: not there, not anywhere else.

'Soon be home,' he said encouragingly.

She huddled into herself, not wanting to hear it, not wanting him to drive her anywhere, her head bent right down so as not to show him how she felt. She didn't want him to think she wasn't better.

'I know it's a shock to the system,' he said, 'but you'll be OK, I'm sure you will. You'll have the group there and you'll have me still, and Dr Rogerson said they'll try and get you some therapy.'

She couldn't think who Dr Rogerson was, then realised it must be Eleanor. Nobody in the house had called her by her surname.

'Will I have to see Dr Greenland?' she asked.

'Yes, you're still under him. But he should listen to what Dr Rogerson says, especially if he can see you're better.'

She wasn't sure Dr Greenland would like Eleanor's way of going about things but didn't say so. Damian didn't know what the house was like. She wished she could have said goodbye to Eleanor and hoped Eleanor wouldn't think worse of her because she hadn't. She'd imagined she would come and hug her too, like Bethan and Leisha, but perhaps she was busy.

For the rest of the way they were quiet. The streets they passed through looked familiar but different, as though she was coming back after many years. There were such a lot of streets. Not just the few she'd been in, which had been vast and intimidating enough, but whole networks full of houses that were full of people, and shops that sold things she'd forgotten anyone bought, like doormats and plastic buckets and barbecues. London was like that, streets and shops and suburbs connected to more streets and shops and suburbs, so that whichever way you looked you couldn't see the end of it. She'd never minded it before but now she felt trapped by its relentlessness. She didn't say so to Damian.

She handed him her keys – Leisha had made sure she knew where they were – and he pushed open the heavy front door. The smell – dust and damp and Eric's flat – hit her as though she'd never smelt it before. When Damian got to the top of the stairs, she noticed he opened her door without using the key. Unlike the hallway, her flat smelt of an artificial scent that wasn't the one she'd bought. There were no letters on the floor under the letterbox, nor was there a smell of old washing-up from the kitchen, and the carpet looked as though it had been swept.

As soon as Jo reached the living room, Emmeline stood up from the bigger armchair and said, 'Hi. Welcome back. I thought you'd need someone to be here.' She smiled at Damian as at a fellow worker.

Jo was so furious that for a moment she couldn't speak. How dared Emmeline park herself here without asking? How dared she keep interfering? At the same time she was relieved; it was comforting that the flat was clean, and at least Emmeline was someone and not no one.

'Thank you,' she said through clenched teeth, glaring at Damian. If this was his doing, he was almost as bad as Emmeline.

'My idea,' he said, his smile so warm and mischievous she had to forgive him. 'I just need to check out a couple of things with you while Emmeline gets you a coffee.'

Emmeline disappeared on cue and Damian was soon done. 'Bye, Emmeline,' he called out as he left, as though he knew her well.

Jo sat back in the small armchair. Nothing had changed and everything had. She wasn't going to let herself be interrogated by Emmeline.

Fran

She sat down at the kitchen table with a mug of tea, enjoying the quiet while Rick was out at his friend Robbie's. Through the glass door she could see how neglected the garden was. She'd have a go at some of that bindweed if it stopped raining. Meanwhile she felt at a loose end: for the first time she hadn't been so keen to come here. Not that she didn't want to see Rick, of course, but what had happened with Stephen had knocked the stuffing out of her. She pictured herself as an old-fashioned rag doll, leaking sawdust from a broken seam. She didn't want to feel sorry for herself; these things happened with people you met on websites. It wasn't like meeting someone by chance in real life and letting things develop, or not. This way there was always competition, knowing that you or the other person might at any moment choose someone who seemed better. She felt like a cheap brand of cereal on a supermarket shelf, picked up and then put back again in favour of a better packaged one. No, that was unfair. Stephen had been kind about it, or at least not unkind, and she too had wondered if they were really right for each other. It hurt, though, that the bright glow of possibility had been so abruptly switched off.

She'd already done her best to tidy the kitchen, tidying away jars of jam and peanut butter, wiping crumbs off the table, scrunching scattered carrier bags into one bag so she could take them for recycling, putting away the contents of those that had been left half-emptied on the floor. She'd swept the floor too, made the heap of papers and magazines on Richard's half of the table into a neat pile and gathered Rick's toys into one place. They might not thank her for any of it, but it bothered her that Richard hadn't seemed to be coping. Not much of a drinker herself, she'd noticed more wine bottles in the recycling box recently and was relieved he'd said he was trying to drink less.

It was harder to bring order to the sitting-room; it had a dusty, neglected look. When she opened the door she was dazzled by dust motes turning in a beam of light from the window. It reminded her of their childhood in the suburbs of York, in a solid mock-Tudor semi the like of which she couldn't possibly afford now, her delight and astonishment at discovering this tiny miracle moving slowly above the latticed shadow from the leaded panes. When she looked beyond the dust in the sitting-room, she saw there was nothing much she could do. Kate's scarf had to stay on the armchair, the books that had been taken out couldn't be put back, even the piles of design magazines were sacrosanct where they were. Everything in the room seemed stopped in time, stagnating in a way that Fran had begun to feel might not be completely healthy. Perhaps it was too soon to say that. She counted back from now, near the end of August, to Kate's death in April. Four and a half months, less than four months since the funeral at the beginning of May. Maybe she was being too hard on Richard. It was beyond her to imagine what it would be like to lose the person you'd chosen to spend your life with – to have them ripped away from you in the space of less than a day.

She closed the door again and looked at her watch. 12.00. Rick would be back in an hour or so and wanting his lunch. She'd agreed they'd have oven chips with Quorn burgers. He said he'd try one, but if he didn't like it she could easily do him some fish fingers. She liked having people to cook for and Rick delighted her. Just the kind of son she would have wanted, if she'd had one. She was glad she'd be there to welcome Richard back later on; it made her feel part of the family. She'd carry the feeling with her on the train back to York; it would warm her as she settled into preparing for her meeting at work first thing tomorrow.

'Fran,' Rick said as he spat out a mouthful of Quorn burger, 'why does Dad keep going to see Jo? Grandad says she's mad.'

Fran couldn't stop herself wincing as she served up the fish fingers – she had them ready just in case. Fond as she was of her father – fonder than Richard, who had always battled with him – she had to admit he was more than a bit of a bigot. Not just about people he called mad, but 'coloured' people and 'those skiving Poles who've come here and taken our jobs'. She dared not mention Muslims to him. She hated it when he talked in those tabloid clichés; they seemed as stiff and unbendable as his arthritic joints. She hoped she'd never become like that.

'She's had a hard time, love. Some people do, and they really struggle. It's not very kind to call her mad.'

'But why is she like that? Mum wasn't, and they were twins.'

She shrugged. 'I don't know. These things happen. Anybody can find life difficult sometimes.' She was careful, not wanting to open up more than he could cope with. 'Looks like you're enjoying the fish fingers more than that burger.' She grinned.

'Eurgh!' Rick's face was a cartoon of disgust. 'How can you eat that stuff?'

'I quite like it.'

'*You* must be mad, then. Fran, my mad aunt, who eats Quorn burgers.'

She had to laugh. 'You can call me mad if you like. I know you don't mean it in that way.'

She remembered Jo at Richard and Kate's wedding, standing awkwardly in a corner in a smart flowered dress that didn't seem to be her style, biting her nails and looking as though she wished she didn't have to be there. There had been something about her, though, an integrity; Fran could see she wasn't just a poor creature to be pitied. That was the only time they'd met properly. Odd to think they'd become family to each other when they had so little in common. Fran hadn't had much in common with Kate either. She'd liked her well enough, but there had been a sharpness about Kate that disconcerted her. Kate hadn't suffered fools gladly, as people said, and Fran knew her well-meaningness could sometimes seem foolish. She'd once said a design of Kate's, semi-abstract flowers on a dark blue background, was very pretty, and had got short shrift for it. She still writhed with shame when she thought about it, though to her it *had* been pretty. Richard, loyal to Kate, had done his best to explain why 'pretty' wasn't OK just then. He loved Kate, there was no doubt of that, and she'd seemed to love him. They'd stayed together for fifteen years. Fran wondered how people managed it; a happy marriage seemed such a difficult thing to achieve.

By the time she heard Richard's key scrunch in the lock she had her bag packed and had stopped trying to find helpful things to do. She was itching to get away but wouldn't leave until she'd caught up with him. Rick had aimlessly kicked a ball around the garden for a while then disappeared upstairs to his room, and Fran was left sitting at the cleaned and tidied table, feeling unnecessary, writing notes for work tomorrow.

As the door opened she stood up, an anticipatory smile on her face.

'Hi, Ricks,' Richard called up the stairs. 'You OK?'

'Yeah,' Rick called back. 'Playing a game.'

She heard the stairs thump and creak under Richard's heavy tread, their two voices in Rick's room, too indistinct for her to make out what they said, and Richard's footsteps, slower and quieter, coming down again ...

'Hi, Fran,' he called out from the hallway. 'Everything all right?'

Her smile, which had slowly sagged, stretched again. 'Fine,' she said. 'Rick didn't like my Quorn burgers!' She laughed gamely.

'Did he have something else?' Richard looked anxious as he came into the kitchen. His face, drawn into deep lines between the brows, reminded her of their mother's when she'd been concerned about them.

'Course he did. Don't worry. I gave him fish fingers.' She moved over to switch the kettle on.

Richard's expression eased, as though that was one thing less to bother about.

'How did it go?' she asked. 'How is Jo?'

'Not too bad, considering. Being there seems to have done her good.' He'd had to let on that it was Jo who was in the crisis house. 'Her mother ...'

Fran remembered the mother from the wedding too: an odd, cold woman who hadn't seemed to like anybody much. Affection wasn't her strong suit, obviously; no wonder Kate had been a bit sharp. 'And how are you?' she asked him.

'Oh, you know. Tired. It's a long way to go. I had a nice walk in Finsbury Park.'

Fran nodded. She didn't know London well and couldn't picture Finsbury Park. 'It is a long way to go for such a short time.'

She heard Richard's faint sigh. Perhaps he took it as a criticism.

'I hope it wasn't too draining,' she said. 'You need someone to look out for you too.'

'Don't fuss, Fran. I'm all right. It was good to see Jo's getting better.'

'I'm glad.' Fran meant it. She couldn't help wishing, though, that Richard would take better care of himself. 'It's not really my business,' she said, 'but I just wondered if...'

'Yes?'

'If maybe you're hanging on to Jo because she's Kate's sister, if you know what I mean. Maybe getting a bit fond?'

Richard shrugged in an offhand way. 'Maybe. But she's herself too, you know. She's got a lot of guts.'

'I'm sure she has.' Fran realised she had stepped over a line she wouldn't normally cross. She looked at her watch. 'I'd best be going now. I don't want to miss the next train.'

'OK. Shall I run you down to Waverley?' He didn't make a move; she could see he didn't want to.

'No need. I'm in plenty of time for the bus.'

When he thanked her she knew he meant it. She wanted to thank him too but didn't know how to do it without sounding sorry for herself. These days they hugged each other warmly, even though for most of their lives they'd hardly touched.

Watching the sea and the wild high cliffs as the train made its way between Berwick and Newcastle – her favourite part of the journey – she found herself wondering what would happen to Kate's ashes. She could understand Richard might want to keep them with him, but somehow she hoped that sooner or later Kate would be set free into the water.

Richard

Grateful as he'd been, it was a relief to see Fran off. She'd slipped upstairs to give Rick a hug and promise she'd be back again soon, and then she'd opened the door for herself and called out, 'Bye, Richard. Take care,' as he emerged from the kitchen. It was always awkward saying goodbye again once you'd hugged and were done with it. Kate had never liked lingering over goodbyes; it was as though a shutter came down over her face, dismissing the other person. Jo was abrupt about it too, he realised, but then she was abrupt at other times. He thought now that she might have cut off from him sometimes because the voices were talking. He couldn't imagine what that must be like – perhaps a scary radio play that you had to keep listening to and couldn't turn off.

He sat down at the table. The kitchen smelt of pine disinfectant and sweetish cleaning spray; Fran had been busy. The table had been wiped and its varnished surface felt smooth, not sticky, under his hands. The order Fran had brought to it made the house feel more peaceful. He sipped his fresh cup of tea and thought he'd give Rick a few minutes before going up to see him. He might even suggest getting out the model railway, if Rick wasn't too scornful of it. The time was long gone when boys had wanted to be engine drivers, or even drivers of electric trains. It was already gone in his childhood but he'd still loved operating the trains, making the points work smoothly, getting down so close to it that the station with its miniature trees and people had begun to seem real. The Carlisle-Settle line, which took him to see his father, always reminded him of it, with its shiny dark-red signs and clean platforms, their tubs and hanging baskets bright with petunias. His model didn't have the green grandeur of the Fells, though, or the precipitous viaduct that had entranced Rick when he first saw it.

Savouring his tea while it was still hot, he took one of the biscuits Fran had left out for him. You couldn't beat chocolate digestives. She must have brought them; he didn't remember buying any. He looked in the bread bin. She'd left some of the bread Rick liked, which came from her local bakery. It was mildly wholemeal and, he had to admit, pretty good as bread went. She'd probably have put a loaf in the freezer for them; she usually did. He savoured the biscuit; as a kid he'd loved to read Arthur Ransome or, when he was younger, Enid Blyton, munching chocolate digestives and drinking a mug of milk. The biscuits had to be dark chocolate; he and Fran agreed about that.

Now he'd started thinking about the model railway, he was impatient to see it again. As soon as he'd finished his tea and biscuit, he ran upstairs and knocked on Rick's door.

'Hey, Ricks,' he called. 'Want to have a go with the railway?' He was surprised to feel so excited about it.

'OK,' Rick said noncommittally, opening his door but looking back at his computer, where a dragon had been frozen on the screen in the act of attacking another one.

'You remember it, don't you?' Richard said, 'And the scenery Mum made for it?'

He and Rick looked at each other for a moment. Rick's wide-eyed gaze seemed to mirror his own eagerness and sadness.

'Yeah,' Rick said, nodding. 'But what about Livingstone? Fran said ...'

'Who or what's Livingstone? And what did Fran say?'

'The dog.' Rick looked at him intently. 'She said was a good idea, and I said I wanted him –'

'OK,' Richard said slowly. 'Well, why don't I talk to your friend's mum about it and then we'll see?'

'Oh, go on, Dad. You know you like Wilkie.'

'We'll see,' Richard repeated. 'Now what about these trains?'

He opened the door of the spare room, which Fran had left neat like the rest of the house. She hadn't stripped the bed, knowing she'd be back soon. The railway, wrapped in polythene sheets, was kept under the bed; he and Kate had deliberately chosen one high enough for it to fit underneath. Grunting slightly, which made him sound like his father, he knelt down and carefully pulled out the big rectangular board, his hands soon grey with dust from its covering. He was aware of Rick watching him from the doorway.

'Here we are, then,' he said with the pride he'd always felt in it. It had been a present from Uncle Bill, his father's younger brother, who had been an ally against his father's sternness and his mother's fussing. He'd had fun with Bill, who had gone off to Canada when Richard was about Rick's age.

'Wow, Dad,' Rick said. 'I'd forgotten how big it was.'

Richard was busy unwrapping it from the polythene. There was just enough space for him and Rick to crouch down beside it on the cheap light-brown carpet that he and Kate had always been going to replace. The station and model people were cruder than he remembered; Kate's scenery looked fresher, more realistic. The trains were in a separate box. Lovingly he took out the two engines and placed them on the track, coupling the carriages to them. By this time Rick was kneeling beside him, gently touching the trains, eager to get them going. Richard had to connect the electrics and plug it in, reaching across the nylon carpet which felt rough under his hands. He pushed the controls towards Rick.

'Go on,' he said. 'You do it.'

Grinning, Rick gingerly pulled one of the levers. A train started to move round a loop of track, slowly at first and then faster as Rick pulled the lever towards him. Richard saw how carefully he pulled a separate lever which controlled the points and then moved one beside the first which started the other train.

'This is so cool,' Rick said, not taking his eyes off the trains as they followed each other, criss-crossing over the points. There was even an old-fashioned signal with an arm that raised and lowered. 'Did you play with it a lot, Dad?'

'At one time, yes. I thought it was the best thing I'd ever had.'

Rick nodded as he moved the levers again, speeding up one train and slowing the other, then stopping it at the signal as the first one went over the points. Every time a train passed Kate's piece of scenery, Richard couldn't help looking at Rick to see how it was affecting him; as far as he could tell, his son was more interested in the trains themselves. Richard remembered the hours Kate had spent with papier mâché, paints and whatever bits and pieces came to hand, making it look as real as possible, and Rick's delight as the hills and woodlands gradually became recognisable. Kate's delight too. When she'd finished it she'd smiled and laughed like an excited child. She had rarely been like that with her fabric designs, though she'd been pleased with them in a more sober way. Even if it hurt, he enjoyed remembering her joy.

Rick was concentrating hard, making the manoeuvres more complicated, revelling in his power over this miniature world. For the first time since Kate's death Richard felt something like happiness. It gladdened his heart to see Rick taking so much pleasure in the railway, and the memory of his own pleasure was surprisingly strong. He could think of few things in his childhood that had pleased him more.

Rick brought the trains to a stop and turned to look at Richard. 'Go on, Dad, you have a go,' he said with a mischievous smile.

'Well, OK, if you're sure,' Richard said. 'But I got it out for you.' It was partly true.

'Yeah. I can see you want to. And it's yours, anyway.'

'It's yours now,' Richard said, as Rick shuffled over to make room for him at the controls.

'Is it? Is it really? Thanks, Dad.'

'You're welcome, son.' Richard started the trains moving again, Rick directing him over his shoulder.

'Look out!' Rick shouted as the two trains nearly collided. 'I don't want you breaking my railway.'

It seemed as though they hadn't laughed together for years. Rick hooted, rolling on the floor, while Richard, shaking and unsteady on his knees, brought the trains to a stop. It was a glorious release, but as his ribs heaved he felt how close the laughter was to the feeling he'd had when his heart broke. When Rick sat up, wiping his eyes, it was hard for Richard to read his grimace.

'Great Edinburgh railway disaster avoided,' Richard said. 'Man's prompt action saves the day.'

'I'd have been prompter,' Rick retorted.

'Course you would. Boy hero saves Edinburgh from train catastrophe.'

Rick stood up, stretched his arms wide and made a deep bow. It reminded Richard so much of Kate in one of her playful moods that it was as if time had gone back.

'I'm glad you like it, Ricks,' he said, wiping his hand over his face. Since that moment at Arthur's Seat Richard had found himself welling up unexpectedly at the stupidest things – the fruit bowl full of fresh oranges, Rick's football boots, a rose flowering through the bindweed. It was so unlike him – emotional incontinence, he wanted to call it – but he couldn't stop it.

Sitting in the bedroom in the early evening, the light on but the curtains not drawn, the trees outside a muted green against a pale sky, Richard looked at his phone, his time with Rick still warm inside him. Shamed by Fran's neatness, he'd put the duvet straight and tidied away most of the clothes. He had to admit it felt better.

Jo had texted: Back now. Emmeline was here but it's OK. He rang her immediately, thinking how lonely she must be in that unwelcoming place. He noticed the 'but' and had the feeling again that she wasn't happy with Emmeline.

'Hi, Jo. How are you?' He'd thought the call would go to voicemail but she picked up straight away.

'Hi.' There was a pause and then she said, 'I thought you might ring.'

'What's it like, being home?'

There was a pause. 'I'm scared. Scared it's all going to come back.'

'Oh, Jo. Is there anyone who can help you?'

'They said I can go to a group every week, at the house. And there's Damian. And Eleanor wants me to see someone.'

'What sort of someone?'

'A therapist, I suppose.'

'Do you want to do that?'

'Maybe.'

'So at least there's something ...' He hesitated. 'And you know you can always ring me.'

'Yes.'

Another pause; he hoped she wasn't ending the conversation. He was afraid of asking unwelcome questions.

'Keep hanging in there,' he said. 'You know how brave I think you are.'

She snorted but sounded pleased. 'Yeah. I'd better go,' she said. 'Running out of battery.'

'OK. But keep in touch.'

The call died and she didn't ring back. He'd hoped she would, for his own reassurance as much as anything. He glanced round at Kate's box on the shelf and felt her there with him. She'd be worried for Jo and rooting for her; she'd love to know about Rick and the trains. He reached into the air to clasp Kate's hand, hungering for its flesh and bone, the soft dry feel of her skin over the prominent knuckles, and imagined his hand moving up her arm to stroke her shoulder and then her breast. No, he couldn't let himself go there – but as always he did.

Jo

She wished Emmeline would go but dreaded being left with nothing but the dreary flat and her own mind. She hadn't bothered to unpack yet but took Squidge out of her rucksack and sat him on the pillow of the newly-changed bed. She felt safer knowing he was there.

'I've left you some ready meals to microwave. You know how to work it, don't you?' Emmeline said for at least the third time.

Jo nodded, forgetting Emmeline couldn't see her.

'I said, you know how to work it, don't you?' Emmeline bustled into the bedroom, the sleeves of her checked shirt rolled up as though she'd been getting down to work.

'Yes.' Jo said vaguely.

'Shall I show you?'

'No. You showed me before.' She wished Emmeline would stop fussing.

'Shall I heat you one up before I go?'

'If you want.' She wasn't hungry but thought she ought to eat.

'Which one would you like? There's...'

'Oh, any.' Just get on with it and go, she wanted to say.

Emmeline bustled out again. Jo sat down on the bed and pulled her journal out of her rucksack. It was nearly finished; she'd have to get another one from the expensive shop in Muswell Hill. Good notebooks were her only extravagance.

Back now, she wrote. *The flat smells of cleaning and Emmeline.* She closed the book quickly as Emmeline reappeared with a plate of insipid-looking macaroni cheese and another plate with two hunks of garlic bread, presumably one for each of them.

'Shall we...?' Emmeline said, waving her hand towards the sitting-room. Without stopping to see whether Jo was following her, she took the plate through and sat herself in the bigger armchair. She put the meal, with a fork beside it, on the coffee table, which she'd cleared and wiped over. Jo noticed she held her piece of garlic bread in a wad of tissues, to stop her fingers getting greasy. Her hands were thick and ungraceful, the fingers bunched close together round the stub of bread.

Jo curled up in the smaller chair, bending over her plate. She found she was hungry after all and the food wasn't bad, but she wished Emmeline wouldn't keep watching her with that predatory maternal stare. It was almost as though she was about to tell her what a good girl she was for eating her dinner. Jo ate as much as she could, until the pale arcs of pasta – like cut worms – began to nauseate her. She put the plate down on the table and said to Emmeline, 'You can finish it, if you like.'

Emmeline did. After she'd washed it up and made them both coffee, she said she'd be going soon. 'Unless you want me to stay?'

Panic flooded into Jo's body. All the molecules in her limbs seemed to be vibrating and there was a cold, relentless thrumming in her solar plexus. Shadows of memories hovered just out of sight and a voice mocked: *Coward. Scaredy cat. Can't manage on your own. Coward.* Emmeline was sipping her coffee, legs stretched out, looking at Jo sideways as if she didn't want to be seen looking.

'I brought my things just in case,' Emmeline said, turning her head towards her. 'I think perhaps ...'

Jo opened her mouth but words wouldn't come. For a moment – just for a moment – Emmeline seemed to grow huge, as big as the man who she now knew was Paul. She could almost feel Emmeline's body bearing down on top of her. Then suddenly she looked normal again, big and lumpy but no more than that.

Jo nodded. 'All right. Damian's coming tomorrow.'

'That's good,' Emmeline said in her soothing carer voice. 'I brought my mattress...' She had an inflatable one with a foot pump, which she used when she and Kirsty went camping – she'd explained it to Jo. 'Unless you want me ...' she said.

Jo almost screamed. Emmeline in the bed beside her, squashing against her, hugging her, stroking her. Emmeline intruding into her sleep. 'No,' she said. 'No, thanks.' She remembered how she and Jans had clung to each other in the night, keeping each other safe. That was different; they'd belonged together.

'OK.' Emmeline gave way surprisingly easily. There wasn't room for her to sleep on the bedroom floor so she'd have to kip down in the sitting room, with the bedroom door shut so that hopefully her presence wouldn't spill out into Jo's space. It would be a squash, but she could move the furniture.

Jo felt utterly exhausted. It was partly the medication, she knew, but the day seemed to have contained more than she could deal with, like a jug filled past overflowing point. Each thing that had happened felt bigger than itself; each person seemed to take up so much room inside her that she felt she couldn't breathe. She was so tired that even the voices didn't catch her attention.

'You going to bed already?' Emmeline called as Jo went into the bedroom.

'Yeah. Tired.'

'You can call me if you need to.'

'Yeah.'

Jo shut the bedroom door and curled up on the bed, clutching Squidge. Her night clothes were still in the rucksack and she couldn't be bothered to get them out. The voices mumbled in her head like a distant radio, dulled by the medication but saying things she didn't want to hear. She pulled the covers over her and slid into a stuporous sleep, forgetting Emmeline, feeling Jans close beside her.

She remembered that she'd woken during the night and Emmeline had come to her. Perhaps she'd called out in her sleep – she didn't know. Now Emmeline, her rucksack already packed, was folding the mattress into its bag. She'd made coffee and toast for both of them – Jo had no toaster and rarely bothered to use the grill – and they sat in their respective chairs eating their breakfast almost as if they were a couple again. Would it have been so bad, Jo wondered, knowing she wouldn't want it. At the moment it didn't matter; nothing seemed to matter. She'd taken her medication and felt as though dense balls of cotton-wool were stifling her thoughts. Damian would be coming soon and she'd ask him to ask Dr Greenland to reduce the dosage. She knew Dr Greenland wouldn't take any notice of what she said.

'Well,' Emmeline said, looking round to make sure she had everything. 'I've got to go now but I'll pop in again this evening – just to see you're OK.'

Jo nodded. It was better to know she wasn't on her own all the time.

Emmeline moved towards her, arms reaching out. 'Bye, Jo,' she said, trying to enfold her as Jo huddled tighter in her chair. 'Take care. You know you can always call me.'

Jo nodded and managed to say 'Thanks' as Emmeline picked up the mattress bag and pushed the door open with her foot. Emmeline's back, broad and slightly rounded, was dependable, reassuring, safe. Jo didn't go to the front door with her. It didn't occur to her until after the Yale lock had clicked shut that Emmeline might have needed her to open the door – Emmeline seemed capable of managing everything herself.

Once she'd gone, Jo went into the kitchen to get more coffee. Sticky splashes had been wiped off the old grey Formica, brown stains had been scrubbed from the enamel cooker top, there were no piles of washing-up in the sink. It was eerie, not like her kitchen, but she didn't feel the usual guilt about having failed to tackle it.

Back into the sitting-room she waited for Damian. The voices were almost quiet and the occasional flashes – the pink skin of Paul's face, so close she could see the open pores, the hot smell of his breath – seemed distant. She was distant from herself too, as though the places inside her where she felt things had been closed up. *After great pain a formal feeling comes*. The formal feeling never lasted. She opened her journal; writing would bring her mind awake.

I'm home now, trying to come through it. It's so frightening and it hurts so much, especially knowing I couldn't do anything, and I have to face it. Now I know what it is and who it is, it's as though my feet have touched the ground. Our brother – our half-brother. We never really knew him and yet he did – a wave of nausea rose up; she put her hand over her mouth, shivering, but then wrote – *those things to us. I don't understand why. Did someone interfere with him? Did they abuse him?*

She stopped and looked up, her head still fogged. She knew these things already but writing them down made them more real. Outside the window a strong wind made the branches of the plane tree shake and shudder. There would be thunder soon. One of the voices said savagely, *You can't do anything for her. She's dead. Just tell her to fuck off.* No, Jo said aloud. I won't do that. Leave me alone. The voice became fainter, almost as though it had heard her. That had never happened before.

Jo

When Damian arrived, he said straight away, 'Remember you've got an appointment with Dr Greenland. I'll take you in a bit.'

'No,' she said, cold with panic. 'I can't see him. He'll make me have more medication. He'll stop me going back to the house, I know he will.'

Damian said calmly, 'He won't. You're expected to go there. They haven't discharged you as an outpatient.'

'And the medication? Will you tell him it's too much for me? I can't think straight. I feel dizzy and my head's full of grey wool.'

'I'll try my best but you know it's up to him. And the medication seems to have been helping you.'

'Being in the house was helping me,' Jo said passionately. 'The medication was only a bit of it.'

'OK,' Damian said. 'You'll have to talk to him yourself, you know. He'll want to know how you're getting on.'

'He doesn't want to know,' Jo muttered to herself. 'He just sits and looks straight past me.'

'What's that? Come on, Jo. We'd better get going.'

She'd hoped Damian would stay with her in Outpatients. It would have made sitting in the waiting room easier. Instead, she was here alone, staring at the orange-yellow walls with hospital notices on them, remembering all the times she'd been there and how crushed she'd always felt coming out of Dr Greenland's office. He had a way of pushing aside what she said and only wanting to hear about what he thought was important. When she'd told him she didn't feel her life had much meaning, he'd asked what activities she was doing and suggested she take up skating. After Jans died, what he was interested in was whether or not she was taking her medication. She knew not all psychiatrists were like that; Eleanor wasn't, for a start. She wasn't just a psychiatrist; she let you see she was a person too.

She'd even said she was a twin. Jo imagined going into Dr Greenland's office and finding Eleanor there instead.

Half an hour or so after the appointment time, Dr Greenland opened the door to call her in. He looked more bulky and bulldog-like than ever and his dark-framed glasses gave him a directorial air. She always noticed how he went in first and expected her to follow, and how the high-backed swivel chair he sat in behind his desk was bigger and taller than the small pink-upholstered one in front of the desk. The neutral pale grey of the walls – supposed to be soothing, she imagined – felt hostile and unwelcoming. Her stomach sank as she waited for him to speak.

'So, Joanna. How are you feeling now you're back at home? No more suicidal ideation, I hope?' He settled his glasses higher on his nose.

She shook her head. 'It's a bit soon to tell how I'm feeling. I feel like I've only just got back—'

'And how are your symptoms?'

'Well, as I said—'

'So no worse at this point? Better, I hope?'

'I think so, but—'

'Good. I suggest we keep the medication at the same level for the time being. No troublesome side-effects?'

Jo didn't know how to begin. 'It makes me feel so heavy. I can't think properly. Couldn't you—'

'Those effects should be manageable, at least in the short term. It's not as if you're doing work that requires concentration. This particular drug has a good record in reducing auditory hallucinations.'

'Yes, but—' Jo sank back in the chair. Her whole body felt overpowered.

'Now, I see from Dr Rogerson's report that she recommends you attend a weekly group at the house. I have no objection to that. However, I would question the wisdom of your having one-to-one psychotherapy—'

This time it was Jo who interrupted. 'But Eleanor – Dr Rogerson – talked to me about it. She thinks it would be a good thing for me to—'

'I understand that's her opinion. I would disagree. Psychotherapy for patients with psychotic symptoms may aggravate the symptoms in a way that makes them harder to control.'

'But I was abused.' She didn't say, we were abused. 'It makes a difference, understanding more about it. Dr Rogerson thinks that too. She thinks people need to be listened to.'

'With the greatest respect, Joanna, I have treated psychotic patients for far longer than Dr Rogerson. And you are still under my care.' For once he stared at her, his eyes impersonal behind the thick glasses, his face more baggy and fleshy than Jo remembered. He looked weary, as though he'd had enough of all these patients.

With the greatest respect, Jo wanted to say, you're not me. You don't understand. One of the voices said to her, *Listen to him. What do you know about it? You're always wrong*, but in her solar plexus there was a burning certainty that she wasn't. She couldn't remember when she'd felt so sure about anything.

He looked away again, sighing with what seemed like exasperation.

'With reservations, then, bearing in mind Dr Rogerson's request and that you are compliant with the medication, I shall write to her agreeing provisionally to a course of six sessions. If there are no adverse effects and Dr Rogerson wishes you to continue, there will need to be a thorough review.'

It was Jo's turn to stare. He hadn't said no, even if his yes felt almost as deflating as a refusal.

'That's all,' he said. 'I shall see you at your next regular appointment, assuming there's no need for one in the meantime.'

He stood up behind the desk and waited for her to leave. Turning her back so as not to show what she was feeling, she picked up her rucksack and rushed out of the room, slamming the door behind her. She would have locked him in if she could.

The waiting area had its familiar smell: sickly cleaning fluid overlaid on body odours and something bitter like rubber. The patients sitting on the orange plastic chairs looked bored or frightened or defeated, or blanked out by medication. She'd always dreaded becoming like them, their bodies so taken over by the drugs that they twitched or jerked or slobbered uncontrollably. Did they know how they looked, she always wondered, or did the drugs numb them to that too? One man was sprawled back against the wall, his belly bulging under a grubby T-shirt, his thighs spilling over the sides of the small chair. Lank brown hair straggled to his shoulders. His tongue moved continually round his grimacing lips and one leg, crossed over the other, swung endlessly backwards and forwards. *You'll end up like that,* one of the voices said in a menacing whisper, *You don't deserve to be any different.* Another voice, which seemed to come from inside her and not beside her head, said, *I'm not going to end up like that. Eleanor won't let me.*

Richard

As soon as Rick had mentioned the dog, Richard had known they would take it; it was just that, somehow, he had to make it all right with Kate. Part of him still couldn't bear to think of bringing an animal into the house, when it would have made her sneeze and run to the bedroom with streaming eyes. Their neighbour Alice, who was utterly devoted to her two labradoodles, had once brought one with her when she popped in and Kate, wanting to be friendly, had leaned down to stroke it. Richard remembered how the dog had gazed up at her while she gallantly tried to suppress a coughing fit. Alice had been sympathetic, but now Richard felt a surge of hatred towards her. How dared she do that to Kate? How dared she cause her suffering?

As if he never had… There were so many times, like when he'd found her crying in the studio, huddled on her chair in the evening dark, because he'd said her new design looked like ice-cream cones. He still couldn't understand why that had upset her. The way she'd been then made him think of Jo: the utter vulnerability, the refusal to be comforted. Then there'd been the time when he'd got impatient with her about Jo. 'Why, for God's sake, couldn't you just have told her to sort herself out?' he'd said, and Kate had shouted at him, 'You don't fucking understand.' He wouldn't say it now. People couldn't sort themselves out on demand. I'm so sorry, Kate, he said to her, his whole body aching to hug her, and then: I'm sorry, Jo. He imagined stroking Jo's hair – it would be like Kate's, fine and silky – and how she'd probably duck away. Oh, why were people so difficult? At least a dog would be straightforward. They didn't take offence at what you said, but you could hurt them – you could see it in their eyes. Like poor old Wilkie if he was pushed away. Well, he and Rick would have to do the best they could.

'Hey, Rick,' he called down the stairs. 'Are you ready? Nearly time to go.'

'I've been waiting for *ages,* Dad. You old people are so slow.'

Richard laughed and ran down the stairs, to find Rick in the hall setting out the things they'd bought, making sure they'd got them all: collar, lead (the dog would surely have those already), metal water bowl, heavy plastic food bowl, padded bed (he hoped they'd got the right size), crocheted blanket, toy bone – Rick had insisted on that.

'You didn't have to put them all out here,' Richard said. 'They go in the kitchen.'

'Yes, I know, but I can see them better here. And, well ...' He wouldn't say he was showing them to Kate, but Richard knew. Light from the front door's glass panel fell on the pale wood floor, making the dog's things preternaturally bright. The water bowl glinted like an object in a Vermeer painting.

'Pick them up, son,' Richard said, 'and then we'll be off. What's this dog's name again?'

'Livingstone. I told you. Like Dr Livingstone.'

'That's a bit of a mouthful.'

'They call him Liv for short. I know it's sort of a girl's name, but that doesn't matter, does it?'

Richard shook his head and jangled his keys in his pocket. 'Hang on. We'd better take the collar and lead, just in case.'

They walked up past the Commonwealth Pool and turned off into a small terrace of Victorian houses, the stone darkened with years of smoke. Most of the houses had black front doors and Richard couldn't tell which one was Kelvin's. Rick had no hesitation. He ran up the black-and-white tiled path and knocked hard on the knocker. There were flower beds on each side of the path, filled with scarlet geraniums that gave it a Mediterranean look.

He couldn't remember Kelvin's mother's name. She was young and pretty, dark-skinned, blue-eyed, with a bright turquoise scarf tied round a mass of curly dyed blonde hair and jeans slit open at the knees. There was no sign of Kelvin but the dog barked and then barked some more. That was the thing about dogs: a cat would have been a lot quieter.

'Livingstone,' Rick said in an excited whisper, just as Kelvin's mum said, 'Hi, Rick.' She turned towards the hallway as Kelvin pushed his way through, not looking at anyone, his face scrunched up. He seemed pale, Richard thought, under his deep brown skin.

'I'm so sorry, Er—,' he said to Kelvin's mother. 'It can't be easy...'

'Amanda,' she said. 'No. I wish we could take him with us, but there you are. At least I know he's going to a good home.'

She went back into the house and brought out an old plaited lead. She kept the door half-shut but Richard saw a bike, coats fallen across it from the row of pegs above, a muddy pair of wellies and a clutter of toys and papers. It would be hard for Amanda, moving to a flat in a street that wasn't as quiet and spacious as this one. Presumably she wouldn't be moving if she didn't have to.

'Hey there, Kelvin,' Richard said. 'Do you want to walk him back with us?'

Kelvin nodded. He and Rick dived into the house to get the dog, who had now started barking again with some force. Richard had a sudden, irrational thought that Livingstone might be huge, so big he'd disrupt their life – so big that Kate would have recoiled from the sheer dogness of him. But Livingstone, when he appeared, wagging his whole body in eager paroxysms, was the spaniel they'd been expecting, black, greying round the muzzle – not a young dog. Rick was kneeling down beside him, stroking him and whispering to him about his new home, while Kelvin clung on to the writhing body. Awful to lose such a close friend. Kelvin's grief hit Richard in the chest. He remembered how he'd felt when the family dog, Spencer, died, the poignancy of that childhood loss made more poignant now by all the losses in his life. Losing his mother hadn't hurt so sharply. Her death was expected, inevitable, in many ways a relief. That sadness had been slower, quietly lingering in the background.

'You can help us take him to our house,' he said to Kelvin. 'And you can come and see him often. It's not goodbye for ever.' Some losses weren't permanent; he had to remind himself of that.

Kelvin looked up at him and nodded slowly.

Once Kelvin had been persuaded to part with Livingstone – with many promises that he could come again soon, very soon – Richard sat at the kitchen table and watched Rick playing with the dog, stroking him, tickling him behind the ears, throwing the toy bone for him to fetch, giggling with delight each time the dog did – or didn't do – what he expected. No stiffness, no solemnity, no holding back. Richard felt himself grinning, his face moving freely as if in warm sunshine.

'You know you'll have to take him for walks, don't you?' Richard asked him.

Rick nodded, so eager his delight seemed bigger than he was.

'Will you do that? Regularly? I'll take him out sometimes but he's going to be your dog.'

Rick nodded again, stroking and cuddling the dog.

'Well, all right then. We'll see how it goes.'

Richard glanced down at Livingstone and found his gaze held by the dog's dark, guileless eyes. It was like falling in love, he thought, secretly as eager as Rick. You see, Kate, it's going to be good for him – for us. You understand, don't you?

There was a lot he'd have to teach Rick about caring for a dog. He remembered well how it had been when he and Fran had first got Spencer, one rainy summer afternoon when his mother had taken them after school to buy new wellingtons. On the way they'd passed a pet shop, and they'd stopped to look at a black-and-white puppy in the window who was curled up quietly, nose on front paws, gazing at them. They'd come back with the puppy and no wellingtons, and Spencer became part of the family. A lot of the looking after had been left to his mother, he remembered guiltily, but he and Fran had loved Spencer just as Kelvin loved

Livingstone. That simple bond had helped to make up for his father's sternness.

Almost for the first time since Kate's death, and despite himself, Richard had a sense that something right might be happening.

Jo

Sitting in Emmeline's car, with Emmeline beside her seeming to take up all the space, Jo wished she'd felt brave enough to go back to the house by herself. It would have meant taking two buses and it had felt like too many streets and people, too much noise, too many different sights to take in after the enclosed world she'd been living in. Emmeline didn't talk much when she was driving and Jo settled back into the car's shabby comfort. Though she knew nothing about cars, Jo could tell it was different from Damian's – the worn grey upholstery, the wind-down windows, the doors you had to unlock separately with a key. 'Twenty years old and still going strong,' Emmeline always said proudly. The car was like Emmeline somehow – functional, sensible, nothing extravagant or unnecessary; Emmeline would keep it going until it died a natural death. Jo understood that. Like Mother, she'd always made do with what she had.

Returning to the house felt strange, even though it had only been a few days. Someone else would be in her room now, going through their own agonies, perhaps being cared for by Bethan and Leisha. She envied that. At least she'd see Eleanor in the group, but the idea of sitting there again with all those women revealing their pain, as though peeling bandages from open wounds, terrified her. She didn't know if she'd recognise any of them, or if anyone would know her. If they did, they might remember things she'd said before about Paul, about Mother. How awful to think she'd said them aloud. *You be careful*, one of the voices said. *They might use it against you. What does it say about you?*

She shook her head to brush away the voice and went inside.

Bethan, who had opened the door, gave her a hug. 'Hi, Jo. Good to see you. How's it going?'

Jo nodded, implying things were OK – which they were, just about, with visits from Damian, and Emmeline making sure she ate, slept and took her medication. She was hovering on the steps behind Jo now and Bethan nodded to her, gently shepherding Jo inside and away from her.

'Right,' Emmeline said. 'So I'll come and pick you up – five-thirty?'

Bethan nodded again, and with a little wave of her hand firmly closed the door.

The group room felt too warm and full of people, nobody saying anything, everyone as preoccupied as she was. It was the darkest room in the house: one small window in the far wall directly facing the high garden fence. Jo wondered why they'd chosen a room so dismal it always needed the light on; it seemed to amplify the dark happenings that haunted people. Jo found a free chair near the corner and sat, legs crossed, biting her nails, hoping no one would notice her.

'That you, Jo?' A voice said from across the room. 'Margaret. You remember me?'

Jo looked up and nodded, vaguely pleased to see her.

'You all right? It's hard when you've just come out.'

Jo nodded again. 'Yeah. You all right?'

'Oh, not so good. Expect I'll talk about it.'

'Yeah.'

Just as Jo had sunk back into herself again, the tall, thin woman in black made an entrance. That must mean she'd only stayed for a week and was already out in the world again. Unlike the rest of them, who had scurried to their seats trying not to be noticed, this woman took her time, looking round to see who might be there. She was just as thin, just as pale as when Jo had seen her before – you couldn't forget someone who looked like a ghost or a nemesis – but the deep craters around her eyes had begun to fill out and her face had a kind of desperate beauty. She pulled down the scarf tied round her head so that it sat low on her forehead and said, in a deep, intense voice, 'I'm Cara.'

Nobody replied. For Jo and most of the others, even speaking their name was an effort. Cara sat down in the only empty chair, directly facing Eleanor, and drew her long black skirt around her, her face tragic. Jo was fascinated. Here was someone who didn't hide herself, who made her suffering visible. She had a sinking feeling that Cara was going to take up most of the time in the group, overshadowing the rest of them. She could imagine Eleanor focusing on her and neglecting the quieter ones – she was so interesting, so dramatic. Jo had an uneasy feeling about her, attracted and apprehensive.

When Eleanor came in, looking calm and welcoming, being there felt better. Nobody had told Jo – or she hadn't taken in – how long she'd be coming to the group. If it was good, she expected it would soon stop. She looked round apprehensively and received a nod of welcome from Eleanor. Then they all had to say their names – not that anyone remembered them. After that it was just as it had been before.

'How was it?' Emmeline asked.

'OK.' Jo didn't know how to answer. The feelings didn't go away, but Eleanor's kindness, the way she listened, made a difference. After the group Eleanor had called her aside to tell her they'd found a psychotherapist for her and everyone would do their best to make sure she could continue for a good stretch of time. From the little she said about Dr Greenland, Jo could tell she didn't care for him.

'Who was that woman in black?' Emmeline asked. She must have seen her come out.

Still hugging Eleanor's words inside her, Jo brought herself back. 'I can't tell you her name. It's confidential. She's a bit dramatic, but ...' When Cara spoke, her voice held the whole room. She'd told a story, and it was a story – of neglect and abuse, like nearly all of them, but the characters were painted more vividly: the glamorous, controlling father, the downtrodden mother who had secret affairs, the kind but abusive grandfather, the aunt who arrived periodically to rescue her. It could have been a novel. She was spellbinding, in a way that teetered on the edge of danger.

'Well, let's get you home, then,' Emmeline said. 'Seems like it wasn't too bad. I hope they're helping you to look after yourself properly?'

'Oh yes,' Jo said, though to her that wasn't the bit that mattered. She didn't tell Emmeline about the psychotherapist; she wanted to keep it to herself.

When Eric Gaines knocked on her door next morning with her post, Jo saw the envelope with 'Chestnut Tree House' printed on it and immediately tore it open, even though Eric was still standing there. He was wearing a stained yellow T-shirt with 'World Mental Health Day 2013' in large blue letters, and idly picking his teeth.

'You all right, then?' he asked. 'Seems like you was away for a bit. That other girl, you know, the large one, she come up here a few times. I seen her opening your door.'

'Fine. Thanks.' She waved her envelopes at him.

'Just asking. So long as everything's OK and that.'

Jo said no more and he heaved himself down the stairs. Why did people always want to know things, she wondered. Everyone in her life – Damian, Emmeline, even Mother up to a point – seemed to. It was Damian's job, of course, but why was it always about how she was coping and whether she was doing what she was supposed to be doing?

The letter from Chestnut Tree, signed by Eleanor herself, told her she had an initial appointment with psychotherapist Lorraine Astley at the house next Tuesday at 10.30. It didn't say much more but told her that what she discussed in the sessions would be kept confidential within the service unless there was serious cause for concern. Their policy of team working meant they would be sharing some of their notes about her with Lorraine, and she was welcome to discuss this with them if she needed to. Nobody before had asked her if she minded them sharing her information – as a patient you expected it.

Emmeline was coming at lunchtime that day; usually she popped in later, on her way home from work. Jo stuffed the letter in her pocket so Emmeline wouldn't see it. Emmeline wasn't keen on psychotherapy; she thought practical help and a good pep talk worked far better. But if Jo didn't tell her, she'd have to get to Chestnut Tree on her own. She rehearsed it to herself: the 102 to Muswell Hill and then the W7 to Stroud Green Road. She knew the way but the place names seemed alien to her, like towns on the map of a country she'd never been to. Then there were all the people, having to sit or stand so close to them on the bus, and the bigness and redness of the buses themselves. She didn't think she could do it.

Just as she started to panic and an accusing voice said, *You're pathetic. Can't even get on a bus now,* she heard a key in the lock. Emmeline pushed her way into the sitting-room, a large carrier bag in each hand.

'Your washing,' she said, plonking one of the bags down on the table, and then, 'Shopping,' holding it up to show Jo before marching it off to the kitchen.

Jo knew she should thank her but said nothing. It was humiliating to rely so much on Emmeline's care.

'Just got time for a quick coffee,' Emmeline said, coming back with two mugs. 'I'll make you a sandwich; I've brought mine. Plenty of ready meals for supper.'

This time Jo managed to mutter 'Thanks.' She felt the letter sticking out of her pocket.

'Everything OK? You're looking a bit ...'

'Yep.'

As they ate their sandwiches – Emmeline had bought wholemeal bread instead of white – Jo felt a surge of panic rise up from the pit of her stomach. She'd have to choose between Emmeline and the buses and couldn't face either. Then she thought: I'll ask Damian; he'll know what to do. What was the matter with her, that she hadn't thought of it before? Perhaps it was the medication. *Come on, pull yourself together*, another voice said, not sounding so nasty. And then Eleanor's voice: *You can do it.*

She had to admit the wholemeal bread tasted better. So did the kind of cheese Emmeline had bought, and Emmeline had put tomato in the sandwich. Jo didn't usually think to buy tomatoes or, if she did, left them mouldering in the fridge.

'Nice sandwich,' she said, less grudgingly.

'I have my uses.' Emmeline laughed, but Jo knew how much being useful mattered to her.

They finished their lunch in silence but it felt less oppressive now. Maybe Emmeline wasn't so bad when Jo stopped resenting her.

After Emmeline had gone she looked at her phone. Three texts from Richard in one day: How are you? Would you like to talk? Hope you're OK. They weren't saying much, but the fact that there were three bothered her. He'd sent two the day before. She was glad he was kind, but it was too much. Her shoulders contracted in the familiar 'keep away' feeling, just as they had before when he'd wanted to touch her.

Richard

It was V who suggested they meet again. Richard had the idea that the monks weren't supposed to ask for things, but perhaps it was OK to want to see a friend. He'd never understood all their rules and regulations, or why V had described a life lived according to them as beautiful.

So here they were with Liv, walking on the lower slopes of Arthur's Seat. The early September day had pale cloud shading into darker grey; a chilly autumnal wind stretched the shoulder piece of V's robes into a wide fan behind him. In the dry weather the sandy paths and bare patches looked almost desert-like, with wind-bent gorse bushes crouched low beside them. Richard was trying to avoid the path he'd taken when he'd had his 'heart attack' but longed to be high up, gazing down over the city he'd come to love and the wide sweep of open grassland below.

V's calm way of saying nothing, as though he didn't mind whether they talked or not, made Richard feel at ease.

'Are we going up?' he said.

'Sure. I was waiting for you.'

'Just deciding which path to take.'

V gave a laugh. 'That sounds momentous. May I suggest the middle way?'

They both laughed at that.

'This one?' Richard said, and headed for the path nearest to them, which was steep and direct.

He took it slowly, not wanting to repeat the experience and still less fit than he should have been. Forty-eight, for goodness' sake. That was no age these days. He let V go ahead and his friend strode up comfortably, while Richard panted behind him.

They were both panting by the time they got to the top, smiling with exhilaration. The sky, gloriously blue, was lightly clouded and the city's buildings seemed to come to life as they glinted in the sun. V spread his arms wide to embrace the whole view.

'When Kate was... with us,' Richard said haltingly, 'We used to play Angel of the North up here with Ricks. He used to love it, careering about with his arms out like that. We don't do it now.' Already it was a story from the past.

V nodded. 'What *do* you do?'

If he'd asked that even a couple of weeks ago, Richard wouldn't have known what to answer. Now he said, 'Well, we've got Livingstone.' The dog was snuffling about in the grass, trotting to and fro, scenting the air.

'You presume.'

Richard could see the joke coming but the way V said it, raising his non-eyebrows, still made him laugh.

'So – walks and pet care. You and Rick both, I imagine. And fun?'

'Yes, Rick is having fun with him. It's good to see.'

'And you?'

Richard wiped his hand across his mouth and said slowly, 'Well, I'm trying.'

'Yeah. You can't force it.'

'Did I tell you about my 'heart attack'?' Richard told him, making light of it so that V wouldn't think he was in trouble. 'I thought I might have another one today, but no sign of it. I was just out of breath. I think it did me good, you know, in some sort of way. I realised it didn't matter if I cried.'

'That makes things a lot easier. You were furiously holding it in last time I saw you.'

Richard nodded. When they'd found a place to sit down, he took out a flask from his rucksack and poured tea into two reusable cups – his dark red one and Kate's blue William Morris one. He'd remembered to leave the tea black, as it was after midday and V wasn't supposed to consume food. He could have had soya milk but Richard loathed the stuff and wouldn't buy it. Richard took out two bars of dark chocolate with ginger and handed one to V, then broke off squares from the other one. Ginger and chocolate were allowed as they were considered medicinal. V had explained that although chocolate hadn't been around in the Buddha's time, carob had – not that it was anything like chocolate. V took out the little cloth from his rucksack so that Richard could make the offering. What a performance, he thought, but he did it as gracefully as he could, the wind blowing through his hair and flapping V's robes.

After he'd eaten his chocolate V said, 'And what about your... sister-in-law, was it? You were worried about her last time.'

Richard ran his fingers through his hair. 'She went into a crisis house for a while,' he said. 'I'd never heard of such places before. They seem to have done her a lot of good but she's still very – you know – very...' What was the right word? Fragile? Wobbly? Vulnerable? All of those, probably. He coughed. 'It *was* abuse, you know. Sexual abuse, I mean. She remembered who did it to them – their half-brother. Awful, isn't it?' Strange how saying something was awful could make it feel less awful.

'To them?' V asked, looking sideways at Richard.

Richard looked down at his hands resting on his knees. 'Kate as well.' He covered his eyes with his hand. 'It's hard to forgive myself for not knowing. I never suspected it with Jo – my sister-in-law – even though she was so funny about being touched...' He tailed off. 'Poor Jo,' he said. 'She's had such a rough deal. And she's so...' Again, it was hard to find the right word.

'You care about her a lot,' V said.

Richard looked down at his hands, fluttering his fingers as though typing on a keyboard. 'I don't quite know how to say this,' he said, 'but somehow it's as though I've started to... have feelings for her.' He couldn't bring himself to mention the sex bit, but occasionally it was there. 'She sort of gets mixed up with Kate in my head – they were twins, I may have said – and... I know it's ridiculous. She could never live with me and Ricks, even supposing she wanted to.'

'Mm,' V said. Richard was afraid he was about to bring out some Buddhist wisdom, but all he said was, 'I can understand that – how you feel, I mean.'

'Can you? I forgot to say there's more tea in the flask.'

V inclined his head. Apparently the monks weren't supposed to say thank you.

Richard was glad of the excuse to turn away. As he poured the tea, strong and fragrant as he opened the flask, he gazed around him at the great expanses of green, the darker treetops, looking like broccoli where they huddled close together, the lighter colours of the grass, vibrant where the sun caught it. He thought of viridian, a colour Kate had particularly liked. Two swans flew up from the distant loch, their great wings rising and falling slowly as if they were heavy to lift. In the distance he could see the pillared rotunda of the Burns monument. While he'd been talking the world had narrowed to the space directly in front of him. Now he breathed in more of it again.

'I keep wanting to see Jo,' he said. 'And I keep thinking she must want to see me. I wish I could go down to London again. She lives in this god-awful flat in somewhere called Bounds Green – I'd never heard of it – and I want to take her away and give her a better life... You won't tell anyone what I've said about her, will you?' He wiped his fingers down his face and looked hard at V.

'No. Why should I?'

Richard shook his head. 'I don't know. Poor Jo – poor all of us. At one time she thought *I'd* abused her. I don't want to risk that again.'

'I'm sure you'll be careful,' V said. 'It sounds as though she's still quite fragile.'

Fragile – yes, she'd always been that, but somehow steely too, like Kate. Richard looked at his watch. 'I'll have to get back soon. Rick will be home from school. We'd better start going down.' He called Livingstone, who came panting towards him, his long loose tongue flapping out of his mouth as he stood wriggling while Richard clipped on the lead.

As they made their way down, V nimble-footed in flapping Birkenstocks over thick socks, Richard said, 'But I haven't asked anything about you.' V must think him not only abusive but egotistical. He always imagined that, as a monk leading what was called the holy life, V was judging him for his unholy life.

'Maybe another time,' V said, smiling. 'I'm all right for the moment.'

He noticed V hadn't said anything about his beloved Buddha. For Richard his quiet presence was enough. Perhaps that was what the Buddha had been like.

Once he'd seen V on to his bus – the monks weren't allowed money so he'd had to be paid for – Richard looked at his phone. He wasn't surprised Jo hadn't texted – he must be careful not to overdo it. Resisting the temptation to send yet another text, he put the phone back in his pocket. Livingstone was tired now, plodding along beside Richard, tongue lolling out.

He'd timed it just right: Rick came crashing in a few minutes later.

'Where's Liv?' he said. 'Can I take him out?'

'He's just been out, son,' Richard said. He didn't say they'd been up to Arthur's Seat; Rick would have been too disappointed.

'Oh, *Dad,*' Rick said.

'He'll need a pee later on. You can take him then, after tea. What do you want?'

'Baked beans,' Rick said. 'With Fran's toast.' For the fourth time this week.

'Wouldn't you like something different?'

Kate had tried to get him to eat other foods and Fran without trying had sometimes succeeded, but since her last visit he'd clung obstinately to what he knew he liked.

'No, thanks.' Rick said it with absolute certainty. 'First of all, I'm going to give Liv his tea.' He looked round and called, 'Liv!'

The dog came bounding in, whimpering with delight, and jumped up with his paws on Rick's shoulders.

'He's not supposed to do that,' Richard said as the dog started licking Rick's face, but Rick was ecstatic. If he had a tail, Richard thought, it would be wagging as hard as Liv's.

He let them get on with it. Rick spooned the nasty-looking brown meat out of the tin and Liv slurped it up, turning to look at Rick with adoration as he chewed.

Well, Richard thought. Things were certainly changing. If David McKinnon could see Rick right now, he might not be so concerned about him. Richard felt the weight of concern lifting from his own heart and realised how burdened he'd been by Rick's pain. It wasn't over yet – how could it be, in so short a time? – though signs of light were showing. But the empty half of the bed, the space beside him where a warm body had been, the useless, fruitless desire for Kate and now, to his dismay, for Jo too – or sometimes for both of them at once, till they blended into one – with nothing to assuage it except the pillow and his own repetitive imagination – none of that had become any less hard. He couldn't understand how V could be so serene and cheerful about giving up sex, even with himself. It wasn't natural, surely. What did he do instead?

Rick liked to get his own tea sometimes. Richard watched him pull open the can of beans and carefully pour the contents into a saucepan, scraping it out the way Kate had shown him; she'd always hated waste. He wasn't great at cutting bread but he liked to do that too, to show he was capable. Richard felt a surge of pride and tenderness. Rick had definitely grown taller and had a leggy, soon-to-be-adolescent look – he was nearly eleven now. His fine hair, like Kate's in colour, flopped over his eyes; the sleeves of his jumper no longer covered his wrists. Time to get him another haircut and some new clothes, Richard thought, hoping he'd know how to go about it. Kate had always taken care of those things. And time to fix the gate, so that it was safe to let Liv out in the garden. Life had its own momentum – the clichés felt true. Perhaps V, in his gentle way, had been hinting at that.

Jo

'No problem,' Damian said when Jo asked him about getting to Chestnut Tree next week. He'd popped in for an extra visit, just to make sure she was OK, and sat in the bigger armchair while Jo perched on the arm of the smaller one. It was good to see him there instead of Emmeline. 'I can't do it, but there's a volunteer service who should be able to find someone.'

Jo wasn't sure she liked the idea of a volunteer. It made her think of Mother and the WI. She stared at him.

'What's the matter? Don't you trust them?'

'It's...' She couldn't tell him about Mother; it sounded too stupid. She muttered something half-audibly.

'Patronising, did you say? Why would they be patronising? They're there to help. Anyway you'll soon be able to get there by yourself. It's early days yet. You're bound to feel wobbly at the moment.'

Jo nodded half-heartedly. Mother thought *she* was there to help. The volunteers would probably be Muswell Hill do-gooders like Estelle – except that Estelle was genuine.

'Well, OK then,' she said. 'Do they know about... mental health?' She hated saying it. People only talked about 'mental health' when you didn't have it.

'I'll ask them to find someone who does. It's OK, Jo. Leave it to me.'

Damian seemed to like saying 'Leave it to me'. So far he'd always meant it.

Stupid cow, one of the voices said. *Think you deserve special treatment?*

After he'd gone Jo fetched her journal and a chewed blue fountain pen from the bedside table. Curled up in the armchair, she slipped the elastic from the corners of the book, opened the pen cautiously to make sure it hadn't leaked and found the page where she'd left off last time.

I'm scared about this therapist. I hope she's not like Dr Rasen. She always looked as though she was curling her lip, holding me up with a pair of tweezers like a not very interesting specimen. I couldn't bear it, the way she never smiled and hardly ever said anything. Mother thought Dr Rasen knew best, just like she thinks Dr Greenland knows best. At least this therapist isn't a Dr anything but just a person. Dr Greenland thinks she'll make me worse – as if he knew how to make me better.

She stopped writing and reached for her phone. I must talk to you, Jans. I need to ask you... She thought of the photographs in her room at Chestnut Tree; how they'd reminded her of the holidays she and Jans had had in Devon. She had to ask: would you rather it was a river or the sea? Richard thought a river, where the water was calmer and the light would shine more gently, but that might just be him. She wished Jans would give her a clear answer.

The voices were coming now, the cruel one saying *You'll have to die.* This morning she'd heard the angel voice again. *The poor little child,* it had said, *she deserves help.* Jo had felt someone stroking her head and for a moment she'd seen a child, sleeping with a blanket wrapped around her. If only the angel would come back.

When Tuesday morning came, staying in bed felt safer than getting up. She'd woken at 9.15 feeling terrified. Supposing this woman Lorraine really didn't do her any good. Supposing Dr Greenland was right. The volunteer – Mick, his name was – was coming at 9.45 and she scrambled into yesterday's clothes. She poured water straight from the hot tap onto sticky granules from the coffee jar, scrunched up a slice of bread from the packet and chewed it in large bites, then swallowed the medication Emmeline had left out for her.

Her bell rang. She ignored it, searching frantically for her rucksack. It rang again. Emmeline had left her a note saying 'Don't forget keys.' She felt for them in her pocket, then stepped cautiously down the stairs and opened the door. A man came in, seeming not to see her, and headed towards Eric Gaines's flat. He knocked and got no answer. She shut the door and stood in the stairwell, taking deep breaths and thinking of Bethan and Leisha. Then she nerved herself to meet him.

He was standing at the bottom of the stairs and grinning at her, casually leaning one elbow on the curved end of the banister – tall, thin, with a black T-shirt and black jeans, his skin whitish against the dark wood. The arm resting on the banister had a large tattoo of a bird with open wings near the wrist. His pale face was almost obscured by thick, wavy brown hair. As he moved closer she saw his skin had deep lines round the mouth that looked like smile lines.

'Joanna?' he said, in an ordinary London accent. 'You ready to go, then? Sorry I barged past you like that.'

'Jo.'

He started talking as soon as they were in the car, in a way that was meant to put her at ease. He'd been a joiner, he said, making upmarket furniture, but had had to give up because of his back. Now he was doing a bit of voluntary work, trying to find another job – something in the craft line, he hoped. Or he might try and set up on his own, making smaller things. He liked making things. He was good at it, he wasn't just saying.

Jo sat biting her nails. She knew most people would have said things like 'Really?' 'That's nice' or perhaps asked questions, but with so much else on her mind she couldn't. The last thing she wanted was to make conversation; the people she knew either talked because they needed to or else didn't say anything. If he was supposed to understand about mental health, she thought he'd realise that. She didn't think he meant any harm, though.

As they came down into Stroud Green Road, he said, 'Now, I'll need you to show me exactly where this house is. I've got it on the sat nav but they do funny things sometimes.'

When they turned into the quiet road where Chestnut Tree was, she immediately saw the geraniums on the steps.

'There,' she said. 'You can't come in; it's women only.'

'That's OK,' he said comfortably. 'I'll go and get myself a coffee. An hour, was it?'

She nodded, slowly undid her seat belt and swung out of the car.

Her legs felt shaky as she walked up the steps. She rang the entryphone and muttered her name.

Stacey opened the door instead of buzzing her in.

'Hi, Jo. Come in and take a seat. You're a little bit early but Lorraine will be here to meet you soon.'

Jo huddled into one of the flowered armchairs. She wished she could smoke but didn't dare go outside in case Lorraine came and thought she wasn't there. She rummaged in her rucksack and found a battered packet of chewing-gum. She'd just started chewing when she heard a door swing shut and half saw, half sensed someone beside her.

'Joanna Brookfield?' the woman said. 'Or do you prefer Jo? I'm Lorraine Astley.'

Jo nodded. 'Jo.' She took the chewing-gum out as discreetly as she could.

'Shall we go through, then?' Lorraine had a normal voice, not a Dr Rasen voice. When she smiled, warm but not overpowering, Jo noticed she had a gap between her front teeth. Jo had an impression of brown hair parted in the middle, light-coloured clothes and a bright orange and brown silk scarf. Lorraine was slightly plump and otherwise unremarkable. Jo instinctively felt safe with her.

It was only an hour, but when Jo came out again everything seemed altered, as though the blue-grey carpet and chintz armchairs had become different versions of themselves. She had cried and stopped crying and cried again, and it had been a relief. She'd told Lorraine far more than she intended – what she'd said she couldn't now remember – and it had been all right. She sat down in one of the armchairs, looking about her, not ready to go back into the world yet.

Stacey looked up from her computer, frowning thoughtfully, and said, 'You can get yourself a coffee, if you like, from the little room by the kitchen. No need to rush off.'

Jo thought about Mick waiting outside but didn't feel able to tell him she wasn't ready. She scrabbled in her rucksack for more chewing-gum and sat chewing and combing her fingers through her hair till she felt she couldn't sit there any longer. On the way out she filled a white plastic cup with water from the cooler and took it with her. While she was working out how to hold the cup and unlock the door at the same time, Stacey came up and did it for her. It felt like magic.

Mick was lounging against his car, peering down the street as though he thought she'd done a runner.

'So there you are. I was beginning to wonder. All right?'

She nodded and hoped he wouldn't notice how her face looked. He glanced at her as he opened the car door but said nothing. As soon as she was in her seat he started talking, seemingly at random. He seemed to think the way to make someone feel less upset was to pretend it wasn't happening and keep on talking. This time it was films, music albums – she'd never heard of any of them – and house prices in Crouch End, where he'd moved years ago, long before it went so upmarket. He talked right till they were at the door, then wished her good luck and said maybe he'd see her again. By then she'd made up her mind she'd go by herself in future.

In the quiet of the flat, drinking coffee and rolling a cigarette at last, she tried to remember what she had talked about – Mother, Jans, Paul, the abuse. And the voices, which was harder, though Lorraine hadn't seemed bothered. She'd sat in her chair facing Jo but slightly turned away, which felt less intimidating, and listened as though she was really interested. Once or twice, when everything was coming out very fast, she'd tried to slow Jo down, but otherwise all Jo could remember her saying was, 'We need to take it very gently. A lot of horrible things have happened and you can't face at them all at once. I'll try to make sure you don't get overwhelmed, but if you feel it's getting too much I want you to tell me straight away so that we can back off. Being retraumatised won't do you any good.' Jo hadn't come across the word before but thought she understood what it meant. She liked the way Lorraine had said 'we' and not 'you'; it felt as though they were equals.

She whispered to Jans that it was safe for her to be there too. Then she texted Richard: Therapist good. I'm OK for now, thanks. One of the voices said, *That's what you think. You just wait. Too good to be true.*

Marian

Ever since she had seen Joanna, Marian had felt uneasy about what her daughter claimed had happened. The more she thought about it, the more possible it seemed – unfortunately. The girls must have been very small: Paul had gone to Australia when they were barely three. Though she was unsure what harm the abuse (there was no escaping the word) had done to them, the idea of his having performed such acts – she preferred not to know what they were – with small children revolted her. He had stopped contacting her a long time ago; no need to find an excuse for not writing.

She had to get ready for the WI meeting. This time Susanna's husband would be giving his illustrated talk on trekking in Ladakh. The pair of them were inveterate travellers and spoke about 'eco-tourism', which as far as Marian could see meant being a tourist while making out you were doing good with it. After the previous talk, on compost making, Susanna had piped up about compost toilets in Ladakh (nobody called them lavatories any more) and said how eco-friendly they were, so people had been eager for the Ladakh talk. Susanna and Geoffrey, her husband, had a permanent suntan and wore walking boots when they went shopping. Marian had dismissed them some time ago as not her kind of people, though they were harmless enough. Whoever the speaker, the WI meeting was an event in the village.

Marian always noticed the hall's smell, a mixture of damp, polish and stewed tea. The floor was dark varnished wood and the wooden ceiling beams were stained dark brown too. The walls were painted a deep cream, which with the dark wood gave the hall a quasi-antique feel, like a pub only less cosy. The curtains had a leaf pattern in brown, green and red which was not unpleasant; they had been donated and were not quite long enough for the windows. Marian had given up wishing someone would replace them. The hall was never warm and she kept her quilted jacket on. Most people were in coats or thick cardigans, even in early September. Often they sat in a circle but today, because of the slideshow, the orange plastic chairs had been arranged in rows. Marian's scraped on the floor as she sat down next to Elisabeth, one of the women she was on friendly terms with. Madeleine and Hilary, the others she knew, were in the row in front. Geoffrey was busy setting up his computer to show the photos on the screen. So far all that could be seen was what looked to Marian like a rather uninspiring list of files. She whispered to Elisabeth, 'I hope this is going to work.'

It did. She saw more than she wanted of a dry, dusty landscape with the occasional green valley. There were mountains, several temples with grotesquely large Buddha statues, and seemingly a lot of donkeys. Geoffrey had said something about blue sheep but all Marian could see was a bluish mountainside. The trekkers had been attended by a team of smiling locals who were presumably paid a pittance for looking after their every need. She had never yearned to go to the Himalayas and after the photographs she felt she had seen enough. She was not sorry when Geoffrey had to cut his talk short because the computer no longer seemed able to cope.

It was her turn, with Madeleine and Hilary, to see to the refreshments, as people always called them. She took care of the tea, filling the huge, permanently stained metal pot with a fistful of tea bags and water that came spitting out of the urn, while Madeleine made coffee in a large cafetière. 'People do like proper coffee,' she always said, as though it would be an insult to give them anything less. Marian usually made do with instant; she had never enjoyed fiddling about in the kitchen. Like most of the women there, Madeleine had an expensive, well-dressed look. Marian didn't have much interest in the detail of clothes – she wore what she happened to have, and if it was too old to go on wearing she replaced it with something similar. Lately she had ventured into trousers, but they never felt right on her thin legs and she wasn't sure whether or not to wear tights underneath. Madeleine had her hair in a sleek bob discreetly coloured a light honey blonde. She had a plump face, the flesh softened and sinking into its lines, and a faint look of disapproval, as though nothing was ever quite up to standard. She and Marian often shared their dissatisfaction with the muddling and inefficiency of the WI committee.

'And how are your family?' Madeleine asked Marian. Like most of the women there, Madeleine had a husband with a good pension, children who had done well for themselves and grandchildren who visited. 'Do you get to see your grandson? Such a pity they live so far away.' She seemed to have forgotten Jancis had died – or perhaps Marian had never actually told her. Now she had even less reason for talking about her family – the word itself felt like a euphemism. She could hardly say, 'My daughters seem to have been sexually abused by their half-brother – my son. One of them is a psychiatric patient and the other has just died of a brain haemorrhage. Her son is being cared for by his father, to whom I have very little to say.' All she said was, 'No, I don't see him very often. And how are *your* family?' So much easier to turn the conversation away from herself. Madeleine's life seemed far more acceptable, and more enjoyable. It made Marian see how little she had, how big a gap Jancis's death had left. She wished she and Joanna could be closer but in all honesty couldn't imagine it.

As Madeleine clattered the blue Sixties cups and saucers out of the cupboard she happily boasted away, to Hilary as well as Marian: the granddaughter's Distinction in Grade 8 violin at fourteen, the grandson's A stars in his A-levels, the other grandson's gap year in Borneo, her son and daughter-in-law's success with their property business... Marian had heard it all before, give or take a few embellishments.

Hilary, who was putting crockery on trays and Taste the Difference chocolate biscuits on plates, had said nothing. She was at least as reticent about her life as Marian.

'That's wonderful, Madeleine,' she said now. 'You must be so proud.'

Madeleine carried on. Marian glanced at Hilary, unsure about her. Hilary was hard to classify, unlike most of them, and seemed to be slightly younger than the rest. She dressed casually, nearly always in trousers, had short wispy hair and wore no make-up. She had come to the village not long after Marian had moved from Oxford and sometimes talked sadly or regretfully about a friend called Nicola, whose death seemed to have been the reason for her moving. That had disquieted Marian. Nicola might only have been a friend, but something about the way Hilary talked of her reminded Marian of the way Joanna had, for a time, talked about Emmeline. One was supposed to take these relationships in one's stride but Marian preferred not to think about them, even though Oxford had of course had more than its share of unconventional people. Hilary, who hardly looked unconventional, seemed to lead a life that was perfectly ordinary. She would no doubt offer to help Marian with the washing-up and was friendly enough, in her quiet way, for Marian to begin to trust her. The nagging discomfort aside, she liked her more than most of them. At least Hilary didn't gloat over her own good fortune. Marian couldn't help wishing she had more good fortune to gloat over.

That evening, having warmed and eaten her ready meal, Marian found herself thinking about Desmond O'Meara. She had reverted to her maiden name after the divorce, seeing no reason to be saddled with an Irish one if she no longer had anything to do with him. A widower, he hadn't come into her life until Paul was eighteen, and she hadn't been in love with him – if you could call it that – as she undoubtedly had with James, for all the good that had done her. Nevertheless he was charming, attractive in a dark-haired, almost Mediterranean way, and had been good with the twins when he was there: more natural and affectionate than she was capable of being. She had liked him and relied on him for that short time, and had believed it would be enough to get them through.

He had left for the obvious reason – he would be obvious, she thought. He had found someone he preferred to be with, an administrator at one of the more obscure colleges who, stereotypically, was younger, prettier and more accommodating when it came to sex – not Marian's strong point. He had not been a don but a Domestic Bursar, at a different college from the woman one might call his mistress, which had at least saved a lot of awkwardness. When he left, with almost no warning, he told Marian he had been having an affair with Diane since soon after the twins were born. She had never got over the shock. They were barely a year old and Marian had been too busy with them, perhaps not interested enough in him, to notice. She had been coping with two lots of nappy changing, two lots of feeding – bottles, of course; the idea of breast-feeding repelled her – and two lots of crying. Often they had both cried in unison and dealing with it had felt impossible. Jancis, who had cried louder, had usually had her attention first, while Joanna lay quietly whimpering. Could that have affected her? Marian doubted it. At the time she had hardened her heart and simply got on with things, doing what was necessary for all of them to survive. She wondered now what difference it would have made to the girls if she had had a husband. Not that she would have wanted to ask him for help, but Desmond had been good at knowing what needed to be done.

She had never subscribed to the notion that a lack of maternal closeness affected people. Not like that man Bowlby, who had seemed to be prominent back in the Seventies. His fat Pelican books with blue spines and titles like *Attachment* had been in Blackwell's on a table just near the door, where one couldn't fail to see them, even though she had no particular interest in psychology. Nobody she knew had wanted to read them: no use crying over spilt milk, surely.

For her people were as they were: nature always trumped nurture. It did seem plausible, though, that what Paul had done could have affected Joanna, and even Jancis too. She was sorry about it – sorry if both girls, especially Jancis, had in some way been handicapped by it. Jancis had been more capable of making something of her life.

Marian had begun to wonder if perhaps she had always been too ready to write Joanna off. It occurred to her that she might have underestimated this second, more difficult twin, the only daughter she had now. Aside from her illness, Joanna too had had certain gifts: she was intelligent; she had done well at school and university; she had always been something of a writer, even if not in an academic sense. It was unfortunate that just at the point when she might have found something worthwhile to do, she seemed to have lost all backbone and fallen to pieces. Marian had viewed it as a failure on Joanna's part. Just as people spoke of fighting cancer, she believed one could fight what was called mental illness. Now, though, she began to realise that the odds might have been stacked against Joanna. It was even conceivable that their father's absence might have affected both of them – she couldn't, after all, deny its effect on her. She had always chosen not to speak to them about him – to stop them thinking of him, but even more because anger and humiliation had silenced her.

Despite Joanna's all too obvious limitations, she was an adult. If adopted children had the right to know who their biological parents were, presumably the same right should apply to absent parents. It might even do Joanna some good to know about her father. Marian couldn't imagine talking to her about it face to face and didn't enjoy long telephone conversations. She could envisage writing a letter, but it would take some time before she was ready. She would have to decide what she could and could not bear to say. She supposed that for the moment Joanna was concerned about other things. This wretched Paul business seemed to be occupying all her mind and it would be better not to cause her further distress.

Marian had a television but rarely watched it. Now she felt in need of it, oddly disturbed and unsettled. Sometimes distraction was best. She had always despised knitting but wondered if she could ask Elisabeth at the WI to teach her. It looked as though it might be soothing. Perhaps she should suggest it to Joanna; this crisis house didn't seem to give them any occupational therapy. In her undergraduate days she had once visited a friend in the Warneford Hospital, and there they had all been busy making baskets. It was a pity Joanna had so few interests. When Marian had said she was unhappy her father had made her learn Classical Greek, and she was certainly none the worse for it. She might even suggest that to Joanna too.

Richard

Unexpectedly, a company Richard had done work for in the past wanted their network updated and had asked him to come down to London to help them overhaul it. It would be good money but he hadn't been planning another trip. Something told him it might be better to leave Jo alone for the moment, but he knew he wasn't capable of going to London without seeing her. She'd texted him a couple of times but hadn't told him much. She'd said something about seeing a therapist and he felt pleased for her – it seemed like a ray of hope. Someone taking an interest in her, at least. She hadn't said anything about what went on there and he knew better than to ask. He'd texted her the date when he'd be coming and asked if she'd like to meet. He thought she'd probably say no, but she'd agreed. He wanted to take her out somewhere but wasn't sure if she'd be up to it.

Livingstone was lying on his feet as he sat at the computer. He felt the dog's warm body heave gently with each breath and was soothed by the small snuffling and panting sounds. In hardly any time it had felt completely normal for Liv to be there, and the need to give him regular food and walks had stabilised Richard's life as well as Rick's. It was comforting to know that in a short while he'd have to go out and pee the dog, as Rick put it, and then when Rick came back from school they'd both take him for a walk, a longish one if it wasn't raining. The days were shorter now – nearly October already – and it was cold, a penetrating Scottish cold. He planned to go with Rick to Duddingston Loch, another place he'd been avoiding because they'd been there with Kate. She'd loved the birds there and had shown Rick great V-formations of wild geese, kestrels hovering wide-winged, flocks of summer swallows, herons stationary as statues. One day they'd followed a kingfisher along the shore as it kept dipping and re-emerging in flashes of orange and turquoise. He still had Kate's binoculars but he usually missed whatever bird he was looking for; Rick was far better at spotting them. Seeing the birds again would surely do him good.

'Come on then, Liv,' he said, lightly nudging the dog with his leg. 'Out we go.'

Liv stirred and sighed, then shook himself and was all eagerness. How wonderful, Richard thought, to be so accepting of whatever life presented.

He'd arranged the London meeting for a Friday, to make it easier for Fran, and would see Jo on the Saturday. Fran would be arriving late this evening. Since he'd resurrected the model railway it had been left out in the spare room – covered with its plastic dust sheets, Richard made sure of that – but he'd had to tuck it away so that Fran could get into the bed. He was amused at how eager she was about it. When they were children it had definitely been his, but she'd loved playing with it, when he let her. She'd never had anything quite equivalent, though she was given a chemistry set at one stage, which she let him share.

She arrived after they'd had supper and taken Liv out for his pee. It irritated Richard to see her hung around as usual with a mess of bags and clutter, trying to unload everything at once.

'Here's the bread,' she said, fumbling in one bag. 'I'll just put some of it in the freezer.' She took out three loaves in plastic bags, dropping one, then shoved two of them into the freezer, not shutting the door properly. 'And here's something for Rick.' She fumbled in another bag, then put the box down beside a patch of spilt tea on the table. 'And I've got something for Liv, too.' A packet of dog treats, which she put in front of his water bowl. 'And for you – us.' Chocolate digestives and his favourite coffee, both balanced precariously on the worktop next to a bunch of bananas.

She put the other bags down, pushed up her glasses, ran her fingers through her fluffy hair, then lunged at Richard in a hug that almost caught him off-balance. He laughed in surprise.

'Where's Rick?' she asked.

'In his room. I think he's got Liv with him.'

She let go with startling suddenness and rushed upstairs. He moved everything to more suitable places and wiped up the spilled tea, which he'd failed to notice before. Once she'd calmed down from her fluster, she'd make sure everything was clean and tidy and take care of the little things he didn't bother with. He could hear her and Rick laughing together upstairs and put the kettle on ready for her. Thinking of her with Rick, he couldn't imagine how he'd resented them getting on so well. She'd no doubt ask him if he was seeing Jo while he was in London, and he felt uneasy about telling her. Fran would only say what she always said, that she hoped Jo was OK and was glad she was getting help, but to him it felt private, as though Jo needed to be protected. Or was it his feelings he was protecting?

'I expect you're seeing Jo?' she said in due course. 'It's good you're looking out for her.'

'Yes.'

'Doesn't sound like she has many people in her life.'

'She hasn't.'

Fran nodded slowly, sipped her tea and said no more about it. Then she said, smiling her wide rag-doll smile, 'Rick loves that dog, doesn't he? Such a good thing for him.'

Richard said, 'I've quite taken to old Liv too. Good to have an animal in the house, especially as we grew up having a dog around.' They slipped easily into reminiscing about Spencer.

The meeting on Friday afternoon was in Camden Town, not far from the top end of Regent's Park. In the few years since he'd been to Camden he'd forgotten just how crowded it got, people shoving their way out of the Tube and barging into each other along the street as they made for stalls that sold rough wool sweaters from South America, colourful shirts made in India and CDs by bands he'd never heard of. That was even before you got to Camden Lock.

Everyone seemed so young it made him realise his age. Here he was, not far short of fifty, a widower (how old did that sound?) dressed in a smartish jacket and trousers and carrying a briefcase. Never mind that the jacket and trousers weren't a suit and the briefcase hung from a shoulder-strap: to the young people he was one of their parents' generation, already obsolescent. The staff of the company he'd been working with were all in their twenties and thirties. By the time Rick was eighteen Richard would be well on the way to sixty. Kate would have been forty-eight by then, as old as he was now. Taking a detour down Inverness Street, through the smells and shouts of the fruit and veg market, he wondered what was left for him, how much longer he would continue. Kate's death had made him acutely aware of his own mortality. He hoped that when the time came he would feel his life had been worthwhile.

He'd managed to find an Airbnb in Muswell Hill and discovered there was a bus from Camden that would take him there. Near the bus stop was a shop selling Dr Martens; they had boots just like the ones Jo wore. He thought of hers, creased deeply across the front, scuffed white at the toes. I'll buy you a new pair, he wanted to say. He couldn't see her accepting them and winced at how inappropriate it would be. He would have to watch himself.

Promptly at 10.30 next morning, after coffee and good croissants in a Muswell Hill café he'd chosen for its olive-green seats and air of quiet comfort, he rang the FRIEDLAND bell. More quickly than he expected the door was opened, not by Jo. A largish woman with a round pink face and light-brown hair in a pudding-basin cut was staring at him with a hostility he didn't understand.

'Yes?' she said, preparing to shut the door again.

'I'm Richard, to see Jo. Her brother-in-law. She's expecting me.'

'She told me you were coming.' She was still staring at him, taking up all the space between the doorpost and the half-open door.

He was forced to ask, 'Can I come in?'

The woman stepped back just far enough to let him into the hallway. He could see Jo standing at the top of the stairs. She waved at him, nervous but confiding.

The woman, who was dressed in a large pale blue sweatshirt and baggy jeans, turned enquiringly to Jo, as though making sure she really wanted to see him. Jo had come farther down, dodging to one side of the other woman so that she was visible to Richard.

'Hi, Jo,' he said. 'Everything all right?' He inclined his head towards the woman, who was still blocking his way.

'Emmeline,' Jo said. 'Richard wants to come up.'

So this was Emmeline. She seemed to take her responsibilities as a carer rather seriously.

Grudgingly, Emmeline stood back just enough for Richard to get a foot on the stairs close to Jo, who was clinging to the banister to make room for him. He was tempted to hug her, or at least put out his hand, but Emmeline looked as if she'd see it as an assault. They went up one by one, first Jo, who ran back into the flat, then Richard, treading steadily after her, then finally Emmeline. Richard could feel her gaze boring into his back; he had no idea what he'd done to deserve it.

He followed Jo into the sitting room. Apart from the two armchairs, the only other seat was a dining chair pulled up to a small table in the window recess. Both table and chair had thick dark varnish that reminded him of his mother's gravy browning. The chair's upholstered seat, a grubby rust colour, was lumpy and sunken. He wished he hadn't noticed it: it made Jo's flat seem even more dreary. As he'd expected, Emmeline had taken the bigger armchair and Jo was curled up in the smaller one. He had to edge behind them to get to the dining chair and sat down sideways on it, facing them. Jo was watching him keenly, Emmeline doing her best to ignore him.

'Shall I get you some coffee, Jo?' she said.

Jo nodded. 'And Richard?'

'I've just had some, thank you.'

Emmeline went into the kitchen. Richard said, 'So, Jo, how are things?'

As she drew breath to answer, he whispered, 'What's all this about?'

'She still thinks you abused me,' Jo whispered back, her face screwed up with discomfort. 'I've tried to tell her. I didn't know she was going to be like this.'

She curled up tighter in the armchair and started biting her nails. Richard wished she wouldn't; it made her look so distressed.

'Would you like to go out?' he said. 'It's a lovely day.' Squares of sunlight, filtered through the window, hovered over the surface of the table, transforming the flat while they lasted. Outside, the leaves of the plane tree flickered bright green and gold in the autumn breeze.

At that moment Emmeline came back with two mugs. Handing one to Jo, she cradled her free hand round the other and sat down, sipping her coffee and eyeing Richard warily over the top of the mug.

'I'm not sure if Jo—' Emmeline began.

Jo cut in, 'That's up to me,' with a flash of spirit that made Richard glad.

'Well, yes, I know that, Jo, but you do need to be careful, especially with—'

'Richard isn't a strange man. He came to see me when I was at Chestnut Tree.'

'I wasn't sure that was a good idea.'

Jo uncurled herself in the chair and sat up. 'For God's sake, Emmeline, you're not my nursemaid.' Richard could have cheered.

Emmeline started to say, 'Yes, but…' then seemed to think better of it.

'With all due respect, Emmeline,' Richard said, his mouth clenched. 'Jo has every right to decide for herself. I'd rather you didn't look on me as a cross between Jack the Ripper and Attila the Hun.'

Emmeline reddened. 'I never… It's just important to me that Jo should be safe'.

'What do you think I'm going to do to her? She's my sister-in-law, my wife's sister.' He couldn't bring himself to say 'my late wife'.

'Well, she did say—'

Jo almost shouted, 'Yes, a long time ago, when I was mad. I've told you it's not true, but you won't believe me.'

'I have your safety at heart, Jo,' Emmeline said stubbornly. 'You're still in a very vulnerable state.'

'You're as bad as Dr Greenland,' Jo said. 'Telling me I can't do this and shouldn't do that.'

Richard had gathered that Dr Greenland was a psycho-something-or-other and had some kind of charge of her. He still wasn't clear about what all these different people did.

Emmeline gave a small, hurt shrug. 'So be it. But you're not up to travelling on public transport. If you want to go out, I'll take you in the car and Richard will have to get you a cab back.'

Richard saw Jo slump back in the chair. The last thing he wanted was to make things more difficult for her. 'Fair enough,' he said, and pointedly turned away from Emmeline. 'Where would you like to go, Jo?'

'We could go to Ally Pally,' she said uncertainly.

'Ally—?'

'Alexandra Palace. You can look right down over London. And there are sphinxes.'

'Oh yes?' he said, mystified. 'Is it far from here?'

'Not far,' Emmeline conceded. 'And there are places to have lunch.'

'What do you think, Jo?' Richard asked, not responding to Emmeline. 'Do you think you'd be OK?'

Jo nodded.

'Let's go, then,' Richard said. 'No point in hanging around. Is it all right if I leave these and pick them up when we get back?' He pointed to his bags.

Jo nodded again; Emmeline looked perturbed.

'I'll have to come back here anyway,' he said impatiently. 'With Jo.'

Emmeline made Jo sit beside her in the front, even though the back seat of her old-style Micra didn't offer much legroom. Richard folded himself in, reassuring himself the journey was only a short one. Any longer and it would be hard to refrain from shouting at Emmeline. To his relief she concentrated on driving. Jo seemed not to want to talk.

Without too much fuss Emmeline dropped them off in the car park near the boating lake. The autumn sunshine came and went, illuminating the trees round the lake and the path muddy with recent rain.

Being near the water was calming. Jo wandered along beside him, not saying much and not biting her nails, he noticed.

He couldn't stop himself asking, 'How on earth do you put up with her?'

Jo said, 'She's not always like that. It's just that she's got this thing about you.'

'Right.' Richard took a deep breath in and blew it out.

'I tell her to go away sometimes when I can't bear it.'

'Good for you.'

'She helps me. I don't really want her to, but sometimes I need it.'

'Isn't there anyone else?'

Jo sighed helplessly. 'I'd rather have Emmeline than a professional carer. She knows me.'

It seemed sad that that was how she had to live. 'Well,' he said. 'At least you don't need her right now. What shall we do, now we're here?'

Richard

The Pedalos on the lake were made to look like swans and dragons, with high, arched necks in garish coloured plastic. Richard pointed them out in mock horror but Jo didn't seem interested. 'Oh yes. They've had them for a while,' she said indifferently.

They ambled on round the lake and up towards the palace.

'That's quite a sight,' Richard said, gazing up at the spreading Victorian building, its grandiosity and patterned brickwork reminiscent of a railway station. At one end was a TV mast – he remembered the building was something to do with the BBC. To the left of the grandiose central section, pedimented like a Roman temple, the rest was a roofless ruin, its colonnade of empty window sockets filled with sky. Like many Victorian monuments, the place was majestic and also faintly comic. He could imagine Kate's delight in it.

'I like it,' Jo said. 'I used to come here sometimes, when things weren't so bad.'

He was pleased to see her interested in something outside herself. 'I like it too. Let's have a look at the view.'

They stood on the terrace, gazing out beyond the green slopes of the park over red roofs and pale rows of houses interwoven with trees just beginning to turn yellow. It surprised him to see how much foliage London had. Beyond what looked like model houses and toy trees, a jagged row of high buildings stood out on the horizon. Some of them reminded him of giant memory sticks or towers made of Lego. He recognised the decorated phallic Gherkin and the tall, elegant point of the Shard, but the rest were just shapes barging into the silvery sky, impressive and inhuman. Beyond them, its misty grey merging into the clouds, was a hinterland of more houses and suburbs, so vast you couldn't see the end of it.

He turned to Jo. She was buttoning her leather jacket and had pulled her jumper sleeves down over her hands. The flowered top she had on under her jumper looked flimsy; its edge was fluttering in the wind. He hadn't seen her in anything like that before. Her leggings and Dr Martens looked as though they'd be thick enough, but she was shifting from foot to foot as though she couldn't get warm.

'Cold?' he asked.

She nodded and moved closer, which surprised him.

'Can we go inside?'

She nodded again and led him along the terrace to the far end of the building, where a pavilion remained intact. They pushed open the heavy blue doors into an indoor courtyard with tall palms in huge tubs and white-painted statuary. It didn't feel much warmer than outside but Jo seemed happier there. Despite the sturdy boots he'd always thought of her as an indoor person, protecting herself within walls.

'This is the palm court,' she said. 'Look at the sphinxes.'

He didn't notice them at first among the palms and statuary, but there they were near the corners, their white gloss paint giving them a sleek, overfed look. They had full, sensual lips and Richard noticed that at least one of them appeared to be wearing lipstick. He laughed, and just for a moment Jo laughed too. It echoed in the big arched space. He tried to remember when he'd heard and seen her laugh before. Mostly she stayed near him, as if afraid of getting lost, but then she wandered off, seeming to forget him.

After a few minutes she came back, saying, 'Let's go on.'

'How about something to eat?' He didn't much fancy the bar they were walking through. It was chilly and high-ceilinged, the beat of the music juddered through him and the lighting was dim except in too-bright patches underneath the lamps. 'Is there anywhere else?'

'There's the café in the park,' she said, as though surprised he didn't know. 'It's much nicer. They do pasta.'

They stood looking down from the top of the steps over a curving road which led out of the park. He assumed Jo knew where she was going. She jump-stepped down thoughtfully, holding on to the ends of her sleeves. At the bottom she turned towards a grassy area planted with trees.

'That way?'

She nodded and strode on purposefully, almost as though she'd forgotten him; he hadn't seen such energy in her before. Her utter focus reminded him of Kate when she was working. Striding up the little slope through the trees, she made for a brick and glass hut with low fencing around it and tables outside. It seemed to be a place where mothers with young children congregated. By the gate she stopped and turned to wait for him, pushing her hair back as the wind blew it over her face. He felt a surge of love for her, tinged with longing. She was brave, he thought, brave and somehow undefeated despite everything. He smiled at her and she half-smiled back, in a puzzled, uncertain way.

There were a few tables inside and he found one near a wall. She still looked cold and huddled her coat around her. As he went to the counter to order, he caught sight of her twiddling a strand of hair the way Kate used to, not realising she was doing it. But she wasn't Kate; he had to keep separating them in his mind.

They sat sipping their coffee, Jo warming her hands round the mug. She still seemed preoccupied, her attention elsewhere; he didn't like to ask if the voices were talking. Then she said, 'It feels different, being out. I like the trees. But all these people…'

He'd seen how she flinched when a young woman seemed to be coming towards their table, though all the woman had wanted was to take the extra chair.

'How's it all going, Jo?' It had been hard to ask with Emmeline guarding her.

She shook her head. 'I don't know. I'm having therapy. Eleanor arranged it.' He remembered the name but not who Eleanor was. 'The therapist is nice. She doesn't keep telling me what's good for me, not like Emmeline.'

'Isn't that what therapists do, though?'

'She says I need to find my own way.' Jo looked at him uncertainly. 'Something about trusting myself.'

Their food arrived. Jo picked up her fork and starting eating with concentration.

'Is it OK?' Richard asked.

She nodded, not looking at him.

After a few more mouthfuls she put her fork down and lifted her head.

'It's the people,' she said. 'Can we swap places?'

Her chair faced into the room: he hadn't thought. There wasn't much space to move but they edged round each other till she could sit down facing a corner with a potted plant on a shelf.

'Better?'

She nodded again. 'Feels safer this way.'

Richard took a bite of his focaccia and chewed, watching her. 'I hope coming out wasn't too much for you?'

This time she shook her head. 'It's OK. Just… things get a bit overwhelming. Don't tell Emmeline.'

'Course not.' He smiled, and saw one corner of her mouth turn up slightly in response. Kate had sometimes done that, but with the other side of her mouth.

'You were saying something about this therapist.'

She took another forkful of pasta and said, before she'd finished chewing, 'Not much else to say. I like her; she takes me seriously. Dr Greenland wants to stop it because he says it'll make me worse, but Eleanor's not going to let him.'

'What does Dr Greenland do? I know you've mentioned him before.'

'Fucking psychiatrist. The hospital one.' She bent her head over her plate again. 'Thinks he knows best.'

Richard was beginning to understand how much control these people had over Jo's life. He felt angry on her behalf. 'And Eleanor is…?'

'At Chestnut Tree. She's a psychiatrist too.'

'I see.' He didn't, entirely. 'And the therapist isn't a psychiatrist?'

She shook her head. 'She's not like the analyst Mother made me see. She talks, and I can see her.'

Richard tried not to look too puzzled and took another bite of his sandwich – avocado, tomato and mozzarella, fresh and thickly filled. Knowing she was vegetarian he hadn't liked to eat meat. He could see why she'd wanted to come here.

She got through her pasta quickly, took a sip of coffee and said, 'You know about the abuse and everything, and Paul?'

He nodded. At least he knew who Paul was. He found it impossible to imagine how any sort of brother could do that. When he and Fran were children they'd played games together that he later realised had had a frisson of sexual excitement, but they hadn't ever *done* anything. Paul had been so much older and bigger. It was literally criminal.

'Not just him, all of it. Lorraine says I need time to process it. A lot of time.'

'I'm sure you do.' That wasn't hard to understand.

'Well...' She frowned at him, her big eyes intent. 'That means... I'm sorry. I don't think I can see you again. Not now. It feels too much.'

Richard sat back in his chair, momentarily winded by the shock. 'You're not still thinking *I* did anything?'

'*No.* It's not about you – not like that. It's just...' She combed her fingers through her hair, pushing it off her face. 'I can't deal with too many feelings at once.'

'OK.'

'I don't think you're bad for me the way Emmeline says.'

That was a relief.

'I just can't handle being with someone who might... you know... might want something from me. It's too much,' she said again. 'Lorraine says people who've been abused need to take care of their boundaries. Phoning or texting is easier.' She looked down at her fingertips and said again, 'I'm sorry.'

Boundaries. He hoped she wouldn't start spouting therapy jargon. 'I think I understand, Jo.' Sadness welled up inside him. 'I probably wouldn't see you much anyway, given that I'm in Edinburgh and you're down here.'

'No. But I want to be clear about it. For myself. To protect myself.'

'I get that.' He felt protective towards her. He didn't want to make things more difficult but he felt he was slipping off a rock into a lonely sea, losing her altogether just as he seemed to be finding her.

'So how do you want to leave it?' He turned towards her, trying not to look anxious though he could feel his body shaking.

'I'll text you and you can text back.'

'OK. And can I text you otherwise?'

'I don't know yet. Not for the moment.'

'Mm. So we'll see how it goes.' He stared at his plate with no desire to eat the rest of his sandwich. 'Had you... had you been planning to tell me this or did it just happen now?'

She looked at him. 'I don't know. I just felt it... This has been nice, but...'

'It has been nice. It's good to see you, Jo.'

'That's what I mean. It matters to you a lot.' She didn't say more but finished her coffee in two big gulps. Then she said, 'It is good to see you. I know you care about me.'

He nodded slowly. 'I do. I really do.'

They walked up Muswell Hill into the Broadway and Jo pointed out the shop where she bought her notebooks. It looked to him like a trendy gift shop, not her sort of place at all, with racks of bright-coloured wrapping paper and displays of the sort of humorous books people only buy as presents.

'Let me get you a notebook,' he said, surprised by the thought. 'So you don't run out.' Giving her a notebook would surely be harmless.

She didn't say anything but followed him as he opened the door.

'What kind do you like?' She had black ones, he remembered, plain and not all that that big.

They walked past shelves of notebooks with gaudy, jazzy covers, twee floral ones and unbearably bright plain-coloured ones. On a lower shelf near the back of the shop were piles of different-sized notebooks with plain black covers, not the most expensive but certainly not the cheapest.

'I get these,' Jo said. 'Not the big ones. Thank you.' She turned to him deliberately as she said it, giving him the sense she really meant it.

He picked one up and noticed a rack of pens on the wall beside them.

'Expect you could do with one of these too. You have fountain pens, don't you?' He pictured her chewing her pen as she wrote, her fingers blotched with ink.

'You don't have to…' she said, not stopping him.

'What kind?'

She pointed to the cheapest Parker pens. He picked out a blue one.

'This one OK?'

He caught one of her fleeting smiles as he hunted for cartridges to fit it.

'Blue or black ink?'

'Black.' After a pause she added, 'Please.'

Kate had preferred blue. Jo's handwriting was almost identical to hers but had a tighter, more cramped look, as though unsure of its right to be there. It was more widely spaced too, keeping its distance.

As he went to the cash desk with her presents he noticed an odd expression on her face. He'd seen something like it when Rick didn't know whether to smile or cry. A young shop assistant with a pineapple hairstyle and pink eyeshadow asked if he wanted the things wrapped; he immediately said yes. He watched her enfold them lovingly in mauve tissue paper and tie the parcel with a strand of green raffia, her hands careful despite long decorated nails.

'Here you are,' he said to Jo. 'Enjoy.'

Jo looked at him, still with the same expression, eyes glazed.

'Thank you,' she said, brushing her sleeve across her face. 'Nice of you. Mother and Emmeline don't give me presents I want, they give me things they think I need.'

'My pleasure. Good to know you'll use it.'

She tried to stuff the parcel into her rucksack, crumpling the tissue paper, then took it out again, smoothed it and slid it in more gently.

They emerged from the shop's bright light into the grey afternoon. Richard put his hand on his head to stop the wind blowing his thin strands of hair.

'I suppose we'd better find a cab.' He searched on his phone.

To his surprise she said, 'I'd rather get the bus.'

'Are you sure, Jo?' He nearly added, 'Emmeline thought it should be a cab' but stopped himself in time.

'The bus stop's just here.' She pointed across the road. 'I want to try. I always used to get the bus.' She took a breath and stood more upright. It was good to glimpse her spirit again.

When the bus came it was almost empty. She huddled into a window seat and he planted himself beside her, shielding her, slightly afraid Emmeline would blame him for doing her some kind of damage. Jo wasn't a child, he told himself sternly, and Emmeline wasn't her mother.

She stared out of the window, seemingly lost in her own world. From the way she moved her head Richard wondered if she was talking to the voices, or if they were talking to her. At one point she gave a start and a shudder.

'All right?' he asked quietly. He stopped himself putting a hand on her shoulder.

She turned to look at him. 'Yes. It's gone now.' She didn't say what 'it' was.

'We have to get off in a minute,' she said, just as the bus announced 'Bounds Green *Station*' in its unnatural way.

He walked with her up the road to the house, not knowing how to break their silence. The light was lower now and the afternoon felt later than it was. As they were nearing the gateway

Jo stopped and said, 'I'm sorry about, you know, not seeing you. I hope you don't mind.'

Of course I mind, he wanted to say. I'm bloody gutted. If you must know, I can hardly bear it. 'I do understand, Jo,' he said as gently as he could. 'You know you can always ring or text me.'

'I know.'

She turned to him as if to say goodbye.

'My things…' he said. 'Will Emmeline be there?'

'She should be at work now.'

Relieved, he followed her up the stairs. When she opened the door, the first thing he noticed was a sheet of paper from a notepad placed conspicuously on the doormat.

'She always leaves me notes,' Jo said, picking it up and staring at it. 'She wants me to let her know I'm all right and nothing untoward has happened.'

'Untoward? What the hell does she mean?'

Jo bit a nail. 'You know. I told you she's got this thing about you.'

Richard bent over the armchair to fish his bags from under the table, grunting as he lifted them out.

'Seemingly she has.' No point in being angry about it. 'Well, Jo. It was so good to see you. I hope you enjoyed our little outing.'

'Yes. Thank you.' She sounded as though she meant it.

'And I'll see you… when I see you.'

'Yes.' To his surprise she added, 'Thank you for coming.'

'You're very welcome.' He decided to risk it. 'Would it be OK if I… gave you a hug? Just to say goodbye, or at least *au revoir*.'

'I don't know.' She edged towards him round the furniture, while he extricated himself from between the chairs and moved closer to her.

He put his arms round her, feeling how thin she was, and held her lightly for a moment. Just as he thought she wasn't going to respond, she freed her arms and tentatively reached out, hardly touching him. Then she leaned in, an unexpected gesture of trust that warmed and moved him. He gently let her go and whispered, 'Don't tell Emmeline.'

He heard her laugh for the second time today, a tremulous, breathy giggle not at all like Kate's chuckle.

'I won't,' she said, and gave him a fleeting grin as she shut the door.

Jo

She had touched Richard. She'd let him hug her and more or less hugged him, and it had been all right. *That's what you think*, one of the voices said. *Untoward. You're untoward.* For a moment she was frightened of it, the familiar dread that those things had happened to her and Jans because she was bad. Then the angel voice came: *You're all right. You've done nothing wrong.* Lately that voice had begun to sound more like Lorraine's, calm and reassuring. Lorraine had said that some of the voices were parts of her that were trying to protect her, and they threatened her because they were so frightened of what might happen if they didn't. Not all of them were protecting her, though. *His* voice had taken root inside her like an unwanted plant; Mother's had grown into her too, criticising and dismissing her. She didn't mind Lorraine's voice living inside her; that one helped.

Perhaps it hadn't been right to tell Richard she didn't want to see him again – for the moment; she hadn't meant for ever. But something she was learning to trust had told her she needed this time for herself – herself with Lorraine. Surely Eleanor wouldn't let Dr Greenland take that away. Emmeline didn't agree about Lorraine; they'd argued about it last time. Jo had been crying after the session, in a way that felt necessary, and Emmeline had thought the worst.

'You know,' she'd said, 'I don't think it's good for you to be looking inside yourself like this. I'm sure Lorraine is well qualified, but that doesn't mean she knows what's best for someone like you.'

Jo had felt hot with fury. 'I'm not *someone like me*. I'm me, and I know if it's good for me. Lorraine listens to me, she doesn't tell me what to do.' She'd decided to talk to Lorraine about Emmeline. She hadn't dared to before, in case Lorraine took Emmeline's side.

'With respect,' Emmeline said with heavy emphasis, 'the illness may mean that you're not always in a position to judge.'

'It's not *the illness* I'm talking about,' Jo shouted. She'd never stood up to Emmeline like this before. 'It's what I've been through. She lets me talk to her about it without telling me there's something wrong with me.'

'Well,' Emmeline huffed, 'in my humble opinion – and I've known you a long time – what you need to be doing is not navel-gazing but getting on with your life. You can go back to the charity shop, can't you, do activities at the centre? You said they've started a yoga class. That would be good for you.'

'It's not either/or,' Jo said, on the edge of crying with frustration. Sometimes she thought Emmeline wasn't very bright – which was just the sort of thing Mother thought about people. 'She's helping me feel stronger about doing things.'

Emmeline looked hard at her. 'So you say. And what does Dr Greenland think?'

'Fuck Dr Greenland,' Jo said quietly. 'He's never listened to me. I always feel worse when I've seen him.'

'He's been treating you all these years. He must know something.'

'Treating me badly,' Jo muttered. She glanced sideways at Emmeline, who was leaning back implacably against the table. 'I want you to go now.'

Emmeline shrugged but didn't move otherwise. 'All right. But don't blame me if you end up worse. You never used to be so argumentative; I'm not sure it's healthy.'

With an obvious effort Emmeline pushed herself away from the table and ambled towards the door, slamming it behind her in the aggrieved way Jo knew well. She always liked to think she was right.

Today was the first time Emmeline had been back since that argument. She'd insisted Jo couldn't meet Richard on her own and Jo had given way, wishing almost immediately that she hadn't. She felt more determined to manage without Emmeline now.

On Thursday morning Emmeline rang to say she would be coming to pick Jo up for the group. It was tempting to accept. The days were getting darker, Jo would have to wait for two buses, she was more likely to be late. But sitting beside Emmeline in a small car would feel suffocating.

'I'm going to go by bus,' she said.

'Are you sure? It'll be getting dark when you come back.'

'Yes,' Jo said quickly, and put the phone down.

She made sure she left earlier than she needed. Standing at the bus stop outside the supermarket, smelling the blood and burnt fat from the butcher's counter, she was seized with doubt and almost called Emmeline. Then the bus came. As she bleeped her Oyster card on the reader she felt a little thrill of confidence. I used to be able to do this, she thought. *You can't now,* one of the voices sneered. *You're not capable. You'll regret it.* She carried on and found a seat in the back corner where she could look out of the window and pretend there was no one else on the bus.

At Muswell Hill it was easier. She'd caught the bus there with Richard, and he hadn't thought she couldn't do it. As they glided down Crouch Hill towards Stroud Green she had an urge to tell him about it. She knew he'd understand.

Despite having left early she was only just in time for the group. Margaret had saved her a seat and on her other side was Cara, draped in black as always, scenting the air with what she said was patchouli. Eleanor invited them to sit silently for a couple of minutes and centre themselves, but Cara could never wait. White-faced and shaking, her husky voice tremulous with emotion, she said, 'I've had a terrible week.' She nearly always had. 'I just can't...' The whole room was silent as she sobbed into the bundle of tissues someone had handed her. Jo couldn't stop watching her. She was beautiful in her haggard way, her voice expressive; she wasn't like the rest of them who sat hunched up in their chairs, nerving themselves to speak. Jo didn't readily touch people but she rested a hand on Cara's arm and felt its bony warmth. She was drinking her in, almost becoming her, as Cara spoke about the things she'd been through, making them sound more vividly terrible than anything anyone else had been through. Jo wanted to be close to her, to share in them with her, but Cara seemed not to notice. After she had sobbed some more she said, looking round the room, 'This is the last time I'll be here.' Jo gripped Cara's arm harder with the shock and felt Cara shake her off.

Eleanor said. 'You haven't mentioned it before, Cara. Is this a sudden decision? Maybe the group would like to know what's happening for you.'

Jo noticed Eleanor was frowning slightly. The other people in the group were either, like Jo, shocked and fascinated, or else looked bored and mildly irritated.

'I'm going back to my father in Norfolk.'

A couple of people gasped. Cara's father had been one of her abusers and she'd said she never wanted to see him again.

Eleanor said neutrally, 'I'm wondering what's brought you to this decision.'

'I can't cope on my own,' Cara said simply. 'I can't bear being alone here in London.'

Jo felt a wrench in her solar plexus. She didn't want Cara to leave and go back to someone who might harm her again. In that moment not seeing Cara felt a huge loss, almost like losing Jans. She nearly blurted out, 'But I love you,' but realised how it would have sounded. All the times she had come to the group it had been Cara, even more than Eleanor, that she had looked forward to seeing. Without her the group would feel lifeless, stifling.

Eleanor said, 'That's quite a surprise. You feel sure it's the right thing to do?'

Cara said, 'Oh *yes,* I'm sure it is.'

'I would feel concerned about you,' Eleanor said, 'and I'm sure others will have feelings about you leaving. Is it OK for them to say how they feel?'

Cara nodded, looking round the room again. Be kind to me, her eyes seemed to say when they met Jo's.

Jo murmured, looking away, 'I'm sorry you're going. I hope you'll be all right.'

Cara nodded and turned to the next person. Perhaps she said 'Thank you' – Jo wasn't sure. She tried not to let herself cry: this was Cara's moment, not hers. She knew how it felt when she was speaking about something and people's attention went to someone else who was upset. It hurt that Cara didn't care about her more but she wouldn't say so.

Going back was harder than getting there. It had turned dark early with the rain and a chill drizzle was soaking into her clothes. She had waited a long time at the bus stop. *You shouldn't have done it,* the voice said. *I told you it was a mistake.* The tyres of passing cars smacked against the wet road and the air smelt of damp pavement and petrol fumes. When the bus came, the light inside it felt exposing and too bright. It was practically empty but she felt vaguely afraid of the few people in the downstairs seats, though they seemed harmless enough: a young couple completely absorbed in each other, an unshaven old man in a frayed tweed jacket whose hands shook continually, two younger dark-haired men muttering in what might have been Turkish. She felt safer when they got to Muswell Hill – being high up was reassuring and the light from the expensive shops shone on the wet pavements, making the street brighter. She had to run for the second bus but getting on it meant she was nearly home. *I can do it*, she said to the voice. It didn't answer.

Emmeline had left a message on her phone. You've only got to call me and I'll be there, she'd said. Jo felt proud that she hadn't called. She made herself a coffee and rolled a cigarette – she felt she'd earned one.

For once she hadn't talked about Jans. Cara's announcement had been such a shock it had stopped her thinking about her sister. It felt shaming to think she'd been a bit in love with Cara, but Cara had seemed so alive, even when she said she'd kill herself.

Other people had said she just enjoyed the drama. But it had felt good to Jo to want someone or something. She knew Emmeline would say it was all her illness, but Emmeline didn't like her caring about anyone else.

In the session the other day Lorraine had wondered if Jo might want to be more independent of Emmeline. She hadn't told her she should, but Jo saw Lorraine hadn't taken Emmeline's side. She was caught in the familiar trap: Emmeline was stifling but no-one else helped her in the same way. Jo realised she felt less capable, not more, when Emmeline did things for her. Immediately she felt guilty for thinking like that: Emmeline had been so good to her.

Lorraine had been doing a lot of wondering in that session; she'd also wondered if Jo would like to know more about her father. Now that Mother had acknowledged Paul was the abuser, perhaps she might be willing to say something about Father too – if Jo wanted to ask, Lorraine added carefully.

Jo wished Jans could be here with her. How different it would have been. She wouldn't have liked the smell of smoke and would have made Jo open the window; she would have wanted milk in her coffee and minded that it was instant. She would have said Jo needed more colour in the room, for God's sake. *No wonder you get depressed, with everything so drab*. I'm not you, Jo would have said to her. Colour doesn't work for me like it works for you. Then they would have laughed, at how alike and how unalike they were.

She saw on her phone that Emmeline had both texted and rung. I'm OK, she texted back, and added Thanks, hoping that would keep her quiet. She thought about texting Richard. Maybe she'd tell him about the bus, or maybe she'd keep it to herself.

*   *   *

Jo

She had no difficulty recognising the handwriting on the envelope, though the scratchy blue address was splodged and distorted with rain. One of the few things she had in common with Mother was that they both used a fountain pen. Eric Gaines had left the letter outside her door and she'd picked it up as she came in from the charity shop. The weather was cold and her hands looked bluish – she'd left her gloves on the bus. She shivered in the minimal warmth of the flat. There was more light in the sky now as she came home. She'd seemed to notice the weather a lot in this first winter without Jans, but to her February was always a hopeful month, despite the cold. She lit the gas fire and warmed her hands in front of the chalky elements as they began to glow orange.

 Out of habit she put the letter on the table, to be opened when she felt strong enough. Mother's letters had become less icy and more communicative, in a matter-of-fact sort of way – the WI, the new estates that were being built in the fields, her neighbour's dog. She rarely talked about Jans and asked little about Jo's life. Jo had got into the habit of putting together some sort of reply; sometimes it almost felt as if they were having a conversation.

 She rolled a cigarette and sat smoking it, then went to get coffee. There was a cluster of mugs on the draining board, ringed and stained or half-full of scummy liquid – she had to see to them herself now she'd stopped Emmeline coming in so much. She rinsed out a mug, shook in some granules from the jar and switched on the kettle. Lorraine had suggested trying to do nicer things for herself and hot-tap coffee was disgusting, even if it was easier. She'd splashed out and bought a cheese and salad sandwich, so she'd have something proper to eat. Estelle, who managed the shop, had tried to feed her but had forgotten again that she was vegetarian. Jo had returned the plastic box of fish balls as nicely as she could – she was getting better at it. Being in the shop with Estelle was like being with the sort of mother she'd never had, who fussed and clucked and called her darling. It felt warm and embarrassing.

Having eaten the sandwich from its plastic triangle, she wiped her hands on her jeans and tore open Mother's letter.

Dear Joanna, – Mother was still incapable of calling her Jo.

There are some things I should perhaps have told you before. I kept them from you and Jancis, not because there was any mystery but because I thought they were better left unsaid. Nevertheless, you both had the right to know about your father, and I regret now not having spoken to you while Jancis was alive. He is not (or perhaps was not – I lost touch with him a long time ago) an exceptionally bad man, in fact not an exceptional man in any way. What he did was something many men do, and women too. I could not forgive him and still cannot, although after all this time it matters less.

Jo stopped reading and put the letter down on the arm of the chair. She looked round the room, noticing the grubby walls and greyish net curtains – she'd never thought to wash them. What she felt was disappointment. She and Jans had wanted to believe that their father was someone special, that he'd had a special reason for not seeing them, and here was Mother telling her he'd been no different from thousands of other fathers who had bunked off. Or, more likely, been sent packing. It wasn't hard to imagine Mother telling him not to come back, and if he hadn't cared that much… That was the awful part. Supposing he hadn't been interested in seeing them. In the stories she and Jans had made up, they'd always believed he would have come back if he could. When they stopped believing in the stories, they were left with the bleak truth that he wasn't there and, as far as they knew, never had been.

One of the voices, a woman's but not Mother's, said, *He didn't want either of you, especially not you. Why would he, you miserable cow?* It hurt so much that Jo wanted to cut. She gripped her arm tightly till she could feel the pain, then let it go, the hurt and shame burning in her chest. She didn't much like cutting any more – the blood and the mess and the scars afterwards didn't seem worth it – but sometimes she didn't know what else to do. The voice didn't say more and Jo remembered what Lorraine had said about it being part of her. She'd always thought Father might have gone away because they were bad – because she was bad, more than Jans. What Paul had done had made her bad. It was so hard to believe it wasn't her fault.

She picked up the letter again. *Your father was called Desmond O'Meara – yes, he was Irish. By the time I married him Paul was more or less grown up. I had struggled to bring him up by myself and did everything I thought necessary. You and Jancis were born shortly after your father and I married, and for the first few months he was devoted to both of you – more so than I was. He seemed to be a good man. Then he found another woman and took her back to Ireland with him. That was all. I chose to cut off from him, for my own sake and yours, and he protested surprisingly little. He sometimes sent money and usually cards and presents on your birthday, all of which I returned to him. Please be assured that I did this in your best interests.*

There wasn't much more. *I am sorry*, Mother said, which was rare for her, *if my withholding this from you caused you both to suffer. I have never been in favour of self-pity, and at the time it seemed to me better for all concerned if I said and showed as little as possible. I hope you will understand. With hindsight I regret it if my keeping him from you deprived you and Jancis of the minimal connection you might have had with him. At the time I did not see that it might have been of benefit to you.*
Affectionately
Mother

Jo still wondered sometimes if Mother really knew what affection was. A familiar anger rose inside her. Why should *she* have to understand, when Mother had never tried to understand her? Then, unwillingly, she saw for a moment how Mother must have struggled in her own tight, remote way, teaching English at one of the language schools, which she had always said she hated, getting odd bits of work from her old college, always doing everything on her own. She thought again of the monkey with the wire mother; in some strange way it felt like a friend. The wire mother couldn't be anything but wire; that was how it was made. Perhaps Mother couldn't have been anything but the way she was. For a moment Jo saw how she and Jans had been the casualties, just as Mother must have been a casualty of her own upbringing. She felt indescribably sad for all of them.

Her next session with Lorraine was tomorrow. She had the money for it ready in an envelope on the coffee table; that came first, before anything she might buy. She saw her twice a week, Mondays and Thursdays, so that the pain didn't get too big in between, and in the gaps she sent emails that Lorraine kept for the next session. She opened up the old black laptop that Richard had given her – a discarded one from a company he'd done some work for – and started to tell Lorraine about the letter. She still felt bad that when Richard had brought the computer round she hadn't offered him coffee, but he'd seemed to understand.

It felt like a miracle that Eleanor had managed to convince Dr Greenland to let her continue the sessions, especially after the review meeting. Jo, Damian, Eleanor and Lorraine had sat crammed round a table in a hot, windowless room, drinking machine coffee from white plastic cups and waiting for Dr Greenland to arrive. When he appeared, his thick file of case notes under his arm, he had looked only at Eleanor and addressed his questions about Jo entirely to her. Damian and Lorraine got a brief look-in later – Dr Greenland interrupting them before they'd finished – then finally he'd turned to Jo, cutting across her as soon as she started to mumble something. They all knew he was waiting to prove the therapy wasn't working, but Eleanor hadn't let him. She had thrown everything at him – trauma, PTSD, the latest research, not least the fact that she'd known Jo more closely than he had – and in the end, grudgingly, he had given way. 'I wouldn't choose to recommend it,' he'd said, 'but there is no evidence of its causing the patient harm.' Damian and Lorraine had both smiled at Jo as though it had been her success, and she'd gazed at Eleanor in awe and gratitude.

Eleanor had been wonderful then, but it had felt less wonderful when not very long after the review Eleanor had told her, as kindly as possible, that she was coming to the end of her time at Chestnut Tree and in a couple of months they would have to give her place in the group to someone else. It still hurt that she wasn't part of it any more, even though Eleanor had said she could always get in touch if she needed. Margaret had gone to live with her daughter in south London and Jo missed her; she had almost been a friend. She was left with the image of Cara – tall, gaunt, black-swathed, fascinating – and the few words Cara had cast in her direction.

'You OK, Jo?' Estelle said as Jo pushed the shop door open, jangling the bell. The wooden floor was swept and the shelves were clean, but Jo caught the familiar old-clothes smell of perfume and bodies. She didn't mind it so much now that she wasn't ironing the clothes all the time. She left her things in the back room and stood ready beside Estelle.

'Do you think you could rearrange those glass ornaments, dear? I'd put them at this end of the shelf if I were you.' Estelle stood back and eyed the shelf critically. 'And you see that funny-looking teapot? That needs to go on the shelf above, so people see it. About time we got rid of it. And then if you could just make sure the clothes are in size order. You know how people put them back all over the place.'

Jo nodded and moved towards the shelves in the alcove. She quite liked being given things to do by Estelle, who always thanked her when she'd done them.

'Oh, Jo.'

She turned round.

'I'm going to have to slip out this morning. I've got to go to a stone setting in Golders Green. No-one close, but I know his family.'

Jo looked at her, not understanding. She noticed Estelle was wearing black, but then she often did.

'John will be here in a bit to help hold the fort, if that's what you're worried about.'

Jo liked John, an elderly man who didn't say much. 'No, I just didn't know what...'

'Oh. When a gravestone has been put up, people have a little service. He didn't pass away that long ago, poor man; it's all been quite quick. It's good to remember someone, you know what I mean?' Estelle gave her a concerned glance.

Jo nodded. A gravestone marked a place where you could remember, but there was nowhere for Jans. Thinking of the photographs in her room at Chestnut Tree, she had a nagging feeling that they were telling her something.

'I'll go down on the bus,' Estelle said, glancing out of the window towards the bus stop. 'No point taking the car. You're sure you'll be all right?'

'Yes, thanks. Sorry to hear...'

Estelle shrugged. 'Well, he wasn't close, as I said, but so sad for the family.'

Once Estelle had gone, the bell jangling loudly behind her, the shop fell into quiet. Jo noticed the light reflected in the shiny pale wood floor, the discordant colours of the clothes on the racks, the boots on the shelf with their legs flopped over. A woman in a shapeless grey coat wandered in, the wheels of her bright pink shopping trolley clattering over the wood. She handled a few of the clothes, leafed through a book and wandered out again.

Jo felt uncomfortable selling people things but Estelle had insisted she try. "Good for your confidence, dear.' By the time John came she had wrapped up a glass ornament for a customer and managed to take the card payment. She let John settle himself behind the counter, stretching out his long legs and straightening the boxes of jewellery on the glass top. He'd been an engineer and touched things delicately, precisely, in a way she liked to watch. He pushed back his longish grey-white hair and adjusted his black-framed glasses, ready for the next customer. He never said much about his wife, who had died not long ago, and Jo would have liked to ask him. She would have liked to tell him about Jans too, but in the shop it didn't feel right. They smiled at each other tentatively and Jo went back to the shelves.

A metal-framed seascape, not a good photograph, reminded her again. She'd become more sure that the right place for Jans should be a river and not the sea. She'd texted Richard last night but hadn't mentioned it, though for some time the question had seemed to hover between them whenever they were in touch. It was as if Jans had started quietly insisting.

Richard

Jo's text was cryptic as always: We need to find a place. He stared at it, not making sense of the words but guessing their meaning from the surge of resistance he felt. There isn't a right place, he thought first of all, there never will be a right place. Kate belongs here, with me. At the same time he knew how she'd hate to feel possessed; she'd want to be free. Jo hadn't mentioned anywhere in particular. He'd have to talk to her, if she was willing and if, as it seemed, the time had now come. Still less than a year; not long at all and such an immensely long time.

It was late afternoon but the pale February light, shining faintly in the office windows, already gave promise of longer days. The little wood-burner he'd had put in was full of blackening embers and he shivered in the cold. As he put the phone back on his desk, he found himself crying again. It didn't happen so often now, that unexpected leakage from body and soul, but he never knew when it would catch him. He never knew when anger would catch him either. Like yesterday: Rick had come in from school in a foul mood. Richard had stopped to ask what was wrong but instead found himself shouting at the boy, 'For God's sake take that sulky look off your face! I can't be doing with it any more.'

Rick had glared at him and shouted back, 'Yeah? What about you, then, looking so fucking miserable all the time?'

'Don't talk to me like that. I'm your father.'

'You're not my *mother*. She's the one that matters. I wish you were dead, not her.'

'How dare you say that to me, you ungrateful, disrespectful little sod. How dare you.' Richard's anger collapsed, leaving a spike of pain. 'Oh God, Rick. Don't you think I wish that sometimes?' He glanced sideways at Rick, who was staring at the floor. There was something about anger being one of the stages of bereavement. He'd read about it a leaflet he'd got from the doctor's surgery and didn't wholly believe it: for him the stages seemed to arrive in no sort of order. The anger had been a long time coming, for both of them, and when it came it seemed to twist them out of shape.

"Come here, son.' He opened his arms for a hug but Rick ran towards him fighting, punching him in the chest and kicking against his feet.

'OK, Ricks, OK. Steady now, you're hurting me.' Richard held him off as best he could.

'Good!' Rick went on hitting out. 'I hate you. I hate school. I hate everybody.'

'Did something happen at school, then?'

Rick's energy gave out and his face crumpled. 'Sandy... Sandy was laughing at me for not having a mother. Just because his mother did a runner.'

'That's awful, Rick. For you and for him.'

'It's not Mum's fault, is it? And it's not my fault either. If someone dies, it's not like if someone goes away. They can't help it.'

'It's not anyone's fault. It happened.'

Rick wiped his eyes with his sleeve and hurled himself into Richard's arms. They'd got used to these moments of grieving together, but each time the pain seemed to sink deeper. Richard held his son tightly and wished for his sake that it didn't have to be like this.

When Rick had had enough, he pulled himself away and said, 'I didn't mean it, Dad. I don't want you to die, not really.'

'I know, son. Sometimes people say things...' He took a risk. 'And sometimes I get angry that she's not here, even though it's not her fault.' He'd ventured saying it because of something V had said. Richard willingly went through the business of offering his friend lunch every couple of weeks in exchange for his – not advice exactly, but intelligent listening. He couldn't remember precisely what V had said, but it was something about being honest and not pretending to be perfect. V had talked about the unskilful ways he'd dealt with his own anger – 'unskilful' seemed to be a Buddhist word. Richard had always admired his honesty.

Rick had nodded as though he understood. 'It's shit,' he'd said in his quasi-grown-up voice, which he didn't use so much now.

This morning, after yesterday's storm, Rick had gone off to school with Robbie as usual. Richard hoped he'd been OK during the day. He'd be back soon and might bring Robbie or Kelvin with him – Kelvin always wanted to see Livingstone. As the evenings grew lighter they'd have time to take Liv for a walk without his needing to go with them.

He shut down the computer, dragged on his warm jacket and shuffled into his shoes. As he did so, he noticed a message on his phone from Fran. She'd got a job interview with a charity in Edinburgh, so could she stay on Tuesday night? As if he'd say no. She seemed to live there half the time anyway, spending weekends whenever she could, not only when Richard was away. Somehow, he wasn't sure how, they both took it for granted that if she could get a job in Edinburgh she'd move to be near them. It wasn't all altruism, he knew – she needed them as much as they needed her.

Livingstone lay beside Richard's chair, whimpering in his dreams. When Richard stood up he shook himself awake and started barking eagerly. Movement usually meant food or a walk, or both. He bounded up and wriggled closer to Richard, propelled by his tail. Richard stroked his head and Livingstone gazed up at him wide-eyed. Having a dog brought its rewards.

Rick and Kelvin came barging in, joshing each other and throwing themselves on to the kitchen floor beside Livingstone, who by this time was an ecstatic bundle, all bark and tail. Kelvin looked up at Richard while energetically stroking the dog, and grinned 'Hi' with a wink of pleasure. Richard liked Kelvin; his disarming cheekiness helped Rick lighten up.

'You lads taking Liv out, then?' Richard asked, once the boys had each consumed a large slice of toast with chocolate spread and a glass of milk. He looked at his watch. 'Just wait for me.'

'Oh *no,* Dad,' Rick said. 'Can't we go without you?'

'I'm not having you out on your own in the dark.'

'But Dad, it's not dark for *hours* yet.' There was a good hour or so, but Richard wouldn't risk it. Since Kate's death he had lost his simple faith in the continuity of life; he had to protect Rick as best he could. He got his coat and made sure they had theirs. As he opened the door the damp chill bit into his hands and face.

'We'll go round the block for a bit and take Kelvin back to his mum.'

The boys exchanged disappointed looks. Kelvin hung on tight to Liv's lead as the dog pulled him forward.

Richard let the boys go on ahead with Livingstone. It was cold and dreich – a Scottish word he was fond of. In late February, the light not only lasted longer but seemed to lift and widen, preparing for spring. They walked up past the Commonwealth Pool towards the road where Kelvin now lived. Each evening as they passed it, the pool's grassy surround and the building's long horizontals emerged more clearly from the winter dark. Kate had always made him notice the comings and goings of the light, but this year the lighter evenings had seemed barely to lift winter's misery. Rick would be eleven soon, a month before the anniversary, and they'd been thinking about secondary schools. Richard had been talking to Kate about it in his mind. As soon as he thought of her the image of the hospital room, never far away, was in front of his eyes again. He tried to do what V had taught him and focus on his feet walking, the movement of his breath, the feelings in his body. Sometimes, for a short while, it helped.

His pace steadied and slowly his breathing calmed. Ahead of him Rick and Kelvin were play-punching and nudging each other. Rick was noticeably taller and thinner than Kelvin; Richard was sure he hadn't been so tall yesterday. If he didn't notice how his son had grown, what else had he not seen? Time was passing. Everything was impermanent, V had said; you couldn't rely on anything to stay the same. Not even grief; not even loss. When Rick was small the family had had a holiday on Mull. As the ferry pulled away from the tall pointed buildings of Oban's waterfront, Richard had watched the lengthening wale, the endlessly churning curls of white water left behind as the boat moved forward. Already, inexorably, their lives were moving away from Kate.

On the way back from Kelvin's in the chilly dusk, Rick said, 'Dad, what are you going to do about Mum's ashes? Are you going to keep them in the bedroom?'

'What made you ask that?' It was unnerving how Rick sometimes echoed his own thoughts. 'What would you like to do?'

Rick thought for a moment. 'I think we should set her free.'

'Why's that?'

'You said she wanted to be by the water.'

Richard had forgotten he'd mentioned it to Rick. 'Mm. Do you think the time has come?'

'I don't think that box should go on being there.'

'I know that, son. But it's about finding the right place.'

'You've always said that.' Pulled by Liv towards a tree the dog was determined to pee on, Rick had to think about other things.

In the lull after tea while Rick was, he hoped, doing his homework, Richard texted Jo, willing her not to reply just yet. He imagined letting Kate's ashes go and decided he had to keep just a little of her. There was an antique wooden snuffbox they'd once bought, thinking they'd find a use for it. He thought it might be comfortable for her.

It was Jo who said, in her reply: Can we talk about it?

Jo

Tomorrow she and Richard would be in Totnes; the day after they would go to Sharpham. Jo hoped it was the right place; Jans seemed to have told her it was. She remembered how they used to go there with Tim and Celia, their aunt and uncle, and swim in the Dart, watching the birds fly over them as they floated on their backs. Once they'd seen a seal in the water, watching them from a distance. It seemed a long way inland to find one but Tim said they came upriver as far as Totnes. Tim was Mother's brother. He'd had a great knowledge of the natural world and a dry sense of humour that was clever, but not cutting like Mother's. Jo didn't think about him often but she had been sad when he died. Celia was in a nursing home now. Jans had once taken Richard to see the Dart and Jo had minded more than she could say. It was a place the two of them had shared; it didn't belong to anyone else.

When Jo told Emmeline she was going in the car with Richard all the way to Devon, Emmeline had seemed to inflate like an odd-shaped balloon. Her face went bright pink and she stood there with her arms folded, shaking her head as if saying 'Over my dead body.' She couldn't stop Jo, though. Damian knew she was going and had told her to take care of herself. Lorraine knew too. She'd suggested Jo might like to bring back something to keep, something small like a stone.

Jo had thought Estelle might mind her taking the time off, but Estelle had just said, 'It'll be cold by the river. You'd better have some warm things.' She'd found a black parka in the shop that fitted Jo and a hat, scarf and gloves set – brand new, probably an unwanted Christmas present. They were light grey, not colourful enough for Jans, but Jo liked them. The hat had a big pompom on top like Mother's old tea cosy, but that didn't matter. Estelle hadn't let her pay for any of the things but had put the money in the till herself. Sometimes Jo wished Estelle wouldn't mother her quite so much.

In the background the voices were muttering: *You can't do it. You can't go that far. Who do you think you are anyway?*

You're not important, not like your sister. She tried to ignore them but they made her doubt herself. Remember they're scared, Lorraine always said. They're frightening you because they're afraid.

She'd been writing a lot in her journal and had already got through the one after the one Richard had given her. Lorraine encouraged her to write but didn't ask about it, so Jo felt safe to read to her from it, even things she wrote for Jans. She didn't think Jans would mind.

It was Richard who had told Mother they were going. Jo had been afraid she might want to come with them, but she'd said it would be too much for her. The funeral service was what had mattered to Mother; she had always liked the formalities, even if she didn't believe in them. Jo didn't think Jans would want Mother to be there. Richard had asked his son – she didn't think of him as her nephew – but the boy had said he'd rather say goodbye at home. At his age she would have flinched from seeing the ashes – death seemed easier to cope with in the abstract. At least they wouldn't have to deal with the boy. Richard's sister, whom Jo didn't remember having met, looked after him when Richard was away.

She knew it was time to get ready and already felt apprehensive: being in the car with Richard, staying in a B & B – which she never did – then both of them going down to the river, each with their different memories. I'll still be with you, Jans. And you'll be with me. She felt Jans near her, real and not real like a phantom limb. She hoped giving her to the river wouldn't mean losing that feeling – all she had left of her.

She was trying not to smoke but went straight to the bedroom for her supplies. Opening the paper, straightening the line of tobacco, rolling it into a narrow cylinder, licking the gummed edge, sealing it up – the ritual was soothing. The taste and smell half repelled her but the first inhalation was a relief. She couldn't find the ashtray so had to stub out the cigarette in the kitchen sink, while she made another coffee and cobbled together a sandwich. She'd be having a proper breakfast with Richard in a café.

When he rang the bell in the morning she was stuffing her nightclothes into her rucksack and swallowing the last cold half-inch of coffee. Pulling on her jumper she ran downstairs to open the door.

His hair had thinned more in the few months since she'd seen him; when he took off his cloth cap his scalp showed pink through the sparse strands that were starting to turn grey. He was wearing a padded jacket and had thrust his hands into the pockets – the wind was bitingly cold.

'Everything OK, Jo?'

'I think so. I'll get my things.' Seeing him shifting about, trying to get warm, she added, 'Do you want to come up?'

As she opened the door to the flat she said automatically, as though he was Emmeline, 'Sorry about the mess.'

'Doesn't matter. I'm used to mess,' he said, and seemed to mean it. 'Let's get going.'

She zipped up her rucksack, put on Estelle's parka – much cosier than her leather jacket – and stuffed the hat and scarf in the pockets. It was good to have new clothes, even if they were secondhand and she hadn't paid for them herself.

'Glad you've got yourself a warm coat,' Richard said. 'It'll be cold by the river.'

She didn't say Estelle had given it to her; it would sound too much like charity.

At another time it might have been exciting, going out to breakfast, but this was simply fuelling themselves for the journey. They walked the short way to the café, wrapped in private silence but comfortable together. Being with Richard again wasn't difficult. He didn't say anything about her not having given him coffee when he brought the computer; perhaps he hadn't minded.

Sitting in the car beside him, full of breakfast that he had paid for, felt more intimate than facing him across a table. She was aware of the bulk of him, his smells of aftershave and washing powder and clean male body, the nearness of his arm when he changed gear. Uneasy memories surfaced: hugging and kissing him, being touched, almost liking it until the terror came. The terror had long gone but she felt a subtle shiver in the narrow space between them.

For a while, negotiating the North Circular and the confusion of lanes at Chiswick, Richard was quiet. Jo sat thinking about Jans while one of the voices nagged at her from time to time, *You shouldn't be doing this. She won't like it. She's the one that matters, not you.* She nibbled her nails and wished she could smoke; all she had to comfort herself was one stick of chewing-gum, half-unwrapped, in her jeans pocket. When they were past the roundabout and heading for Richmond – she'd once wandered about in the park looking for deer – Richard asked her again, 'You OK, Jo?'

'Mm.'

'I know it's hard. For both of us.'

Jo said, 'It'll be better when we've done it. For her and us.'

'I hope so,' Richard said doubtfully. 'Listen, Jo. I hope you won't mind, but I've kept a few of her ashes in a little box. I couldn't let her go completely.'

'It's not up to me,' she said, pulling back in her seat. 'I just wanted to let her go.' She chewed her gum harder; she couldn't say how wrong it felt.

'You and she were special to each other… Maybe I haven't respected that enough.'

You haven't, she wanted to say, but kept chewing. The gum already had a sour taste. 'She was special to you too,' she said flatly.

They were on the dual carriageway now, London beginning to fall away behind them. He said, 'You knew, Jo, didn't you, that I kind of had feelings for you?' He wasn't sure if they were really in the past. 'Not just because you're like Kate, though that was part of it. You weren't just a substitute for her.'

She nodded. It was easier to talk about it now that he had said it. 'That was why I didn't want to see you; I didn't want you to mix me up with Jans and think I could be her. And, well... If you had feelings for me, how did I know you wouldn't try to take me over, like Emmeline?'

'Oh, Jo. I wouldn't do that. I don't want to control you.'

'No, but sometimes people think they're being kind and really they're just being bossy.'

'Promise me you'll say if you feel I'm being controlling.' He seemed to mean it. 'I have a lot of respect for you – the way you've been facing all of this. It takes courage.'

She bit her nails hard. *Don't believe him,* a sarcastic voice said. *He doesn't mean it. Why should he care about you?* Then Lorraine's voice: *Can you let yourself take it in*?

They were quiet again. As they passed through a wooded area, bare trunks slipping past as if on a conveyor belt, her eyes kept closing and blinking open again. Jans appeared to her, with windblown waist-length hair – neither of them had been able to grow their hair much below their shoulders – and a strange flesh-coloured garment with a triangular flap of material joining each sleeve to the side, so that when she raised her arms it looked as though they were webbed. *Are we going swimming?* Jans asked, opening her mouth silently like a fish. She started swimming towards Jo, though there wasn't any water, and Jo caught her in her arms and said, *I'm not going to leave you. Not ever. Don't leave me.* At this point Jans disappeared and Jo was left holding a tiny box, no bigger than a dental floss container, with DO NOT OPEN written on it.

The car stopped, jerking her awake. They were in a big car park surrounded by trees, facing a large EXIT sign. She stared at Richard. 'Where are we?'

'Just a service station. I thought we'd get a coffee and a sandwich; it's nearly lunchtime. Took us ages to get out of London.'

Still dazed and yawning, she said, 'How long did I sleep?'

'A good hour and a half.' He was smiling at her. 'Sorry I had to wake you.'

'Oh...' she said. 'I dreamt about Jans... Kate. It was horrible.'

'Do you want to tell me about it?'

'No.' She couldn't, though she did want to. She swung her legs out of the car and stood up, gazing round the car park at people hurrying in and out of the big glass doors. 'It looks weird. Too crowded.' She ducked her head and pulled up the hood of her parka.

'It is a bit weird. We could be anywhere.'

'Do they have toilets here?' Surely they must have, but these places seemed to be their own worlds with their own rules.

'Course they do. You'll see the signs when you go inside. I'll get the sandwiches – something veggie for you.' He waved at her as he headed for the coffee stall.

She pushed the revolving glass door. Inside, the bright windowless space with wall-less cafés and open-fronted shops confused her. She had always hated shopping centres. She wandered from one end to the other and back again until she found a short corridor with a red square and a blue square on the wall. The white figures drawn on the squares were squat and cartoonish, like gingerbread people. On the back of the cubicle door in the Ladies was a poster asking for donations to help refugees. All you had to do was text – if you had spare money. Jo had never known what it was like to have money to spare.

She came out to face a sea of shiny beige floor. There wasn't an obvious exit, just the same cafés she'd wandered past before, seemingly in a different order, and people weren't heading in any one direction. She looked back, recognised the Burger King, turned round again, looked for the door, then stood for a moment in utter panic, trapped inside this artificial palace full of nasty food and things she didn't want to buy. She nearly texted Richard but was afraid he'd think she couldn't look after herself.

She turned in the other direction and, to her relief, saw a set of glass doors at the end of the corridor. When she came out, she was faced by a steep grassy bank with a narrow paved path in front of it. Her body vibrated with panic again. *Look how pathetic you are. Just pathetic,* one of the voices said. *Why don't you just go and lose yourself?* She felt the way she had when she'd got separated from Mother and Jans in Oxford's Westgate Centre - she would have been about four – running backwards and forwards, screaming for them. I'm screaming for you now, Jans. Can you hear me?

The path seemed to lead round the corner of the building. She was still panicking, but somewhere in her she could feel Lorraine's calm presence. There was no voice but it was as if Lorraine was saying, 'Come on, you know you can do it.' Jo was sure the path would come to a dead end, or else that Richard would have given up and gone on without her, but then there were the front doors and there he was, holding two cardboard cups and a paper carrier bag, turning his head from one side to the other.

'Where were you?' he said. 'I was getting worried. Are you all right?'

'I got lost,' she mumbled, weak with relief.

'Never mind. Let's have these in the car.' He waved the bag towards the car park.

He'd got her a cheese and tomato toastie. The cheese had begun to congeal and the wrapping was translucent with grease, but it was still good. She never thought to have toasted sandwiches.

'What about paying for everything? I've got some money here.' She pulled her rucksack on to her lap.

'Shall we talk about it later?' he said through a mouthful of sandwich.

She unzipped her rucksack and felt for her purse inside it. She wanted to give him the money now; it didn't feel as though it belonged to her any more. She put the rucksack on the floor and sat with the purse on her lap. Sixty pounds. It had accumulated over time, helped by the occasional gift from Mother, in an envelope she kept under the seat of the armchair. She'd forgotten about it until yesterday.

'I want to pay what I can,' she said.

'That's OK, Jo. I know you don't have much.'

'It's important,' she said. 'Doing this matters to me – and it's for Jans.'

Richard took the notes with care, thanking her.

He gave her a steady look, which felt to Jo almost like respect. Instead of turning away she looked at him back. Now she'd given him the money she felt more equal, more like everyone else. Lorraine kept saying she was just as good as other people but she'd never believed it.

'Let's go. I hate these places,' Richard said.

When they were on the road again he told her about his dog. She and Jans had always wanted a dog but they were both allergic to them, Jans more so. Yet another thing in their childhood that they hadn't been able to have.

'And what have you been up to?'

She could have muttered something about the charity shop but took a risk. 'Not much. I'm writing something. It's about me and Jans and – you know – the abuse and everything. Us growing up.'

'That sounds good. You seem to like writing.' He paused, as though he'd been about to say something and thought better of it. 'I hope you don't mind me asking, but did you ever find out anything about your father? It always seemed strange there was nothing of him in the house.'

'Mother wrote to me. He was Irish; he went off to Ireland with someone else. Mother told him not to bother us, so he didn't. Except she never let us have the presents he sent us.'

'How awful, and very sad. He might have wanted to keep in touch with you... You say 'was' – do you know if he's still alive?'

'No.'

'And you haven't tried to find out?'

'No. I wouldn't want to see him. It wouldn't do any good.'

It was enough having to deal with Paul and the way Mother had been. Some people talked about forgiving as though it would be easy, but right now she didn't feel up to forgiving anyone. Lorraine had said forgiveness wasn't about pretending it didn't matter: you couldn't really forgive until you'd felt how much you'd been hurt.

She drifted off again while Richard was talking. As her eyes closed, she saw the photo of her and Kate under the apple tree and remembered the Saturday afternoon when it had been taken. She and Kate had been to Port Meadow on their bikes, taking bags of windfall apples to feed to the horses. When they came back they saw Mother sitting in the overgrown garden with a visitor – they never had visitors – whom Mother introduced as their aunt Rosalind. She looked a lot like Mother, only nicer. Mother hadn't told them she was coming, they didn't know why. They'd never seen Rosalind before and never saw her again – she lived in Canada – but she had talked and laughed with them and taken the photo as a souvenir. The afternoon had been happy.

Richard

'OK, Jo?' Richard glanced across at her; she was rubbing her hands over her face. 'Been asleep? We'll be in Totnes soon.'

'Mm.'

He steered carefully round the bends in the road, minimally noticing the Dart's wooded banks, the hedgerows on one side and the sloping fields on the other. Even at the bleak end of winter it was good to be out of the city. The fields were greener than he'd expected – people always talked about Devon rain. Rain was pelting the car again now, darkening the road and obscuring the bends. He saw the lights of another car too close behind him and flashed it irritably.

He noticed she'd nodded off again, head to one side, mouth slightly open, childlike and unguarded in sleep. She was still vulnerable, probably always would be, but as soon as he'd seen her he could tell she was handling herself better. She was more *there* – he didn't know how else to put it; she didn't flinch away so much. Perhaps this therapist was making a difference. How much could a few months of therapy do, though, after all she'd been through: the horrible abuse, the thought of which still made him shudder, that odd, cold mother, the missing father, the breakdowns themselves? It amazed him how well Kate had survived such a childhood, but he wished he'd understood her struggles better. So often learning seemed to come too late.

We're all work in progress, he thought: Jo, Rick and me learning to live without Kate, Fran wanting someone of her own and not having anyone. Nothing goes away: you just learn to accommodate it till gradually it becomes small enough to bear and you become big enough to bear it. He smiled as he thought it; he was sounding like V.

He had the radio on, quietly so as not to disturb Jo, but the news bothered him. There had been talk of a new disease for some time, and he noticed how frequently words like 'lockdown' and 'pandemic' were being used, softened by the newsreader's measured voice. His first fear was that something might happen to Rick, then that he might die and leave Rick without either parent, with Fran not able to travel to look after him. It all felt palpably real. Then came another pang: not travelling from home would mean he couldn't see Jo, just when they were beginning to become part of each other's lives. He wanted to say something about it to her but decided not to. She had enough to contend with.

They were coming near the town now, past the Cider Press shops – which looked like the sort of place Kate would have enjoyed browsing in – along an even more winding road bordered with trees, with a glimpse of river beside them. The rain had turned to battering hail and sharp gusts of wind slapped the sides of the car. He drove under a high blue-painted bridge with 'Welcome to Totnes' across it in gold letters.

'Nearly there,' he said to Jo, loudly enough to wake her. She sat up and looked around.

'I remember this,' she said. 'We used to like it here, when we stayed with Tim and Celia.'

'Your aunt and uncle? Did they live here?' He watched the wipers push heaps of hailstones, like small peppermints, to the sides of the windscreen, the water running down as they melted.

'Bridgetown. They had a big house with a walled garden. They took us out to places and gave us nice meals.' She smiled as she said it. He didn't know Bridgetown but pictured a warm, comfortable, colourful house near a row of snug cottages.

The B & B was in a small turning off the Plymouth Road, which Richard found thanks to the sat nav. An ageing man in a grey pullover opened the door just wide enough to peer out.

'Yes?' he said, staring suspiciously at both of them. His face was gaunt, his eyes sunken behind thick lids, his temples hollow, with thick blue veins. 'My daughter's not here. Are you booked in?' He hobbled away, shoulders bent, arms moving stiffly, and came back with a clipboard and two sets of keys. 'Johnston and Brookfield? The two singles – or was it a double room you were wanting?'

Richard thought Jo would be thrown by this, but when he glanced at her he saw the shadow of a grin.

'The two singles, please,' he said as neutrally as possible.

'Sign here, then,' the man said, taking a pen from behind his ear.

Richard signed in the space the man pointed to and handed the pen to Jo. Seeing her signature close to his, the writing unmistakably like Kate's, reminded him for an instant of signing the register when he and Kate were married. It was as if he and Jo were married in spirit, for this strange time at least.

The man handed them each a set of keys, grasping them awkwardly in his arthritic fingers, and pointed up the narrow staircase which, like the entrance hall, was carpeted in purple – a flat, sweetish colour, not the deep, rich shade Kate had loved. 'You' – he nodded at Jo – 'on the right, you' – nodding at Richard – 'on the left. You'll see the room numbers. We don't have no smoking in the rooms' he glanced at Jo's stained fingers – 'and no smelly take-aways.'

Richard caught more than a trace of a Yorkshire accent but decided not to mention it. Jo looked uncomfortable and started biting her nails.

'You'll have to vacate the rooms by ten,' the man said, as though he couldn't wait to be rid of them. 'Anything you want to know, all the information's in the room.'

'Thank you very much,' Richard said, trying to sound grateful.

'My daughter should be here soon. She's the one as deals with guests. I'm just doing her a favour.'

Richard smiled and inclined his head.

'I'll leave you to it, then.' The man opened a cream-painted door with a large PRIVATE sign and shut it firmly behind him. Richard glimpsed a red swirly carpet and a small Highland terrier, which barked as the door closed.

He glanced at Jo, glad she didn't seem bothered. Perhaps she was used to people being like that with her. They opened their respective doors and she slipped into her room. His was so cramped he could barely squeeze round the sides of the bed. The ensuite bathroom had a sliding door and was painted a sickly purple that matched the hall carpet. He had to manoeuvre himself into it sideways and sit on the toilet seat to use the washbasin.

In a while he'd take Jo out for a meal. Before that he must make sure the box was safe. Sitting on the bed, he unzipped his suitcase and felt under a thick jumper for the hard-edged shape wrapped in the delicate scarf. Strange to think it would no longer be with him. He and Rick would bury the box in the garden with a ceremony of their own and Rick would make a memorial – he'd said he wanted to do that. Richard would plant Kate's favourite rose, a scented white one called Boule de Neige. For a moment he was flooded with guilt: perhaps he should have buried all her ashes there. He left the larger box in the case and felt under the scarf for the wooden snuff box, gently stroking its smooth surface before he lifted it out, cradling it in his hand like a precious, exceptionally fragile egg. That was his bargain with her: he'd release her into the river if she'd let him keep these fragments.

After their hurried pub meal – he could see Jo didn't like being in pubs and got her out as soon as he could – he found it hard to sleep. His room was hot, the bed uncomfortably soft, and he drifted in and out of dreams where Kate turned into Jo. At one point he tried to throw her into the river, clothed and alive, and watched her shocked face as she sank under the water, mouthing at him, 'Don't let me go.'

He showered, shaved and dressed, observing what he was doing as though he had no connection with it, and wandered down to breakfast because his room was so suffocatingly small. It was barely eight, the time when breakfast began, and he found himself alone in a basement dining room with too much lighting and glass doors that looked out over a bare patio. It had rained during the night and the concrete paving was still glistening. In one corner, away from the other tables –he knew Jo would prefer that – was a small table for two. It was covered with a pristine white cloth which, when he touched it, turned out to be plastic.

Everything on the table was clean, orderly and standardised, from the packaged portions of marmalade and sauces to the thick white china crockery. He supposed he'd better eat something but could summon up no interest in the glass-shelved servery set out with fruit and cereals. Why on earth had he told Jo he'd meet her here at 8.30? They didn't have to leave till 10.00 and he was sure she didn't get up early.

Just as he was fingering the handle of his empty cup, a plump woman with dyed dark brown hair and too much makeup for so early in the morning came bustling up to him, her face creased into an ingratiating smile. Richard couldn't bring himself to smile back until she mentioned coffee. She stood, pen poised over her order pad, reciting all the options for cooked breakfast, and looked disappointed when he said he'd wait till his sister-in-law came down. The woman gave him a curious look and bustled away. By this time other people were taking their seats; smells of frying and muffled sounds of Radio 2 were coming from the kitchen. It was all so cheerful.

Huddled over his coffee, he was aware of a presence beside him, like the other times when he'd sensed Kate, rather than imagined her there. The contact felt soft and poignant; it didn't overwhelm him with grief. In fact there was something joyful about it, as though she was telling him to be happy. He saw how determined he'd been that this should be a sad occasion, but a space under his breastbone seemed to have opened up, a warm feeling that let him know it didn't have to be so. *It's all right*, Kate seemed to be saying. *Just let go and it'll be all right.*

When Jo came in, nibbling a thumbnail and staring at the floor, he knew she hadn't had a good night either. She sat down opposite him and stared blankly somewhere beyond him, as though she didn't know where she was. The landlady, whose name he'd discovered was Ruth, was hovering nearby, ready to take their order. Jo obviously needed coffee, but neither of them could decide what to eat. To Ruth's disappointment they settled for toast, and sat silently spreading it from the little white plastic pots.

'Low tide's just after eleven,' Richard said. 'We'll need to get over there by about ten-thirty. It's a bit of a walk down to the river, as you know.'

Jo nodded, still looking blank.

'There may not be much bank to stand on if we leave it too late.'

Jo nodded again. He didn't know if she'd taken it in. Then she said, 'I'm glad we're doing it together' and looked round to one side, as if she might be sensing Kate there too.

As they packed their bags into the car it started raining again. The icy wind pinched their cheeks.

'What a day!' Richard said with a helpless shrug.

Jo said nothing but pulled down her woolly hat. It suited her, he thought, even with that ridiculous pompom that made it look like a tea cosy.

'We'll need wellies,' he said, 'for walking across the field. I don't suppose you've brought any?' Of course she wouldn't have; she wasn't an outdoor person.

She shook her head and said, 'I've only got these boots.'

'I've brought Kate's, if you'd feel OK about wearing them. At least they'll be the right size.'

She stared at him for a moment, eyes wide in what he took to be horror, then softened and said, 'OK. It'll be nice to wear them for her. Feels more like she'll be there.'

'That's what I thought.' He didn't say how he'd struggled with knowing Kate would never wear them again.

He followed the sat nav through narrow lanes with high hedges, last scraps of autumn leaves still clinging to the wet branches of the trees. Passing the granite cross in the centre of Ashprington village, he wondered yet again if this was the right place. Jo seemed to have no doubts. She was gazing out of the window, as intent as a child on everything they passed.

'I remember this,' she said. 'We're getting near now.'

The high hedges gave way to fields and trees. As they followed the road down towards Sharpham, Richard glimpsed a generous curve of river with gently sloping green fields on the far side.

'It's beautiful,' he said, forgetting momentarily that that was why they'd chosen it.

'Yes,' Jo said. 'We loved it here. We used to go and see the vineyard and the place where they make the cheese.'

'Cheese?' He'd forgotten that too, even though he'd been told they couldn't park near the shop that sold it.

'Yes. Where are you going to park?'

They'd said he could park opposite the farm gate and walk down from there. The rain had slowed, and by the time they got out it had almost stopped. The business of dragging on thick socks and boots and watching for signs of more rain kept him from thinking about what they'd come to do, but then he pulled out a small sports bag from the back of the car and cradled it in his arms.

'Are we ready, then? It's down there, isn't it?'

He opened the metal gate and began following the path down towards the river, making sure Jo was behind him. Everything shone with water and the air smelt fresh and earthy. The grass was a deep, bright green and the hedge a tangle of rotted rosehips and shrivelled blackberries. Richard found himself loving the walk and turned back to Jo, who was close behind him.

'You OK, Jo?'

'Yes. It doesn't rain like this in London.'

He knew what she meant. He noticed a gateway to a muddy sloping path, at the bottom of which he could see the river. 'Is this it?'

'Yes,' Jo said. 'I remember it. This is where we used to come. We saw a seal in the river here once.'

'A seal? I bet that doesn't happen often.' He started down the path. 'Careful you don't slip. Those boots are quite old.'

Turning towards her again he saw her edging carefully down, picking her way among the tree roots. Kate would have been less cautious. He'd been holding the bag in his arms most of the way but now he slung the handles over his shoulder as he squelched down to the river bank.

'So here we are,' he said as Jo came up beside him. They trod carefully between fallen branches towards a half-submerged stretch of grass and water plants, but stopped before they reached it. They stood on a small muddy promontory, their feet half in the water.

'Right here?' Jo said.

'Seems as good a spot as any.' They were in the middle of the river's wide bend, the larger curve to their right and the narrower part to the left. A few gulls soared and screamed overhead and two cormorants stood on the bank, wings held out as if in an ancient rite.

'So how shall we do it?' He held the bag in front of him by the handles as though that too were part of the rite. 'Can you undo the zip?'

Jo unzipped the bag and together they took out the box, Jo gently unwrapping the scarf that had cushioned its journey. While Jo held the box Richard slung the bag back on to his shoulder so that he had both hands free. What now? he thought, and for an awful moment he had no idea. Then, Jo's hands still round the box, he opened the lid. He didn't look inside; nor did she. For a moment they both stood clasping the box, their hands over each other's. Then, as if they'd both heard the same command, they lifted the box and tilted it, waiting for a gust of wind. When it came, some of the ash blew back towards them, the dark grey gritty powder flying over their heads as it dispersed. A little of it landed on Richard's shoulder; it felt like Kate's blessing. He shook the box, making sure it was empty. Kate was free now, and something in him felt freer too.

They stayed with their hands together until Richard gently pulled his away. He closed the box, which now hardly weighed anything, and put it back in the bag.

Jo had dropped her hands to her sides, but he took her left in his right and grasped it firmly for a moment. Then he reached into his pocket. He hadn't forgotten it – the stone he'd always meant to give her. He squeezed her hand again, pressing the stone into her palm.

'You'll need this,' he said. 'To remember her by. And to remember I'm still here.' He paused. 'As a friend.' He would be a friend to her no matter what.

She nodded slowly and then said, 'Yes. A friend.'

She turned away for a moment, making, he guessed, her own private farewell. There was a ripple in the water and a small sleek dome appeared above the surface. As Jo turned back, the seal lifted its head and opened its round eyes in a kindly, enquiring gaze.

Author's Biography – Susan Jordan

Susan Jordan moved to Devon in 2011, having spent most of her life in London, and loves being close to the countryside and the coast. She worked as a psychotherapist for many years but retired in 2022. She also worked for a branch of Mind, in projects committed to helping users of mental health services lead fuller lives. Part of the inspiration for **The Box** comes from her work at Mind. The experience of abuse she describes in the novel is also based to a large extent on her work.

Susan has always wanted to write. She read English at Oxford and has an MA in Creative Writing from Bath Spa University, where she wrote both fiction and poetry. She has published two full-length collections of poetry and two pamphlets, one of which won a competition, and her poetry has appeared in magazines and anthologies. She has been involved with Buddhist practice since the 1980s and regularly goes on retreat. She has various interests, including music, and sings in a local choir. She shares her home with a cat called Koala.

Support and Advice

If you or someone close to you have been affected by issues described in this book, here are some websites that you may find helpful:

- AtaLoss: https://ataloss.co.uk (information about bereavement support)
- Cruse Bereavement Support: https://www.cruse.org.uk
- Mind: https://mind.org.uk
- NAPAC: https://napac.org.uk (supporting recovery from childhood abuse)
- National Hearing Voices Network: https://www.hearing-voices.org

Palewell Press

Palewell Press is an independent publisher handling poetry, fiction and non-fiction with a focus on books that foster Justice, Equality and Sustainability. The Editor can be reached on enquiries@palewellpress.co.uk

Milton Keynes UK
Ingram Content Group UK Ltd.
UKHW020706070824
446656UK00009B/155